RENÉE BRANUM

Renée Branum holds MFAs in Fiction from the Iowa Writers' Workshop and Creative Non-Fiction from the University of Montana. Her stories and essays have appeared in the *Georgia Review*, the *Gettysburg Review* and *Best American Non-required Reading*. She lives in Cincinnati where she is pursuing a PhD in Fiction. *Defenestrate* is her first novel.

RENÉE BRANUM

Defenestrate

VINTAGE

1 3 5 7 9 10 8 6 4 2

Vintage is part of the Penguin Random House group of companies whose addresses can be found at global.penguinrandomhouse.com

Penguin
Random House
UK

First published in Vintage in 2023
First published in hardback by Jonathan Cape in 2022

penguin.co.uk/vintage

A CIP catalogue record for this book is available from the British Library

ISBN 9781529114485

Printed and bound in Great Britain by Clays Ltd, Elcograf S.p.A.

The authorised representative in the EEA is
Penguin Random House Ireland, Morrison Chambers,
32 Nassau Street, Dublin D02 YH68

Penguin Random House is committed to a sustainable future for our business, our readers and our planet. This book is made from Forest Stewardship Council® certified paper.

MIX
Paper from
responsible sources
FSC® C018179

To Richard for giving me Buster.
To Liana for giving me Prague.
To Sara for giving me my most ideal reader.
To Faye for giving me sisterhood.
To my mother and father for giving me life.

Golden Years

WHEN I PICTURE the city now, I see it from overhead. Bird's-eye.
A long, lonely aerial view looking down onto orange clay
rooftiles curved like the shells of snails. The city shrinks, small
enough to be covered with a palm—my palm, my twin brother's. We both seem to remember those years from above, as if
we were often sailing out over the streets that opened up into
squares, the ice skating rink dusted blue, that high clocktower
with its windows sealed shut, the bridge a long spine of black
bone straining across the bread-colored water. And I guess it's
true that the city rises, tiered, made up of slopes and heights,
spires and hilltops and towers—all these high places you could
climb, to get a better view of things, and I guess it's also true
that I was always climbing them.

I remember once wandering home drunk and coming upon
a bit of scaffolding along the back wall of a church and starting
to climb it without even blinking. My brother was there too,
but he didn't follow. He stood with his hands shoved into his
coat pockets, whistling "Golden Years" and rocking forward
and back on the balls of his feet. Always so careful, my brother—
it's strange that eventually he was the one to fall.

I stood up there with the frost in the air hitting me just right
so that the skin on my face came awake for a moment and then:
my cheeks went all sleepy and numb, and there was a faintly
greenish mist coming up off the snow that sat in gutters, tram

lights glancing upward. Nick waited down below, until finally he called up,

"Hey, sis. You get your kicks yet?"

And I guess I had.

I don't know what it was I hoped to see from up there—the street getting smaller as though I was looking at it through the wrong end of a telescope, the spires at the base of the hill poking holes in the tame rounded skyline. I was always daring just a little too much in those days, putting space between myself and the ground, myself and safety, myself and my cautious slope-shouldered brother who was singing under his breath, *Don't let me hear you say life's taking you nowhere, angel. Come get up, my baby,* the whole time I was climbing dizzily back down to him.

The Curse

THERE'S A SUPERSTITION in our family about falling—a kind of tight-lipped joke that's no longer a joke because it's happened too often over the years: cousins leaning against railings that wouldn't hold their weight, uncles losing their footing while cleaning leaf debris from slimy gutters, aunts toppling from ladders, their spines folding up on themselves like coat hangers. Something in our bodies wants to fall, blood magnetized to pavement, iron and concrete greeting each other across a stretch of air, the downward plunge and crack, like a pink Easter egg dropped from a window—we splinter that easily.

We can trace it back a century or so—the story of our great-great-grandfather Jiří in Prague who was said to give a gentle push to the back of a Roma stonemason where he stood placing chunks of limestone smooth and flush to form the bottom sill of a paneless window in a high church steeple. It was 1895 and there was a resurgence of new architecture, renovation, the city preening and polishing itself like a vast peacock with slate and granite and sandstone feathers. Jiří oversaw many of these building projects, gained a reputation for precision and efficiency. The stonemason, it was said, had seduced Jiří's youngest daughter, but who knew anymore if this was true. What was certain was that the stonemason landed below on rain-slick cobblestones, and his body bent into a hook, curving strangely like a treble clef and, according to legend, witnesses afterward reported that the body didn't bleed. No, they said, not even a trickle.

I couldn't tell you what Jiří felt looking down at the question mark the stonemason's bloodless body made against the wet cobbles, the slice of October light that fell across him like a sash, whether our ancestor felt triumph or shame or a rage that still itched in his palms after the suddenness of the shove. But I can tell you that it was the end for him of his hard-won reputation, the end of a long and respectable career, and he fled with his wife and children to the American Midwest where he found work as a mule driver in a coal mine. It was there the family stayed, and there my brother and I grew up.

The belief is that the stonemason's fall has somehow been handed down through the years, that for generations our family has held on to this death and never been forgiven. You could call it a curse, but that's a word we never seemed to use.

"It's only a story," our mother always told my brother and me, but I remember some nights her superstition would get the better of her, and she'd line the floor around our beds with

3

pillows, tucking the blankets so tight around our little bodies that we struggled and thrashed after she switched off the lights, straining against our cocoons like Houdini escaping from a straitjacket.

Someone, some relative perhaps, had given our mother a coffee mug that showed a simple cartoon illustration of a man and woman perched on the edge of a deep swimming pool, peering into it. The pool had been drained of all but a foot of water, and, standing in the shallow water down below, the pool's high walls looming around him, was a little boy with a tiny rubber inner tube around his middle. The image's caption read *Better safe than sorry, son.*

It was this mug that often rested on the squat nightstand between our twin beds while our mother kissed our foreheads, made the blankets tight around us. A smell came up from the mug like leaves going soft at the bottom of a well—mint, citrus, chamomile—as deep and unfathomable as the earth's molten center. And I remember turning my head on the pillow to stare at the mug: the two parents side by side, their legs dangling into the emptiness of the drained pool, and I remember hating them a little for their stifling caution.

I think a part of me always longed for the fall. I know it's morbid, but I remember growing up with a kind of envy for that sweet, endless plummet—how your body can be given a measure of grace as it greets the air, feels its own heft and buoyancy.

Some members of the family are so superstitious they will not go higher than the second floors of buildings—will keep far back from balcony railings or the sharp sudden edges of hiking trails. But I've always dared more than the others, climbing up onto steeply pitched roofs, looking out at towering views with an arm slung loosely around a chimney, skirting close to ledges, daring my own weight to pull me down, daring a phantom push from behind, feeling the height lift through me, all the way from feet to forehead.

When I was a little girl, I wanted to be a trapeze artist, a stunt pilot, a high-dive champion, a female Evel Knievel.

"Your mother will *not* go for it. Not a chance," my father said when I showed him a flyer for a circus camp when I was eight— glossy pictures of arched bodies poised on high platforms, lifting their arms above their heads as if straining to get even higher before rising into the air like gaudy smoke, ruby sequins dusting the air with light.

"It's safe," I protested, showing him pictures of padded mats on the internet, showing him harnesses and cables.

A year or so later, I showed my mother an article in *National Geographic* about cave divers. "Now, don't you go getting any ideas," she said, shaking her head a little wildly, her earrings tinkling like tiny bells. She held me and I squirmed in her lap. She sniffed at my hair and I imagine that it smelled like the high branches of elm trees, like sap and sunlight and too much air.

We all make our way through a world of so much danger; I could never believe that our fear should be any greater than anyone else's. I didn't want to believe that my body would be asked to pay any consequence for the actions of a relation I'd never met, of whom not even a single photograph exists. Not that I couldn't imagine him. I felt at times that I knew his face, craggy and sunken-eyed, heavily shadowed from the sight of the stonemason stumbling forward into all that air, swallowing gusts of it on the way down, and on the pavement below, his chest swollen with that huge final breath.

Defenestrate

ONE THING THE city of Prague is famous for: throwing men out windows. The word for this is *defenestration*. Tourists can climb the narrow stairs to the room where Catholic noblemen were defenestrated because of a religious dispute in 1618. You can look down from the window to see exactly the length of their fall. Catholics say these men were saved by angels, cradled in the arms of the Virgin herself, lowered gently to earth. Protestants say the men survived because they landed in a dung heap piled below the window. Looking down from that window, it is easy to imagine an angel in the expanse between sill and cobblestones; easier still to imagine a pile of shit, and easiest of all to conclude: the city holds both of these in the loose clasp of its hand.

The Patron Saint of Sudden Death

OUR MOTHER. SHE lined the walls of our house with crosses of different shapes and sizes. Elaborately filigreed wrought iron, wood, even animal bone. She matched the ends of her fingers together, held the tips beneath her chin, and breathed small prayers, pleas that gravity would no longer wreak havoc on our little clan. From her bedroom, clouds of incense sneaked through the crack under the door and still managed to make us choke as we tiptoed past on the way to the bathroom.

"God," she told us, "will show us the way to live."

By which I now think she meant: survive.

At the stove she stirred thick soups as if making potions. Her cheeks puffed around the spells she muttered as she halved garlic, crushed rosemary in her hand. We passed behind her through the rooms like stocking-footed ghosts, and she'd turn at every shift in the air to reach for us. She patted our hair. She wiped at our faces. Even my father's. She wanted evidence, the proof of touch, before she would allow herself to believe that, yes, we were alive, unhurt. Yes, we were surviving. A cut, a bruise, and she tended it, always thanking God himself that the gash was no deeper than it was, the scar a temporary bridge toward healing.

I think that, as a deeply religious woman, painfully devout, our mother always felt a bit guilty about her belief in the family superstition—as if these legends of falling could somehow replace her faith, grow upward through thinly lit cracks like a tree pushing aside slabs of sidewalk as it aged and spread its roots. And this was why she continued to tell us,

"It's only a story."

But she was thorough. She wrote out psalms on fluttery pastel Post-it notes and stuck them to the walls above our beds. The notes lifted and trembled in the gusts of private cyclones that the ceiling fan kicked up: *Though he fall, he shall not be utterly cast down; For the Lord upholds him with His hand.*

Certain saints she thought could be of particular help. Rita of Cascia or Jude Thaddeus, these patron saints of lost causes, impossible cases, desperate situations.

With every step, we were in danger. And so she prayed.

She prayed in English. She prayed with the feeble scraps of Latin that she knew. She prayed the only prayer she'd ever learned in Czech: the Lord's Prayer. I liked hearing her tongue enter the sharp-angled maze of consonants when she got to the line: *přijd' království tvé*, "thy kingdom come," then drop into the open loop of vowels at the end: *ale zbav nás od zlého*, "but deliver us from evil," the final word, *zlého*, like its own deliverance—all breath.

She prayed to martyrs who, in life, had known all kinds of strange and elaborate pain—tangled limbs, jutting bones and stretched skin. She prayed to Saint Andrew Avellino, who, because his brain filled up with blood one morning without warning, is traditionally invoked against sudden death.

If any of us came upon her while she knelt and murmured, we would back away slowly, as if from a crouching panther. We would hush our breath and soften the fall of our feet. The creak of the floorboards blended with her whispered entreaties like weird, wobbling notes of music. Sometimes our father would shake his head as if he felt sorry for her.

She'd grown up in a household driven by fear, and prayer was the only weapon she had against it. If any family member should fall but survive the fall, this success was attributed solely to the power of prayer, and candles were lit in gratitude to Saint Andrew Avellino, who had intervened on behalf of generations of sinners. And while she lit those candles, I was climbing up to the bird's nests in backyard sycamores, adding locks of my own hair to the soft interiors so that some small piece of my body could always be up high, surrounded on all sides by air and light. And while she prayed, I breathed down onto clusters of turquoise eggs the single word *zlého*, again and again. To me, it sounded like air and light.

She lit candles for every fall, for cousins she barely even knew.

What I do not know is whether she lit a candle after my brother fell, or whether she had stopped praying for him years before.

Builder of Small Worlds

OUR FATHER. OVER the years, he meticulously built a very small town for his model train layout. Every single stop sign and mailbox was painful in its smallness, hard on the eyes. He glued together tiny trees like tufts of broccoli. He built, tree by tree, an entire miniature forest that he placed beside the closed loop of the railroad tracks. In the branches of some of the trees, there were nests. In the nests, eggs so minuscule they made the eye shrink, made you blink and squint, each one just the faintest oval of pale blue, each a contained world the size of a dust mote, without the faintest hope of ever hatching.

While he worked, he kept his breath small in his chest so as not to shift the branches before the glue had dried. He took careful sips from the plastic cup full of caffeine-free root beer going flat and warm at his elbow. He hummed, the melody so soft it barely made it past his lips, and if you bent close over him, you could make out the song, could sometimes even hear a faltering brush of words: *Joy to the fishes in the deep blue sea, joy to you and me.*

He kept himself busy, building that tiny world. And I sometimes wish, now that he is gone, that I'd tried to understand this a little more.

About the train tracks, about the teeny eggs in the trees, I never once asked him: *Why?* Never asked if this was his way of accessing a high, towering view from the safety of a kitchen chair.

Our father was always a frail man, never dared much. His own father, our Grandpa Frank, was an airline pilot who never once crashed and who died unglamorously of heart failure in his late seventies. Perhaps this was one of the reasons our mother married this man—trying to work something tame and earthly into our bloodline. To ground us a little.

She told my father about Jiří and the stonemason on their wedding night, as if she were afraid the story might drive him away.

"Why are you telling me this?" he asked, their bodies close in the glow of white sheets, and years later I would think of this whenever I'd tell the weird stories of family deaths and injuries to strangers in bars who often paused afterward, swallowing their beer, confused, to ask: *Why are you telling me this?*

"I'm telling you," my mother told my father grimly, "because it happened."

She paused, rubbing her hand over one side of her face, unclenching her tight jaw.

"And some of us believe that it's still happening," she added. It was ominous but sweet and strange, and so my father nodded and kissed her forehead and told her that maybe they should've asked for helmets and mouth guards as wedding presents.

"Don't joke," my mother said, but she laughed anyway. And my father did not ask her if she was one of those who still believed in the superstition, because, I suspect, he already knew.

Miniature Museum

IN PRAGUE, NEAR the Strahov Monastery, there's a brown door tucked back from the street with a sign just above it: MUZEUM MINIATUR. The museum is a single room. You bend over low-power microscopes, peer down to see, tucked safely behind little glass windows: a flea wearing infinitesimal shoes made of copper, a train of camels in the eye of a needle, a grasshopper with a minuscule violin propped beneath his chin. These things, too small to be understood by the naked eye, were made by a man who had to practice breathing exercises, had to "work between heartbeats," because even the blood pulsing in his fingertips would make the flea's shoes tremble, could cause the camel's slender neck to break. The smallness of these things was terrifying—inscriptions on a shaft of hair, a micro-scopic book with pages that could be turned but were too fragile to be handled by anyone but the maker. I was told by the curator, "Some miniature artists go blind after only a few years of work." I was told that some of the tools needed to make these things were themselves too small to be seen without magnification. My body, bending to look, seemed massive. Outside, the city itself was impossibly, scarily vast. Lost within it, I held my breath, tried to still my pulse, looking through the curved lens.

I would like to ask the miniature artists who went blind from looking: *Was it worth it?*

I would like to ask my mother if she believes her God went weary and squint-eyed, piecing our world together.

I would've liked to ask my father, who spent hours at the kitchen table, sculpting a landscape that he loomed above, gigantic—the only time he was ever so giant—if this tininess put strain on his body, if maybe his heart went weak and tired from his attempts to quiet its beating. I wish I could've asked him, the only truly sane one among us: *How will any of this possibly keep us safe?*

Master of the Pratfall

MY TWIN BROTHER, Nick. Winter was always his favorite season—ice on downward-sloping sidewalks when we'd walk home from school together, skating on the soles of our shoes. He was always primed for a fall, my brother—keeping his muscles loose and relaxed. We tossed ourselves down into the safety of snowbanks, practicing the pratfalls we picked up from watching hours and hours of old Buster Keaton films.

Nick was very good at that one-legged slip backward, as if his tilted shoe might reveal a smear of yellow banana peel underneath. His rear end would meet the piled-up snow with leg extended, and no matter how quickly they happened, his falls always seemed slow, measured. He'd pinwheel his arms for comic effect, waver lengthily over his own fall as if making up his mind whether to surrender to it.

He tried to teach me: "The trick is to learn your weight. Lean back into the air, and feel the angle of the fall rising up to you."

The snow was mashed and flattened by our attempts—our slides and rolls.

I envied him. Grace was always so easy for him—how he'd be carried forward through slowed-down seconds just by the force of his own stride, then go down quick in a sweet backward flail, as if he'd known all along the exact instant it would come: that inevitable clutching of gravity.

As for my own falls, I could never seem to keep a straight face. I laughed each time I went down—laughter that was loud and sudden and shocking, neighbors staring at us from their porches and driveways, snow powdering down from the ends of their shovels.

Nick's mouth remained thin and grim while he fell, as if he were studying for an exam, measuring his body's strange geometry. His face was so beautiful and still, a point of calm in the midst of those arcs and flurries of movement.

He saw each fall as a thing he could make perfect. And if there were times when his rhythm was off, or he landed too hard on an elbow or shoulder, often he would spit and curse, dusting himself off angrily. He came close to real rage at times, when his falls weren't quite right—though this strain toward perfection was never something he tried to force on me. My falls could be loose and sloppy and oafish, and he would only nod and offer quiet advice.

Once, not long after we'd returned home to the Midwest after our years in Prague, I saw him go down hard as he was coming up the little half flight of stairs outside his apartment building, and I laughed, seeing him flatten out and books spill from his arms. I almost wanted to applaud. It was a good fall, there was abandon behind it, clumsiness and grace married in the way he greeted the concrete steps with a comical shrug of surrender: afraid, startled, and then—unhurt. He knew the miracle of it, I could tell. There was no one else around, only me there, laughing. And he looked up, met my eyes, surprised by me, surprised by himself, by gravity, by the sweet solid lump of his own body, and he said:

"I'm glad you were here to see that."

And I told him that I, too, was glad. I loved him then—the way that, as a child, watching Buster Keaton fall over and over, so many times, made me feel I knew him, made me feel he was no longer a stranger.

The Longest Fall

THESE DAYS, SLEEP comes on gradually, lifting its face to mine, offering the kind of solitude that consoles—no one else there with you, your dreams so vibrantly unwitnessed.

I've dreamed of my own fall so many times. But each time is a little different, and so it's difficult to know which one is really mine.

In Prague, Nick once told me, "There are some of us who just never seem to get over how strange it is that we are here," and I knew what he meant. He wasn't talking about the city and our lack of belonging there; he was trying to get at how odd it is that our lives ask us to live them, that the world is so dense and clammy with all these lives being lived all at once.

Walking is a lot like falling—or at least like waiting for a fall. We risk that fall with every step—onto our faces, the heels of our hands. This is why our mother used to pray so unceasingly. To pray against *zlého*.

Last night, it happened. I'd been visiting Nick in the hospital, and I stopped at a bar on the way home. I drank beers one at a time, letting them coat me from the inside, like a chemical poured down a drain to break apart a clog, and then I walked the rest of the way home at two in the morning, thoroughly coated.

I stumbled and fell in the street, and the pavement scraped a layer of me away. I was all spread out, one arm reaching up above my head like those old pictures of circus girls, and I rolled onto my side, lifting my chin from the asphalt to see if anyone was around. No one. Another dream unwitnessed.

My shoe had filled up with blood, and afterward I lay in my bed and that sentence kept coming: *My shoe filled up with blood.* I thought maybe it would be with me forever, like those people who, after a head injury, will hear over and over, for the rest of their lives, a pocket-sized marching band constantly playing "The Stars and Stripes Forever."

Eventually I surrendered. I counted out a trio of sleeping pills from the bottle on my bedside table. They formed a cluster in my palm like the miniature eggs in the trees of my father's elaborate train layout. I swallowed, and the repeating sentence left, the throbbing in my chin left, the last beer-heavy faces I'd seen at the bar left. Sleep grazed me lightly all over, and in dreams, my fall was made more lovely—perfect almost, a fall that Nick could be proud of, telling me through the dense curtains of sleep: *I taught you well.*

Today, in Nick's hospital room, I lifted a corner of the Band-Aid to show Nick the carnation-shaped wound on the heel of my hand. I angled my chin like a woman trying on a hat to show him the purple cloud climbing up my throat. He whistled.

"Good thing you weren't five stories up," he said.

I told him that a Serbian flight attendant holds the record for surviving the longest fall with no parachute. Her fall was slightly over 10,000 meters after a small bomb exploded in the luggage compartment of a twin-engine jet airliner that went down near Srbská Kamenice, Czechoslovakia, in 1972. She was the sole survivor of the crash, and although she spent several days in a coma and sustained injuries to her skull, spine, ribs, legs, and pelvis, she eventually made a complete recovery except for a minor limp when she walked.

"Stop trying to steal my thunder," Nick said.

Hymnal

AS A LITTLE girl, I joined our church choir only so I could sit up in the loft and feel my voice rise into the high vaulted ceilings, then sink downward to settle like snowflakes on the hair of the congregation. I warbled, my voice doing cartwheels in the air, my own private trapeze act, while the choirmaster frowned and waved his hairy hands.

Down below, my mother's face was always turned toward me—vigilant, as if afraid I might suddenly lurch out into the arched space below that domed height, shoot through the clerestory windows like a beam of light, swing wickedly from one of the silver hanging chandeliers. She watched my mouth shape itself around the music, nervously twisting the church bulletin in her hands until the pastel-tinted paper became a pair of small, distant wings.

I sang. I sent my voice out through ripples of multicolored light: *Though the mountains may fall and the hills turn to dust, yet the love of the Lord will stand as a shelter for all who will call on His name.*

Some days, I'd watch my brother down below carefully ripping pages from the hymnal, one by one. He scratched out words with a stubby little pencil, replaced them with his own longings, rewrote the hymns until they became earthly love songs, luscious and unholy, and these he delivered to only the most beautiful of the altar boys, the one that glowed like dew.

My mother never noticed my brother's scribblings, because she was always looking up at me.

The Followers

STARTING AT THE city's center, it took Nick and me a full year to build any kind of useful map, to stop moving through the ready-made underground tunnels of the metro and find instead where the alleyways spit us out. The streets unraveled, stray threads from spools of city squares that always offered assortments of easy landmarks: the statue of a saint about to be burned alive, the ornate clockface hung with sapphire planets and gold numerals, the red awning of a cart that sold halved rolls and slim bricks of fried cheese. We learned to orient ourselves by these fragments, and eventually we no longer needed to look for them, didn't need to scan the face of the tower for the small window near the top where the head-and-shoulders outline of a man could always be seen, unmoving.

Sometimes, in the days when it was all new, Nick and I would set out, passing a flask of whiskey back and forth between us. We'd grow careless, indifferent—drowning so slowly in the city's intricacies that we scarcely noticed. We'd follow the curled lips of the streets for hours, their tugging little currents, until one of us would say, "Are you sure this is the right way?" and the other would say back,

"What do you mean? I've just been following you."

Hospital Visit

IN THE HOSPITAL, my brother and I talk about Prague. He is beautifully bandaged, snowy and clean beneath sheets that are almost as tight around him as the tucks our mother used to make in childhood.

"You look good," I tell him.

"Why are people always telling the sick and injured what they look like?" he asks.

I open a pudding cup for him and lick the foil lid clean.

The only real evidence that the fall has addled him in any way is how our conversation always seems to circle back to our Prague days—"Remember that New Year's Eve I was so drunk I thought it was the Fourth of July?" It makes me uneasy, as it borders on obsession, as if a light in his brain has come on that can't be turned off again.

"Remember? We went out on the bridge to watch the fireworks and there were so many people packed together that the press of bodies smashed our bottle of champagne?"

"Yes, Nick. Of course I remember."

Yes. The shattered green glass stuck to the wool of our coats, the sparkling wine fizzing against our legs. Yes, Nick and I—dense and solid in the midst of so many other dense and solid bodies, moving with the crowd like the slowest, thickest tide. Like oil. I could feel Nick's ribs against mine, rising and falling with breath, and on the other side of me, some stranger's ribs—also rising, also falling.

We lapped champagne from the palms of our hands, brushing flecks of glass from each other's shoulders—so drunk that we looked up into the fireworks coating our faces with a hazeled glow, the colors licking like candlelight, and I heard my brother start to sing—*Oh, say, can you see by the dawn's early light*—his voice booming stupidly out of him, reckless and even a little bit ugly. But he threw back his head and the crowd seemed to make the slimmest halo around us, stepping back from this new heat coming off him in waves. And he kept on singing right up into the droop and spin of the dangling sparks, *the rockets' red glare*, with such abandon that I loved him entirely. I loved my brother, and I knew the love I felt had something to do with home, but I was too drunk for anything to matter except what was inside that moment: the neon exploding into green that drooped like the leaves of ferns, the song and the cigarettes roughening our throats so they rang like dirty chimneys. I pulled my arm free from where it was pinned to my side between us, and I slung that arm across my brother's shoulders and I threw my voice up to meet his in the air, shrieking to be heard above the *bombs bursting in air*, singing to crack our lungs open, and we could feel the crowd hating us, these drunken loud Americans, but we didn't care, not then, not while we leaned together with our pants soaked through with champagne, too drunk, too happy, to feel the blind reach of the cold.

"That," Nick said, closing his eyes and slumping back into his pillows, "was a good night."

And I wonder if he is remembering, also, the Canadian tourists that tried to hush us, throwing their voices against ours, and Nick shouting back at them across the sea of heads, "Fuck you! Canada is America's *hat!*"—all slur, but enough to bring the Canadians wading through the crowd toward us as Nick angled for the bristle of violence, clenched and unclenched his champagne-dampened fists, his body hungry for the blow, the perfectly calculated fall that would follow—until I yanked him deeper into the tide of the crowd and, fortunately, blessedly, we were able to fade. Lost again.

In the hospital, I don't touch him. I don't want to jostle him, to see him wince behind his bruises. He has always been the beautiful one, long-lashed and silky beneath his stubble.

His left hand was crushed to pulp in the fall, pinned between him and the scrap of lawn where he landed. He lifts the other one toward me to take the pudding cup, the hand that dangled above him like a flag of flesh when the paramedics came and talked hurriedly about the best way to lift him. We know without saying it that this was the emergency we'd been waiting for—the fall that has been hanging over us our whole lives, before that even, since the moment Jiří's palms met the rough fabric of the stonemason's shirt and sent him flying out into a soft drizzle that he outpaced as he fell, faster than water.

And of course the thing I could not ask Nick, could never ask no matter how many hours or pudding cups passed between us, was whether he had meant to fall, had wanted it, had planned for it, had felt the green and gray lure of the ground rising quickly to fill his eyes and had given himself over to it.

The Great Stone Face

NICK ONCE TOLD me that Buster Keaton was the first man he'd ever loved. His idea of romance began one night when he dreamed of kissing the thin black-and-white line of Keaton's mouth, pulling back to watch him reel away into a bright backbend—like a rainbow without color.

"That makes sense," I told him, thinking of all the times that Nick and I sat close to the TV in the living room as kids, noses almost touching the screen, drinking in Keaton's constant motion. Fall after fall, each one existing without any harm, a kind of immortality building up over time. We watched Keaton's small impassive face and thought: *Maybe magic is really that easy, just takes practice, takes patience.*

To practice for the fall is like practicing for death, but smaller. Keaton knew this, I think. He must've. He was built for the fall, small as a flightless bird, a little contained world of muscle and bone.

My brother, I think, also knew this.

Keaton spent his whole life falling—down stairs, through windows. In one film, he kisses his hands to his mouth as he falls backward from a high ledge, bidding the world a cheerful adieu after his heart is struck and pierced by the sight of a girl kissing a mouth that isn't his, and then: fate intervenes in the form of a soft pile of hay that bears his weight and, just like that, he is spared. He's lost something, sure, but not the thing he thought he was losing. Not: everything.

Aunt Petra

WHEN I TELL strangers in bars about the falls, the deaths of family members, I sometimes rush through the list, bored by the sound of my own voice. The stories go all flat and pale over time like something that's been run over by a car many, many times. I don't know when it started to make me so goddamn tired, telling these stories. But they're still in me, like a yolk in an egg, and I find myself wanting to needle a tiny hole into the base of the shell and drain myself clean.

"I had an aunt," I tell them, and her story rises up through the liquor, slantwise, like daylight through a dust-grimed window. "She was attending a women's college in Virginia in the sixties, studying music—piano."

And I tell them: the music building had three floors, and on the third floor was a series of crowded rooms with nothing at all inside but a baby grand piano and, if you were lucky, a window. The building stayed unlocked at night so that the girls could go up to run scales or play the same phrase from a sonata over and over until their hands started to match up, like a jigsaw puzzle falling together. I've always imagined that the music coming from that building late at night was never sweet, never easy, but sounded somehow both frantic and tired, like someone who privately, deep down, longs for sleep but has just ingested a significant quantity of some illegal stimulant.

So this woman, my aunt Petra, was practicing there late at night, at the weird hour when one day mixes with the next and you start to feel a little lost because of it. She was up in one of those small rooms, her hands shaping to the keys, and after maybe an hour, she glimpsed a little quiver of movement at the corner of her vision. She looked up from her music and there, just beneath the window, was a puny man, maybe three feet tall, bent and leathery and goblin-like and white-haired with over-sized hands. She noticed his hands in particular, because he had them out in front of him, wriggling his fingers as if he was playing an invisible piano. She took her fingers off the keyboard, lowering her arms to her sides, and the small man did the same. She stood up from the piano bench in terror, and he straightened up to his full stature. She moved to the door and he mirrored her in this, mimicking all of her movements, his shrunken face showing her fear back to her. She shook the knob of the door and he rattled the pane of the window across the room, but she couldn't get the door open. It was jammed or locked or the knob wouldn't turn or her hands were too moist or she was just too fearful and trembling to properly work the door. At that point, her terror was so great, rattling the knob and screaming for help while the small man did the same on his side of the room, that she was ready to get out of there at any cost. So she flung herself through the closed third-story window, glass tinkling down around her, and broke both her legs in the fall. Afterward, they took her to a mental hospital where she spent the next three years, but she never saw the little man again, and she never afterward could stand to be in the same room as a piano.

And sometimes, as I talk, the strangers beside me at the bar start to get antsy. "What are you telling me?" they ask at the end.

"I'm telling you," I say, "that the world is too much for more of us than you think."

Pigeons

IN PRAGUE, NICK and I lived in an airy whitewashed apartment where the river coils back from its banks. I kept the curtainless window of my bedroom cracked during the summer months, waking some mornings to find gray feathers flurried across the floor, sometimes crustings of white and purple bird shit just beneath the sill. I swept and scrubbed. There was a dirty magic to the act of cleaning up after these visitors. Once, sifting through the feathers in the dustpan, I found a single pinion, brilliant green and shimmering.

Above Nick's desk, he'd taped a quote that he'd written out on yellow legal paper:

> *I am accompanied always by my guardian angel, my little guardian angel, because this guardian angel of mine wants me to remain in this world as yet, in order to reach the final bottom, to go down yet one more flight, to the place of the ultimate pit of despair, because the whole world hurts, and even that guardian angel of mine hurts, how many times I've felt like jumping from the fifth floor, from my apartment where every room hurts, but always at the last moment my guardian angel saves me, he pulls me back.*

These words belonged to the Czech author Bohumil Hrabal, who died in 1997 after falling from a fifth-floor hospital window. He fell while attempting to feed the pigeons gathered on his sill.

The Golden Tiger

AFTER BOHUMIL HRABAL fell to his death, his doctor made a statement saying that he had "no doubts" that Hrabal's death was intentional. A suicide.

No doubts. Not even one.

In Prague, Nick and I would sometimes end up sitting at the end of one of the long tables in a pub called the Golden Tiger that Hrabal used to frequent when he was alive. The ancient, weathered men that gathered there, sneezing into their pints, did not like to make room for us at the tables; they'd slide down the bench a mere inch and let their beer slop over onto our seats. We'd sit in their puddles and brood.

Above our heads hung a bronze cast of Hrabal's face, made directly after his death. This mask was the only decoration of any kind in the pub. It was hung on the wall close to the high ceilings, nearly twenty feet in the air—a mask with eyes gently closed, cheeks sagging into slight jowls, and the mouth turned down at the edges. Tired but serene. He looked like all the other old men who sat at the tables and drained their beers without looking at us.

My brother looked up at Hrabal's death mask, raised his glass to it. "*Na zdraví*, my good buddy," he said. Every time. Or sometimes: "Cheers, *strážný anděli*."

His Czech was better than mine. I asked him once what that meant, *strážný anděli*, and he told me. It meant "guardian angel."

Uncle Ivan

I BUY A man at the bar a shot of Jameson, and he swirls it around as if he's afraid he'll find a bug in there.

"My great-uncle Ivan," I begin, once he's swallowed the liquor, "tried to kill himself once, but it didn't work."

I tell the stranger how Ivan had crawled out a window onto a high ledge above a busy street in Chicago. The height had startled him, made him feel sick and dizzy, so instead of jumping, he decided he would roll off the ledge, as if from a bunk bed to the floor below. So with his back to the city, he lay down on his side, waiting for the moment, as if he wanted to die in his sleep.

But when Ivan tried to will himself forward and over, he felt hands pressing against his back. Afterward he told anyone who would listen: a pair of hands had kept him in place like a door in a dream held shut against some pursuer. He said the heat held him there, the weight of those two palms pressed, burning through wool to touch him. He thrashed, threw his weight against them. But eventually he gave up, defeated.

"And then what?" the stranger asks, tapping his glass with a dirty finger. "What did he do after that?"

And I tell him: "He climbed back in through the window and kept on living."

Mother and Son

I BRING THINGS to the hospital: plain chocolates that Nick and I hold on our tongues, letting them melt there so slowly it feels somehow geological.

I bring him our tattered copy of Buster Keaton's biography with its frayed dustjacket, Keaton's watery-white face like a single unblinking eye on the cover. I read aloud to Nick from the "good bits," as he calls them, those odd stories Keaton's father used to tell him about the storms that sought him out among coils of cornstalks.

I bring a deck of cards that have scenes of Prague on them. My mother had shoved the cards into the toe of my Christmas stocking one year, and as a little girl I used to spread them out across the floor, try to build the city, piece it together.

Our mother still has not come to see Nick. She still has not returned my calls. I call and leave her long rambling messages:

"He's got his color back, the doctor says there might be some damage to his spleen but there's probably no need for surgery so that's good. He's being himself mostly except for when the pain meds make him a bit loopy . . ."

I keep talking until a beep cuts me off, and the current running beneath all my words is just: *You have a son, you have a son.* This is all I know to do.

Lucifer

MY MOTHER, SO fierce in her love, would pull us into her lap to show us pictures from the massive family Bible—images so bright and liquid the ink seemed to still be drying. The edges around an illustration of Lucifer's fall were smeared and worn, his wings like black lightning bolts, an elbow crooked in front of his face as if to shield his eyes from the brightness of the earth's curve.

"You know that saying *pride goeth before a fall?*" my mother asked us, pleased to be teaching us some biblical truth, seeming to cluck and preen.

We stared at the picture. She tapped it, as if momentarily uncertain what lesson to impart. "Pride is ugly," she said. Our eyes had not left the glossy illustration. It was gorgeous. "It turns angels into devils," she told us. We listened, politely.

"That," she concluded, turning the page, sounding suddenly nervous, "is what happens when you think you know more than God."

It wasn't long afterward that the Lucifer illustration went missing, ripped from the Bible's frayed spine along a jagged edge. Days before, I had seen Nick folding up the picture into a paper airplane, sending it sailing out into the yard through the open window when he saw the handsome mailman passing by. But I said nothing, kept his secret. As always.

Cyclone

MY FATHER, so quiet in his love, seemed better able to read his audience, was more willing to pander to us. When we turned nine, our father bought us Keaton's thick hardback biography; that pale, looming face filled the dustjacket like milk in a glass. Our father used to read the book out loud to us as if it were a collection of fairy tales, bedtime stories. And then he began to embellish, to make the stories his own, to *tell* them.

We'd nestle together in a deep armchair, and Nick would make his request: "Tell us," Nick would pipe. "Tell us the one about the cyclone."

And our father would begin.

The year was 1898, and Buster was three years old. A cyclone whirred like a great engine through the town where Buster Keaton's parents were performing in a traveling vaudeville show alongside the famous escape artist Harry Houdini. The cyclone's breath reached young Buster where he slept in the upstairs room of a boardinghouse, easily puncturing the glass of the street-facing windows and lifting him through. And little Buster, waking in the arms of the storm, must've thought that he was still dreaming, since he so often dreamed of flight, the streets and treetops gray and gusty down below as he turned onto his belly to better see the world bent beneath like stalks of wheat in a gentle breeze. He moved with all the poise and pliancy of a well-made kite, recognizing other shapes that moved with him: steeples and linens and crates of chickens squawking and flapping to make him laugh. The cyclone carried him gently, finally setting him down, cautious as a new mother, in a blank field where he was found by his parents without a single bruise or scratch.

Buster's father, Joe Keaton, swore this story was true. But many were skeptical, claiming that he invented it as a publicity stunt for their vaudeville act. People wanted magic back then, paid money to get close to it. True or not, Buster grew up believing in it, being told, again and again, that he was born with luck on his side.

And anyone could see it, watching his films: Buster's body always remembering that very first flight when he'd been suspended in the cyclone, muscles poised to navigate any distance, no matter how great.

For us, these stories were closer to religion than religion ever was. Buster was our own private patron saint, our guardian angel: Prince of Pratfalls. If our mother should ever find out where our devotion really lay all those years, it would likely break her heart. But not, I suppose, any more than it's already been broken.

And through the miracle of Keaton, this is what I've come to know, to believe, the thing I always wanted to tell Nick but could never find the words for: this naked fact that disaster is so often our only path to grace.

Hloupá

IN THE HOSPITAL, Nick keeps remembering. There are some absences, blanks, and I resist filling them in for him, because, I think, I want his memories to be his own, to not be colored and weighted by mine. It was all almost a dream anyway—those years in Prague—each season like a separate sleep, every path through the city its own fall in miniature.

I'm convinced, while he drones on about our time together in Prague, propped up in his hospital bed like a limp puppet, that he's making up some of the details, inventing them on the spot. And it frightens me a little, thinking that, yes, maybe his fall *has* muddled his mind after all. But mostly I just nod.

"Oh, sure," I say. I can't deny him. Not now. I can't take any single piece of it away from him.

"Remember," he says. "It was that same New Year's Eve that the champagne bottle exploded. But earlier in the night. We were crossing the Charles Bridge toward New Town, and they'd taken down some of the statues from their plinths to have them cleaned. And you scrambled up onto one of the empty plinths and posed like a statue?"

I blink at him. Empty.

"You were very drunk," he says.

But then the memory does start to slip forward. Or maybe it is just so easy to visualize: the plinth above the bridge's stone railing wrapped in ice and my feet somehow finding just enough grip to get up on top of it; how I felt held by a giant blue palm up there, held by the lantern light flickering like winged insects across it, that light shaping everything, molding all the miniature tide pools of history into a river shape. I knelt up there. Ten feet, maybe twelve, above the heads of tourists and the tilted face of my brother. Yes. I replaced the stone body of a faceless saint with my own. I put a rigid, flattened palm to my forehead to shade my eyes as though I was looking into some greater distance, and the people scuttling across the bridge down below stopped to look up at me, at the figure of a girl stiffening into pure spectacle.

There would've been two ways to fall: forward onto the loaf-like stones at the foot of the plinth, or backward into the Vltava, water that had likely swallowed so many bodies over the years that one more would scarcely mean much. I think both falls were in me then, though I didn't think of either as something that could happen without my choosing. I didn't think of the height of the plinth or the slither of the frost beneath the worn-smooth soles of my boots as real risk until—yes that's right, I remember now—until a police officer stopped just beneath, watching me in disbelief, screaming up at me in Czech, *Jsi hloupá?* And I said something down to him so that he switched to English, and what he said then, cutting through the ice in the air, was:

"Are. You. Stupid?"

"Oh, yes, sir," I said, trying not to laugh down at him. I was drunk. Drunk and so happy because I'd never smelled the river quite so nakedly, never known the horizon quite like that. But through the blur of the liquor, I began to feel the slip of my feet, feel the pull of the river beneath me on one side, the faraway stones of the bridge on the other. The two shapes my fall could take.

"Ano, pane," I said. "Stupid, yes. Definitely."

Fuck You, Jiří

It may be stupid to dare so much, to risk yourself because some part of you refuses to believe in prophecy while another part wants to fulfill it. It gives shape to a life, even if the shape is just the space between a height and the ground. We feel our own frailty by measuring it against the frailty of others, the ones closest to us.

Nick had always been the one to keep his feet on the ground, but even so he wasn't safe. We can believe that we are well armored because so many of us survive, but did Nick get the curse out of his system when he fell, or is it still hungry for him, still unfulfilled?

What is it, even, that has borne us up over the years—these bright patches of strangeness in what would otherwise be an ordinary life?

We both wanted to see Prague, to return to the scene of our ancestor's crime, as if this could help us make sense of the shape our lives had taken. We wanted to see where it happened, sure: the exact window. We wanted to measure that height with our eyes, looking up from the ground. Then measure it again, looking down from the steeple.

But all through the city, almost every day, this feeling followed us—the feeling that, had the stonemason never been murdered, had Jiří never given in to his stupid rage, we could've been born here instead. We could have belonged here. I know it's a fiction, that whole alternate history: the years calcifying around the moment when Jiří reached a hand toward the stonemason's back, feeling the urge to send him sailing down like a leaf from a tree, feeling the urge to end him, and then letting his hand fall back to his side and turning away, returning to the life that waited for him below.

There came a day in October when Nick and I stood in that church steeple, the one where it happened, and the air was striped with a yellow light, liquid and slinky—like a rain-soaked tabby circling a lamppost. We stood up there looking out at the dusk, so softly golden, and Nick called down from the window, cupping his hands around his mouth,

"Fuck you, Jiří!"

I echoed him, sending my voice out into the gingered air: "Yeah, Jiří, you murdering piece of shit!"

A man below looked up at us, shielded his eyes with his hand just the way I had on that empty plinth when I posed like a statue. I pointed down at him.

"That guy's name is probably Jiří," I told Nick, and we both nearly fell over laughing.

Filling In the Gaps

THERE ARE PARTS of the story we still shy away from, parts we can't possibly know: for example, how the stonemason's rough hands might've fallen down the length of Jiří's daughter's naked back. She would've been sixteen or so at the time—the age when it is easiest to fall in love, the age when Nick announced to me that one day he would marry a man who looked exactly like Buster Keaton—with eyes like that, softly lidded almonds, lit up beneath with liquid sorrow.

We can fill in the gaps. We can invent their lovemaking—the stonemason twined up with my great-grandmother. The stonemason was used to handling stone, but here he was now handling a whole miniature world of such soft skin—his fall written in the lines of his palms as they moved up and down her thighs.

Maybe I am inventing too much.

I do not know what my great-grandmother wanted. I know that, in America, she married a carpenter named Paul and they had eight children together.

I do not know whether the stonemason was a good man or a bad man, whether my great-grandmother even wept for him, or who helped to carry his body home to his family.

I do not know what Jiří knew. Perhaps he felt a growing suspicion when he watched the stonemason pass by his house, hungry eyes flitting toward an upper story window, the girl's bedroom where a single oil lamp sat on the sill, flickering wetly.

I imagine that all of it was confirmed later when he saw the stonemason kneeling reverently beneath the church steeple windowsill to place a stone that this man had worked and shaped until it was as smooth as his girl's skin. I imagine Jiří watching the stonemason crouched there, and a small shard of flint appearing in the stonemason's hand, its end sharp enough to carve with. Perhaps Jiří saw the stonemason mar the block of limestone with the letters of his daughter's name, and then, holding his breath, watched the stonemason begin to deepen her name, letter by letter.

This, I suspect, was too much for him. A blinding light may have flashed behind his eyes. Jiří stepped forward just as the stonemason was standing up, his work finished for now. It was almost unwilled, like batting a fly. And perhaps afterward he knelt for a moment, running his fingertips over the shallow grooves of his daughter's name, weeping soundlessly, before finally turning away.

The Splat Calculator

THE STONEMASON'S FALL from window to courtyard was a little over a hundred feet.

In my high school physics class, our teacher, Mr. Wecker, told us that falling from a height of a hundred feet was the equivalent of getting hit by a bus going 55 miles per hour. We watched Mr. Wecker work out the math on the board, writing out the equation, showing that a man weighing 200 pounds and falling from a height of a hundred feet would spend 2.47 seconds in the air before reaching the ground. The classroom was silent while Mr. Wecker counted, "one Mississippi, two Mississippi," then clapped his hands to mark the moment of impact.

He referred to this equation as "the splat calculator."

My brother fell from a height of only fifty feet and so, according to "the splat calculator," he spent just 1.75 seconds in the air. But that is more than enough time to assemble a thought about what is happening to you.

Parroting

I WASN'T THERE when it happened so I don't know what it looked like, but I can picture it—the world tilting to meet him, the ground wavering in his eyes like lines of heat above a blacktop. The noise he heard while he was in the air: a whooshing, almost a whistle, like the passing of a train, like a cyclone forming, but also almost like no sound at all.

He hit his head on the way down, falling through tree branches that helped to slow his fall. The doctors said it was the tree that saved my brother's life; they said that perhaps, in knocking his head lightly against the trunk, he was unconscious when he hit the ground and thus rendered limp and yielding and loose.

"That is the sort of thing that can *really* make a difference in these situations," Nick's doctor said.

"Oh," I said, dumbly. "Oh, good."

In Nick's version of events, he was standing on the little balcony of his fifth-floor apartment. It was a west-facing balcony about the size of a large sofa. He saw a bright green bird land on one of the near branches of the elm tree, its feathers shimmering like melted glass. It was the type of bird that has no business flying around free in the midst of a Midwestern autumn, that doesn't belong outside a cage or pet store. The small-bodied parrot cocked its head at my brother, and Nick ran inside searching for some scrap of bread to tempt it with, to lure it back to safety. He grabbed a half-eaten glazed doughnut off the countertop and rushed back to the balcony. The bird was still there, its eye following Nick's movements, beaded and black like an ink droplet. He reached out his arm, leaning forward into the tree's limbs to offer the doughnut. The bird hopped toward it, curious, but would come no closer. Nick leaned out farther, stepping up onto the railing and cooing at the parrot, calling it "sweetheart" and "little bud." And that, I suppose, is when gravity caught him, trapped him in its net, and he thrashed his way forward, losing himself by degrees until, all at once, it was over.

I can't bring myself to tell him that I don't believe him—that it resembles the death of his favorite author to the point of absurdity, the point of suspicion. I only nod, ignore this blatant plagiarism of Hrabal.

About his attempt to lure the parrot, I tell him, "That was pretty stupid."

"Hindsight is always pretty stupid," he tells me.

"Did the parrot finally get hold of the doughnut, at least?" I want to know.

"Not at all. It was still in my hand when the ambulance got there. I offered it to the EMTs, but they said they'd already eaten."

His eyes are bright and inky as that parrot's must have been. There's something like laughter in them, but also something I can't name. I'm frightened but I will not show it. I will not.

"Nick, you were passed out when the ambulance got there," I remind him.

"Well," he says, mulling this over, "that's what I would've done if I'd been awake."

"We should get that doughnut bronzed," I say, deciding it's better to keep the joke going.

"You can send it to Mom," he says. "She can put it on the shelf with our baby shoes."

Mirror Maze

AT THE TOP of the city, on Petřín hill, there's a labyrinth made of mirrored walls. You enter at one end and are faced the entire time with the image of yourself, lost, wearing whatever you've chosen to wear that day, the little banner of red scarf around your neck.

On New Year's Day, I went alone. I watched myself, constantly tricked, thinking a passageway opened only to be greeted by smooth glass, finally maintaining the faintest touch on the surface, fingers trailing against the reflected image of fingers trying to find the maze's edges. With my shape shoulder to shoulder with me, I turned to glimpse the bend of my eyebrows, thinking: *This is what you look like when you can't find your way.*

Parking Lot

FINALLY. THE PHONE rings in my hand, and it's her, and I answer. All at once, she is there. Her voice is big, tearful. I imagine I can hear the click of rosary beads in her nervous hands.

"Where were you?" I ask, trying to make the *w*'s hard and accusatory, but they come out wobbly, wavering.

She is apologizing, and I don't know if I believe her when she says, "I'm so sorry, my angel, I was out of town all week at this craft fair in Springfield, and wouldn't you know it, I'd been driving for two hours before I realized I'd left my cell phone at home."

It has the edgeless smoothness of a lie, but perhaps she is too pious for such practiced deceit. Or perhaps she weighs the sin of her lie against the sins her son has chosen to commit in the years since we left her. True or not, I cannot forgive her absence. The phone feels hot against my ear, and I say nothing. She draws in a sharp breath between her teeth and says, curtly, "How is he?" She doesn't wait for me to answer before she adds, "I've been praying," and she doesn't pause at all before going on: "I've never stopped praying for him. You know that, right?"

I didn't know it, but I don't tell her this. I am crossing the hospital parking lot on the way to the nearest bar—my usual route—and with no warning at all, the words are suddenly there, in my mouth, fully formed and horrible:

"Mom, I think he may've tried to kill himself," I blurt out. "And I don't know what to do."

There's a long dizzying pause, then I hear my mother's tongue click against the roof of her mouth, her "that's-a-shame" noise, and I realize that I am sobbing.

I hold the phone against my ear, crying into it, standing in the middle of a parking lot while cars maneuver around me, the red sign above the emergency room swimming behind my eyes like a rise of blood. I expect her to say that she's sorry, that she's coming, that she'll be there as soon as she can. But she says none of this. She waits for my tears to quiet a little, and then she says, her voice faint as spun sugar,

"My poor little girl. You've been so very alone."

The Most Beautiful Suicide

AT MY USUAL bar, I take the empty stool next to a solitary man who is dressed like a bearded lumberjack. It takes me a moment to realize his outfit is actually a costume, catching sight of the little stuffed blue cow he holds very gently beneath his arm. It is still nearly two weeks till Halloween, but the costume parties seem to have started early this year. Holding the stuffed ox that way, he looks like a woman keeping her expensive handbag tucked close, on constant lookout for the threat of thievery.

"Somebody shrank Paul Bunyan," I say, hoping to hear what his laugh sounds like. Instead, he shows me his teeth in a neat smile and offers, without hesitation, to buy me a drink. I tell him what to order, but the bartender is already setting a glass down on the bar in front of me.

"I guess that means you're a regular," he says.

I shrug. "Not regularly sober, I suppose."

He asks me all the things he's supposed to—about what I do for a living and what part of the city I like best, and I answer, but I'm anxious to get out from under the small talk as quickly as possible. It takes three or four drinks before I feel myself hitting my storytelling stride—sentences stretching long like taffy, my voice deepening just a pitch, the honey-bright whiskey getting into my words. He seems receptive enough, and I have a feeling he'll make a good audience. For the first time today, maybe the first time this week, I feel somehow *correct*—that sweet little click of fate, the day aligning so that the lumberjack could be here to receive whatever it is I've come here to say.

It's an easy enough transition, we've gotten onto the subject of family, so I begin telling him about my distant cousin, a twenty-three-year-old bookkeeper named Evelyn Frances McHale who in 1947 took an elevator up to the 86th-floor observation platform of the Empire State Building and jumped to her death. I give him the facts: how her body landed on a car parked on the street below, and, four minutes after her fall, it so happened that a young photography student by the name of Robert Wiles was walking past and snapped a picture of her body with his Minolta Rangefinder camera.

The lumberjack orders more drinks while I take out my phone and look up the famous photograph to show him. He spends some time squinting at it, frowning as if the image were difficult to make out, or as if he needed reading glasses.

"You say she was your cousin?" he asks, not sounding skeptical, more surprised at how strange and specific the reach of family can sometimes seem.

I nod. "My third cousin twice removed," I tell him, and it is the only detail of the story I'm allowing myself to invent, not even entirely sure what "twice removed" actually means.

He looks down at the image on the screen for a long, silent minute, as if wanting to spend a little time alone with it. "She's very pretty," he says innocently. Then he looks up at me and adds in a rush, "Oh, and so are you."

I ignore his comment, tapping the phone's screen with a finger to return his attention there, telling him that the reason Ms. McHale's body appeared so undamaged by the fall—so "pretty," to use the lumberjack's own word—was that her feet hit first, the impact knocking her shoes free and tearing the delicate weave of her pantyhose. It's the only damage to her body that's evident in the photo, and since, we, the viewers, are looking at her lengthwise and head-on, the damaged feet are farthest away from us, receding into the distance—the last thing that catches our eye, almost an afterthought.

"You see," I'm telling him, "everyone remarks on the serenity of the face, how it looks as if she might wake up at any moment—stand and walk around, like an enchanted princess in a fairy tale. This is the most obvious aspect of the image—its peace."

"Sure." He nods, and I hear him mutter, almost inaudibly, under his breath: *"Rest in pieces."* It doesn't seem as if the utterance is something I'm meant to hear, so I go on.

I point out where the violence of the image resides—in what the evident force of the impact of her falling body has done to the hood of the car she landed on, the rumpled metal forming around her like the silken sheets of a deep soft bed.

At first glance, you could almost think that the sheen on the car's hood is light rippling on the surface of moving water—a modern Ophelia, grasping with a gloved hand at the white beads of her necklace. The photograph has been famously deemed "the most beautiful suicide," and it's an image that's hard to get away from. By which I mean: it is everywhere. Andy Warhol reproduced the image in one of his series prints in 1963. The picture is referenced in music videos by David Bowie, Radiohead, even Taylor Swift. The image appears on the cover of a Pearl Jam album and has been featured as the cover art of lesser-known bands such as Saccharine Trust and Machines of Loving Grace. It is an image that is returned to, again and again, in popular culture. As a society, we can't seem to take our eyes off it, I tell the lumberjack, and I'm not entirely sure what it is that everyone is trying to glean: some reassurance that a willed death can still serve as a container for beauty; an awareness that, on some level, aestheticizing death is our only real recourse against it—our only hope toward any immortalization; a promise that, yes, the thing we feared all along is just a sweet, endless sleep—I mean: *Just look how restful she is.*

The lumberjack snaps his fingers, and his face lights up a little. "*That's* where I've seen this picture before," he says, my phone resting on the bar in front of him. "Pearl Jam."

I smile. I was right about the lumberjack. He is proving to be a nice, sturdy vessel that I can pour all of this into.

I pick up my phone and find another image to show him, Andy Warhol's green-tinged rendering of the print in sixteen repeating panels—four rows of four.

"See how the Warhol prints don't rest quite so easy on the eye?" I ask him. He peers down at the fingerprint-smeared screen. Nods dutifully.

We're making good headway on the most recent round of drinks and the lumberjack is nestling in a bit closer to get a good look at my phone, his upper arm brushing mine, and I can feel the vague steady heat of him even through the flannel of his shirt, through the wool of the coat which I still have not removed, or even unbuttoned. He has positioned his soft plush Babe the Blue Ox so that it can also have a view of my phone screen, as a child might do, and I'm charmed by this. I try to think of the last time someone's arm has rested, just like this, against mine—both gentle and insistent—but no memory springs readily to mind, so I keep talking, keep telling him what I know, or think I know, about the image before us.

I tell him how, in following the spread of different exposures of the same image repeating, our gaze, at times, loses track of Evelyn's body entirely. She gets absorbed into the darkness of the car—her face, in some of the reprintings, too dark or blurred to be recognizable as a face. We lose our sense of it, of her. Her death doesn't stand up under the test of sustained *looking*. Her suicide then morphs into a kind of visual nonsense through repetition. It's comforting in a way; disturbing also.

The lumberjack stares down at the screen. He puffs out his cheeks, lets loose a long breath of air. "I see what you mean," he is saying. "I get it. But"—he takes a loud sip from his glass of whiskey and ice—"but why did she kill herself?"

I feel an odd sense of relief at his question—perhaps only because it means that I get to keep talking about the woman in the photograph, and the talk is somehow cleansing me, is creating the only white noise able to erase the sound of my own fear—and so I tell him about her life, about how Evelyn Frances McHale was the sixth of seven children born to a well-off bank examiner and his wife. Evelyn's mother, who struggled throughout her lifetime with depression, left her seven children in the care of her husband and departed the family for whereabouts unknown when Evelyn was nine years old. After high school, Evelyn enlisted in the Women's Army Corps and served throughout the war in Jefferson, Missouri. After her service was complete, her friends at the time recollected, she burned her uniform. She lit a fire and spread the uniform out across the flames as though she were laying the thing carefully out on her bed before putting it on. When asked why she did this, she answered only, "It was ugly and uncomfortable."

In 1945, I went on, Evelyn moved to New York, where she worked in Manhattan as a bookkeeper at an engraving company. It was there she met her fiancé, Barry Rhodes, a college student working toward his degree at Lafayette College, a ninety-minute train ride from the city. Evelyn rode the train back and forth many times to see Barry. Once, she took the train to serve in Barry's brother's wedding party. After the wedding was over, Evelyn tore the bridesmaid's dress from her body and burned it, just as she had her Army uniform, crying out, "I never want to see this thing again."

At this point, I pause, relishing the detail of the burning clothes. "Have you ever had that impulse?" I ask the lumberjack. "To burn clothes like that?"

"Well, no, I don't think so," he says, making a big show of being overly thoughtful about it. "But I do remember a pair of pants that I hated as a child. These stiff khaki slacks. Sometimes my mother would make me wear them to school, and once, in art class, I pretended to spill a jar of red paint all over them. It wasn't an accident, though. I hated those pants."

His story doesn't really seem to shed much light on Evelyn's habit of incineration, but I feel reassured by it anyway, its simplicity.

"Why do *you* think she burned the clothes?" I ask him.

He lifts his drink to his mouth again. "I dunno," he says casually. "Sounds to me like maybe she was crazy."

I'm disappointed by this response, disgusted even, and I almost want to abandon the whole affair. I feel drunk enough now, cleansed enough by talk, to walk myself home, but he is ordering me another drink, his arm pressing against my arm, and the story isn't yet finished. So when the bartender sets another round in front of us and the lumberjack asks me, "Well, what happened then," I go ahead and tell him.

I tell him that on the day of her death, May 1, 1947, Evelyn took the train back to New York from Easton, Pennsylvania, where she'd been visiting Barry. Barry said afterward, "When I kissed her goodbye that morning, she was happy and as normal as any girl about to be married." The wedding date was a little over a month away.

The train arrived at Penn Station around nine, and Evelyn promptly disembarked and walked across the street to the Governor Clinton Hotel, where she asked the clerk at the front desk for some stationery and a pen. She sat in the lobby writing a letter for an hour and a half, and when she was satisfied, she walked two blocks east to the Empire State Building, where she bought a ticket to the 86th-floor observation deck.

At ten-forty, a patrolman by the name of John Morrissey, who was directing traffic at the intersection of Thirty-Fourth Street and Fifth Avenue, saw a white scarf drifting down from the building's upper floors. He then watched a larger, heavier fall of white and heard the crash of impact, a noise, he said, that "sounded no different from a car accident." Evelyn had landed on the roof of a United Nations Assembly Cadillac limousine that was parked along the curb of Thirty-Fourth Street. A horrified crowd quickly gathered. Among them was Robert C. Wiles, whose documentation of the event would appear later in *Life* magazine and be included, throughout the years to come, in a wide number of photography anthologies. While considered one of the most iconic images of the twentieth century, it was the only photograph that Wiles ever published.

On the observation platform, the security guard who, at the moment Evelyn jumped, was standing a mere ten feet away from her, found a tan coat folded across the railing along with a brown makeup bag filled with family photos and a black pocketbook with the letter that she had written earlier at the Governor Clinton Hotel. In the note, Evelyn specified that she wished to be cremated so that her family members would be spared the pain of seeing her body. She wrote that her fiancé was better off without her and ended with these words: *"Tell my father, I have too many of my mother's tendencies."*

"Her one wish," I tell the lumberjack, "the only thing she asked, was not to be seen. And we, a world of onlookers, could not honor even that small request."

The lumberjack is looking at me in a patient way, as if still waiting for a punch line. "I still don't think I see *why*," he says then. "Why she killed herself, I mean."

The story I've told him suddenly feels private. And there's nothing more that needs saying. So I shrug. "Maybe it's like you said before," I tell him. "Maybe she was just crazy."

I finish my drink in one messy swallow. The lumberjack's breath has gotten heavy, his face a little slack. Drunk now.

There's a long, hefty moment where we're just there together, confused and pleased in each other's strange company.

"Look," he says. "Do you wanna go to this costume party with me or what? It's really not far."

Family Resemblance

NO, SHE WASN'T really our cousin. Although I suppose she could have been. The family is vast and widespread and we have trouble keeping track of one another. The family tree that sprawls across the opening pages of my mother's Bible is crowded with branches and crammed with illegible handwriting so that the tree looks as if it is trying to survive some kind of blight.

I remember, as kids, Nick and I finding the photograph of Evelyn's suicide in one of those *Century in Photographs* anthologies, a collection of "the most influential images of our time" that our mother used to keep on the coffee table. Many of the pictures were already so familiar to us—workmen eating lunch on a high beam, a sailor dipping down to kiss the mouth of a woman in a white dress. It was strange to think that these iconic images actually had a beginning; their familiarity made it seem, to us, as if they'd always existed. There was nothing surprising about any of them, though. It was a rainy day, a lengthy wet afternoon, and we turned the pages, bored. And then there was the photo of Evelyn, of her fall.

Nick and I looked at the image, stunned by it. We were maybe nine years old.

"Is she dead?" Nick asked in a hushed voice.

"She must be," I answered him. Neither of us could fully believe it.

I remember fixing my gaze on the gloved hand that was holding on to the pearls of her necklace. It almost looked as if she were still worrying them in her fingers, fidgeting absently, like our mother working through the beads of her rosary. And as I was having this thought, Nick said a bit raspily, "She looks just like Mom." And I saw then, with a jolt: Yes. Yes, she did.

Visitation

I CHECK THE time on my phone, and it isn't as late as I thought. Too early, even, to switch to beer. The bearded lumberjack squeezes my hand, and I nod blankly, staring down at his hand on mine.

"What do ya say?" he pretends to make the blue ox speak in a high-pitched voice.

"But I don't have a costume," I say, hearing myself slur a teensy bit.

He looks me over. It's been unseasonably cold and I'm wearing a fawn-colored coat and a blue scarf. He ties the scarf around my head and knots it in such a way that it falls down my back, leaving my ears exposed. He waves the bartender over and asks for two cocktail onions.

"Take your earrings off," he says, and I comply. He spears the onions onto the small simple silver hoops as if he is stringing a candy necklace.

"There," he says, once the stinky jewelry is affixed to my earlobes. "Girl with a Pearl Earring."

"I smell," I say, "like pickled onions."

"That's okay," he says. "I doubt you'll be the only one."

We walk together up two flights of stairs, and the closed world of the dim apartment is achy and feverish—all these strangers brushing sleeve to sleeve, trying to share some kind of glow. A couple dressed as a moth and a lightbulb pass a bottle back and forth between them, taking tidy sips, like humming-birds dipping toward a blossom.

In the corner, a single lamp is draped in purple cloth. The hostess has taped cardboard bats to the wall. At one end of the living room, a TV plays *Nosferatu* silently, for atmosphere, to remind us of the old-fashioned shapes of fear. No one really watches it.

Guests huddle in the kitchen, keeping as close as they can to the booze, the source of their shared glow. I pour gin into a plastic cup and pluck one of the onions from my ear to drop in there. It rotates toward me like a pupilless eye. I go stand beside the fridge and almost immediately lose myself. Everyone here has a bright edge, but I am all blur. A man dressed as the Phantom of the Opera ladles green punch from a hollowed-out pumpkin with care and precision, so as not to spill any on his white gloves. I am dizzy watching how slowly he moves.

I plunge back into the living room, and I see those familiar dim, placid eyes before I see anything else. Keaton. It's his face and not Nosferatu's on the TV screen now. Time must've passed. I have a strange urge to drop to my knees, immediately recog-nizing the scene. *No*, I think, *not here*, as if this should be private. I know the film well. I can tick off the seconds frame by frame like the movements of a dance. I watch the screen where a storm, a cyclone, is trembling and whirring like machinery.

Keaton is in its midst like the mast of a tiny ship. I look around, trying to catch someone's eye—the sweating astronaut, Pippi Longstocking with her wire hair, my lumberjack. Everyone is looking elsewhere. It is only me and Keaton meeting eyes through the screen, like a ghost that only I can see. He is here, I am here—this awful miracle.

I watch, and in the film, he stands stationary while the house behind him creaks in gusts of wind, the whole front wall tearing away like paper. It is both slow and quick, Buster this oblivious beacon, rubbing the back of his neck as if to demonstrate for me his frailty, and then the front wall of the house drops down around him, a solid slab like a drawbridge lowering, and an upper story window perfectly frames this lone man's intricate smallness like thread through the eye of a needle.

You can almost *see* the loudness of it, the crash of beams, the hunger of gravity like a screech, and Keaton is there—a visible patch of silence, the sound of my brother's path through the air—defiantly alive, unscathed, untouched.

The urge is strong to cross myself, just as my mother taught us—forehead to chest, touching the center, then left shoulder, right, measuring the height and depth of my body—but all motion has drained out of me. No one else is looking at the screen, but I don't know why this should shock me. Even the cameramen, when the scene was filmed in 1927, closed their eyes when that house front fell, unwilling to meet Keaton's eyes should the angles be the least bit wrong, should anything be miscalculated by even an inch. They all looked away, hiding their faces, while Keaton did not flinch, did not blink, the camera's lens the only eye to meet his.

And I see it now, my eyes going dry because my lids will not close. I see, in the midst of this defiant refusal of harm, a kind of surrender.

Wreckage

IF I HAD been in any way brave, if there was any courage left in me at all, I would've said to our mother, I would've said into the phone, moist and slipping against my cheek:

"I am *not* alone, because Nick is still here. And he is not alone because I am here. You, you are the one with nothing left."

Is she proud that she still stands, I wonder, even with the house's jagged walls pulled down around her?

In this imaginary conversation with my mother, she could easily return my honesty with cruelty. That's the danger. I could say, "I'm not alone because my brother is here, alive." And then she could say back, I can hear her voice:

"Yes, but didn't you just tell me that he tried to leave you?"

Rift

NICK AND I left for Prague at the end of a summer so milky and humid that walking felt like swimming. We were young then, fresh from college, and both of us were living at home trying to save money on rent, working a series of dumb, ugly part-time jobs and squirreling cash away.

The air was very good that summer, felt clean in spite of the humidity, and after Nick and I got off work, we'd drive out to a field at the edge of some empty farmland, coat ourselves in a film of bug spray, lie down in the grass, and make our plans. Sometimes we'd build a fire. Once, we lit off a couple of fireworks. We'd already started talking about Prague, lazily dreaming. It was in us. We'd always wanted to go. Maybe just for a month or two. Just to see it, drink it in. Climb the steps to the top of the tower. It gave purpose and shape to the slow, arduous days. Maybe if we loved it we could even stay awhile, get jobs there, teach English out of shiny textbooks. We had no other plans.

We borrowed outdated travel guides from the library. We memorized maps. We asked our mother to teach us Czech phrases, though she couldn't remember much—mainly the words for animals and food. *Holub* meant pigeon. *Pivo* meant beer. We even practiced the Lord's Prayer with her to get the shape of the words right: *Přijd' království tvé*, "Thy kingdom come," and we held those words in our mouths like shards of eggshell, while our mother beamed.

The good we felt in those days seemed inexhaustible, until abruptly it exhausted itself.

The boy's name was Alex, and he did look a little like Buster Keaton around the eyes. The word *limpid* came to mind. He was a slender, smooth-faced film student who made zombie movies with a clunky old video camera, a decade out of date. For the movies, he mixed blood from corn syrup and red food dye and occasionally there were lidded buckets sloshing in the backseat of his red Buick, sugary trickles of gore running down the sides. He lived in town beside a squat building that used to be the old train depot but was now a dingy local bar called

Sidetracks. And that's where we met him—smoking a cigarette in the alley while boxcars rattled past.

"Wanna be in my movie?" he shouted to my brother, straining to be heard above the scream of the train's whistle, the clack of its wheels. Nick beamed, already in love.

At first, Nick asked me to tag along. Maybe he wanted me to bear witness to this thing that was happening to him. And so I watched them together, Nick suddenly shy, his fingers inching toward Alex's open palm. I remember the two of them hugging a lot, playing a game of shyness, Alex turning his face away from Nick's at the last minute, delaying the kiss. They'd stand beside Alex's Buick holding each other's skinny bodies for a while, then pull apart. Nick wrote poems that he tore from his notebook and left in Alex's backseat—odd, flailing, rhythmless lines about fossils and feathers and cathedrals built of ice. I wasn't worried, though. I thought, "It's time he fell in love with someone real. Someone reachable."

Once, Nick curled up in Alex's lap like an awkwardly large cat while we all watched *Night of the Living Dead* together at Alex's apartment.

Once, the three of us went hill-hopping—an activity that consisted of driving recklessly along unpopulated backroads on the outskirts of town and getting up enough speed to lift off from the crest of a hill. If you're going fast enough when you reach the top, the vehicle's wheels will leave the ground momentarily, and for a few dizzy, weightless moments, you'll be airborne. I drove. Squeezed together in the backseat, Alex pressed against my brother, stroked my brother's hair back from his forehead while we lurched and soared and I watched them in the rearview mirror.

Eventually, I left them to it. I liked Alex well enough, but the trio didn't feel sustainable. So I stayed home with my stack of guidebooks. I tallied my earnings. I looked at flights. I didn't know quite what it all meant—Nick's romance, what new form things might take. But I told myself that I would go, even if I had to go alone.

Then, toward the end of the summer, Nick started getting sloppy, spending nights at Alex's place, driving home to our parents' house at dawn reeking of candy-sweet fake blood and foreign cologne. Not even bothering to sneak in.

"We were filming," he said by way of explanation, his voice dense with romantic excitement. "Night scenes."

I don't know exactly how we expected our mother to react when the truth finally surfaced. Maybe, we thought, she would go a little wild at first with crying and praying, her knees chafed and rug-burned, the beads of her rosary giving off a glow from the heat of her fingers. Maybe, for a week or two, she'd leave the heavy family Bible open on my brother's bedside table with passages marked, a Post-it note underneath flapping like a tongue. And then maybe there'd be a period when she and Nick would be unable to speak about what she'd surely deem my brother's "lifestyle" without erupting, and during that period my father and I would serve as their go-betweens, delivering assurances to my mother of "No, Nick doesn't *hate* you, he just wishes you would *chill*," and to my brother of "She'll come around, just give her time." Then it would all blow over, and we would have just enough time to resume our familiar shapes before Nick and I left for Prague, started our own life together. Then he could write long, amorous letters to Alex. He'd be very good at that.

But that is not what happened. It was somehow much smaller and uglier, and it happened very fast. When my brother finally told my mother where he'd been spending his nights and with whom, told her, "This is what I've been wanting all along," she shook her head slowly. She couldn't seem to finish her sentences:

"No," she started to say, "no son of mine . . ." and her speech seemed to tumble forward into a pattern of old-fashioned cliché, her eyes going narrow. "I can't have you under my roof, if you want to live like that."

Just like that. We were all shocked by her coldness, like touching your hand against a surface you didn't know was coated in ice. She didn't need to say anything more. Nick turned away, a neat, angry pirouette. My father and I were fretful and silent, hovering at the edges of the room while Nick snatched his car keys off the table and left.

Usage

OUR SPEECH IS so full of *falling*. It follows us around all day long.

We fall down laughing, fall apart, fall away. We fall prey to things. Things fall by the wayside. We fall behind, fall flat on our faces, fall back on things. We fall in line, fall from grace, fall in step, fall in love, fall on our swords. We fall out with our friends. We fall afoul of the law. Our words fall on deaf ears. We fall down dead.

We say, "Let matters fall as they may."

We say, "Things fall apart."

When the house fell down around the hapless character that Buster was portraying in the film, he did not want to die, but neither did he want to be spared. He wanted nothing at all, because he did not know that the house was falling.

Bird's-eye View

NICK DID NOT return home for three days. He told me later how he'd parked on Alex's street, sat with his hands gripping the steering wheel unable to stop shaking, even afterward when Alex held him, stroked his hair, actually said the words "There, there," as if Nick were a child in an old-timey stage play.

In Alex's apartment, they baked dense buns with jam and custard piped into the centers. They made love while they waited for the dough to rise, then made love again while the rolls baked and hardened in the oven.

Nick told Alex about our mother's rigid Catholicism, about how darkly and firmly she'd spoken the words "Not under my roof," and Alex tsk-tsked, his eyes taking on a sheen of tenderness. Nick dropped a couple of tentative hints about staying with Alex for a while, but Alex seemed to become distant and elusive then; until eventually, the buns sat steaming on their plates, and Alex said vaguely, "I just don't know if I like where this is heading. I don't like the idea of being involved with something like this."

My brother's rages were almost always directed at himself—his own failure to put a word right in a poem, to lend the correct angle to his snowbank pratfalls. Sometimes he swore at malfunctioning objects—toasters too hot or too slow. Once he dropped his reading glasses into the crack between his bed and the wall and raged while he tried to retrieve them. I was so shocked by the fury and loudness of his anger that I laughed. And then, seeing his face and sobering, I thought, "This is ugly," already becoming a prediction of uglier things to come.

I can imagine Nick's rage rearing up between him and Alex, tinting the room red like the glow from a traffic light. He told me later, putting his head in his hands, how he'd wanted to hit him, and how, instead, he'd swept Alex's kitchen table clean with his arm—the floor a sudden mess of spilled salt, white shards of plates, smears of jam in vibrant clots. They both stood looking at the mess, and Nick had knelt to scoop up some of the broken porcelain into his hand, when Alex said, "You need to go," and he went.

For the next two nights, my brother slept in his car, drove out to one of the fields where he and I used to dream our Prague dreams. Finally, his phone battery dead, the backs of his hands riddled with mosquito bites, he decided to drive home, to start the slow, unwieldy process of making peace, or, failing that, to talk over with me what to do next.

He came home well after eleven that night, but our parents were still awake, my mother agitated and sleepless, her rosary clicking like teeth inside her fist, my father keeping her company at the kitchen table while he shaped miniature boulders and green hillsides out of modeling clay.

And so when Nick came inside, closing the door gently behind him, my mother sprang up to greet him like a frantic dog, and her face was twisted, making me think of how she used to knot the church bulletin up in her nervous hands while she watched me in the choir loft. The sound of her own voice seemed to give her pain when she said, "Nickie, I'm so glad you've come back to us," thinking his presence was evidence that he'd chosen her, or God, over the new life he'd been building for himself in the sugary bloodstained backseat of Alex's Buick.

"I knew you'd come to your senses," our mother went on. "I just *knew*." Her voice sounded so false and strange, and she seemed to draw inward, away from her own words. She wavered, her eyes wild and tired—uncertain even. There was a moment when I thought she was going to drop to her knees, but instead she pressed a hand to Nick's chest, and it seemed almost to burn him; he grimaced but let her hand remain there.

"You were always such a good boy," she said then, her words pushing him into smallness, shrinking him down to boyhood, the unseen hymnal pages folded into the sleeves of his blazer. It was the sort of thing one said at the funeral of a very young person or even a dog, and Nick's face tightened in horror at the sound of her words, her sudden admission that she had never really known or seen him.

He drew away from her touch, and her arm dropped. He opened his mouth, closed it. Shook his head. Our father's hand was still poised in the act of gluing a tiny leaf to a tiny tree, waiting, rigid. My mother's face seemed somehow larger than usual, expectant, every inch of it showing strain.

"Nothing's changed, Mom," he said, as placidly as was possible for him. "I'm not here 'cause I've 'seen the error of my ways' or something like that."

Her face crumpled. "But," she said softly, leaning toward him, "I can't just stand by and watch you live in sin."

Nick bristled a little. There was a staticky sharpness in the air of the room, like the electricity that prickles the undersides of leaves before a thunderstorm. "Well, Mom," he said, his voice tense but reasonable, "I don't believe that what Alex and I have been doing is a sin."

That shook something loose in her. All at once, my mother was full of words that streamed from her mouth in a kind of rabid torrent. A memorized litany, empty and ugly, quoting scripture: *"Take care, my son, lest there be in you an evil, unbelieving heart, leading you to fall away from the living God."* She hissed like a snake: "It's an *abomination*"—perhaps the ugliest word in the English language. I'd never heard her speak this way; it was strange, foreign—as if she might be possessed by some cruel priestly ghost. She was already beginning to sob, overwhelmed by her own vitriol. *Zbav nás od zlého*, she jabbered, shaking as though she contained her own private storm, and Nick knew what the words meant, knew the darkness that her belief breathed into the final word of the prayer: *zlého*, evil.

My brother seemed to realize that to her, this was even worse than the fall she'd been dreading for him, and he hardened, weariness draining from his face, replaced by a stiff rage.

And where was I? I know I was there. But in memory, the room shrinks down, and I am hovering above it from ceiling height, as if perched like a small bird on a blade of the slowly revolving ceiling fan.

My mother couldn't see the anger building up in Nick. She kept pressing: "Why are you even here?" she asked. "Did the little deviant you were seeing get tired of you so soon?"

My brother erupted. He started shouting into our mother's face a vivid list of all that he and Alex had done together in the backseat of his Buick, all they'd done waiting for the bread to finish baking. His dick going hard in Alex's tightening grasp, then gripping hard the edge of the countertop while Alex dropped to his knees, the strain and release with the heat from the oven coating the room and an egg timer ticking the strokes in rhythm with the heavy smack of flesh against flesh. He spat it all out at her, biting the words into pieces, all the ways they touched each other. As Nick's rage crested, my mother seemed almost fueled by it, leaning forward as if waiting to receive a blow. And then the blow came:

"You'll never know that," he said. "With your candles and your rosaries. You'll never know the real grace there is in being fucked senseless."

My mother slapped him hard across the face, and Nick writhed away from her hand. There was a moment when, like a boxer, he seemed to ready himself for more violence, shifting his weight back onto his heel, coiling up with fury, his hands all knuckle, all bone, right on the brink of retaliation. My mother reached behind her, groping along the surface of the kitchen table and felling a number of my father's clay trees, her hands feeling for some small implement that might make her as strong as her son, might show him that her rage was equal to his. There was a pair of needle-nose pliers on the table that my father had been using to carefully shape and tweak his miniature landscape. The pliers had pale blue handles, I remember. She brought the weapon into the space between her body and Nick's, and the thing in her hands was no longer recognizable to any of us, like a word you say over and over until it loses its meaning. There was a pause, a hideous moment of possibility, and then Nick reached out and knocked the pliers from her grip with a ringing slap, taking a step toward her to erase the gap between them. The pliers spun and clattered, and it was in that moment my father stood up from his chair.

"That's enough!"

My father's voice, not mine—though I'd been thinking that word: *enough*. I remember its edges, soft and sharp at the same time, like the rough shape of a torn leaf. Like *zlého*. Our father stood up so fast that the kitchen chair where he'd been sitting for years and years fell over onto its side. He took a step toward them, he said my brother's name, and then he put a hand to his chest, as if he still felt the slap in there, a flutter behind his lungs.

And all the while, I watched from up high, spiraling slowly above the tops of their heads.

A Catalog of Deaths

ONE THING I'VE begun to realize: from a certain point of view, every single death contains a fall. Even if it is only the fall your upright body makes on its way to the ground.

As we say: *fall down dead.*

Even Grandpa Frank, most ordinary of men, slid heavily from the padded swivel chair in his study when his heart gave out on him.

In this way, it's easy to see the fall everywhere. Easy to find deaths that satisfy the superstition: my great-aunt Flóra, who "fell ill" quite suddenly and did not leave her bed until she died two weeks later. In her delirium, she was said to address herself by name, offering strange advice,

"Flóra, darling," she warned herself, "don't go down there."

And if death can really be compared to sleep, then wouldn't it, like sleep, be something we fall into?

In a museum of medical curiosities that Nick and I once visited, rows of skulls are displayed together in a glass case. Each skull states the person's name, age, occupation, and cause of death. My eyes scanned the skulls busily in search of falling deaths. There was only one: *Girolamo Zini, age 20. Rope-walker.* But his cause of death did not mention a fall. Rather, the card says he "died of atlanto-axial dislocation"—in other words, a broken neck. We are left to fill in the rest, to imagine his body's angle as it split the air.

Invocation Against Drowning

IN PRAGUE, SEVENTEEN bridges span the Vltava River, connecting one shore to the other. The bridge where, on New Year's Eve, I climbed up onto that frost-crusted plinth is the oldest of them all. Construction began in 1357. It's hard to believe man-made things can last this long.

The stone is dark, in some lights almost blue. The air, as you look up or down the length of the river, also goes blue in the distance where the current narrows to a blunt tip. The water is ink in any weather—a darkness that invites looking, like the pupil of an eye.

It was one of the first places we went to, or rather ended up at, following the idle procession of dawdling tourist bodies. I carried a ragged little guidebook under my arm, where it had turned damp and gluey from my sweat. I read to my brother about the city around us, trying to bring him back to the surface.

On the Charles Bridge, we stood in front of a greenish statue of a bearded man holding a cross in the crook of his arm like a baby. In his right hand he held an impossibly long gold quill, and his head was ringed behind with a gold halo, five stars strung along a hoop of gold.

"Here," I said, feeling the statue's eyes on me when I looked up from the moist book in my hands. "Right here, in 1395, the king had that guy thrown into the river." I pointed up at him.

Nick removed his sunglasses, wiped them on his sleeve, put them back on. I waited for him to ask me more about the statue, but he just stood there, hands in pockets, very still.

I told him anyway. I told him that the man had been a priest, the personal confessor to the queen of Bohemia. The king, suspecting his wife of infidelity, had commanded the priest to reveal all that she'd told him in confession, but her priest refused. "The seal of confession," he told the king, "is sacred." And so he was thrown from the bridge, tossed into the river by the king's guards under cover of darkness.

And yes, things were still sacred back then, and so legend had it that the moment the priest's body hit the water, a ring of five stars rose from the spreading ripples made by the fall—rose and kept rising, high above the city. Maybe it was still rising, the way we thought, when we were kids, the balloons we let loose could make it to some outer world.

Nick still wasn't saying anything, and so I kept on, and I realized that a handful of tourists standing behind us were listening to me read from the guidebook—a well-dressed couple had their arms linked, heads tilted attentively.

"He was sainted in 1729. Now the patron saint against calumnies, invoked against floods and drowning—"

"Isn't that fucked up?" Nick broke in. "You're murdered and then it's your job once you've drowned to protect everyone else from drowning?"

I moved a step closer to him, closing the gap, but his voice rose a pitch higher. "They put up a goddamn statue of you, and isn't that just a way of sentimentalizing injustice?"

I could feel the tourists behind us stiffening a little. "I'd be *pissed* if I was this guy," Nick said. "Five stars? Five fucking stars rising up into fucking heaven—just sprinkle a little magic on it, and then the last moment of your life gets to be *such a pretty little story.*"

He took a small silver flask from the inner pocket of his jean jacket, and it sloshed while he unscrewed the cap. *Oh,* I thought, surprised that he'd kept the drinking private, wanted it only for himself. That was something new.

I thought I understood Nick's anger, but then I thought of our own family legend, how someone at some point had offered up the strange and chilling detail that the stonemason's body hadn't bled after the fall. *Not a drop,* all the aunts and uncles had said. And I wanted to tell Nick that maybe it wasn't wrong to want things to be holy. But his anger still hadn't burned itself out.

"Who was even here to count those five stars?" he went on, taking a swallow of the liquor. It smelled a little like rancid plums, and how had I not heard it until now—the slur in his voice? "Can you just promise me one thing, sis, I'm serious: when I die, don't you dare let them call it a miracle."

I put a hand on his arm, leaning into him, the crescent of tourists shifting uncomfortably behind us. "Nick," I said, speaking directly into the small dark space of his ear, trying to make my voice soothing. "Nick, it's just a story."

History Lesson

THESE ARE THE facts. I've been keeping track, running through them, because I think some part of me believes it's my task, my duty, to make sense of these things.

1. It was October 4, 1895, when Buster Keaton was born in a dried-up nowhere town called Piqua, Kansas.
2. Keaton shares a birthday with the Russian poet Sergei Yesenin, also born October 4, 1895. Same day, same year. Yesenin was a favorite poet of Bohumil Hrabal's, and, alongside Hrabal's prose, lines from Yesenin's poetry written out on yellow paper covered the wall above my brother's desk in our Prague apartment, these lines among them:

   Home shall I go again,
   delight in others' happy health,
   then in the green dusk beneath the window
   go and hang myself . . .

3. Although historians believe that Saint John of Nepomuk was most likely tossed from the Charles Bridge in late March of 1395, a five hundredth anniversary celebration of the saint took place on October 4, 1895, when the current statue was erected at the west end of the bridge.
4. We lost track of the exact date over the years, but we do know that the day Jiří pushed the stonemason out the window was in the autumn, quite likely in early October, of 1895. There don't seem to be any newspaper articles

about the event, possibly because Jiří paid to keep his name out of the press, or possibly because the church he was renovating made efforts to cover it up, or possibly—probably—because in those days the death of a Roma laborer was hardly considered news, even if it was a murder. The only way to verify the date would be to track down the death certificate, and no one, not one member of my family going back to Jiří, has bothered to remember the stonemason's name. Perhaps (I am forced to consider the possibility), perhaps it never happened at all. Perhaps it is, as my mother always insisted, "only a story."

5. It was October 5 when my brother fell, leaning out over the railing to offer a scrap of something to the branches. He waited a day, or maybe miscalculated, mistaking the date. Either way, perhaps the date was built into him all along, into the calendar that is our body—how we, by being born, by being here, can hold time, its imprint, pressed like a coin into clay.

Am I an idiot for thinking these convergences could, in themselves, mean something? Or am I an idiot for not realizing that there is definitely some meaning here? And which idiocy is more dangerous?

Another Version

SOME MEMBERS OF the family have been known to suggest that when Jiří fled to America with his family, my great-grandmother was beginning to fill out softly around the middle, a slight swelling pressing the buttons of her brown travel jacket. They say that really we are not descended from Paul the carpenter at all (*sweet, steady, simple Paul,* they say), but rather from the Roma stonemason, that we carry his death with us because our blood refuses to forget the injustice of it, not because, as others wanted to claim, his surviving family members put some kind of vengeful curse on our clan.

"There is always more than one version of things," our great-grandmother Agáta used to say to our mother, and our mother would nod, pretending this was profound.

Another thing she used to say: *"Nemůžete si vybrat svoji krev."* In English: *You cannot choose your blood.*

If I could choose, I would choose the stonemason over Paul, the sweet, steady, simple Midwestern carpenter. I would choose to think of the fall as something that remains in us not as a curse, but rather as the stamp of something that happened, that somehow persists because stories are meant to persist. It would be a way to keep hold of him, clinging to this memory that none of us could recall—a memory contoured by all the lives and deaths that came after—the stonemason, like all of us, like anyone, resisting his own death by passing it on.

Big Bang

MAYBE IT ALL goes back farther than we think. The world is old. Sure, maybe not old in the greatest, grandest scheme of things. Maybe not as old as the universe. And this, our current universe, is maybe not as old as the one that came before it—the one that collapsed like a pair of lungs expelling breath, squeezing everything down to the size of an atom, and then, *in the beginning*, breathed in deep again, filling the lungs back up and pushing everything outward.

Can it even be considered a view, when the thing you're looking at is too small to be seen? Or too large?

Is the belief that a single atom sprang into *everything* really less strange than the things my mother believes? Is it really so much more plausible than the idea that a man pushed another man from a high window, and we, his bloodline, must fall and keep falling, through the years? I don't know.

Here's what I do know: I know that, in telling this story, I've left my father there, stranded in the moment of his shouting "Enough!" while he crossed the kitchen toward his wife and son. I know I've left him poised, midstride, hanging in that moment between the lungs squeezing down and filling back up. He begins to fall, but has not yet fully fallen. He's still suspended there, cushioned by the air around him, while I look on, while I remember, while I stagger across the living room at the costume party blind drunk with a single cocktail onion still wet and putrid against my left earlobe.

I leave him there, because that is the only way to keep him alive.

Canyon

I TRY TO leave the party. There's nothing there for me after Keaton has come and gone, after I've drained my plastic cup of gin. But at the door, the lumberjack stops me, puts a hand on my arm.

"Are you leaving?" he asks, and I can't really tell, beneath the noise of the party, whether his voice is gruff or sorrowful.

"Maybe I just need some air," I say, by way of appeasement, and he follows me down the stairs to the little courtyard where I take a pair of cigarettes out of my bag and light them both together. He is handsome in his plaid flannel with one suspender beginning to drift down the breadth of his shoulder, blowing smoke from his nostrils in a dragon-like way. But there is something about his face I don't like—a hunger behind the beard, a resentment toward all that stands between him and the things he wants. I understand this look, but that does not make it a pretty sight.

The nicotine sends me spinning, the air a funnel touching down on me, and I can feel my drunkenness showing on my face. He sees it instantly and latches hold: "Should I help you get home?" he asks.

"That won't be necessary, thank you," I say, speaking like a character from a Jane Austen novel in an attempt to feign sobriety. It is all laid plain—my body drifting free from me, and the suspicion that maybe it doesn't matter if the lumberjack follows me back to my apartment; maybe it doesn't matter if I let him undress me while the room spins bright as a carnival above us. This is exactly what large quantities of gin always do to me—replace resistance with indifference. But what, I sometimes wonder, can change indifference into wanting? Whiskey, perhaps, or a couple of deep glasses of red wine.

I have been here before—this moment when the body, *my* body, seems to reach beyond itself, to catch the notice of others, stirring up some stranger's hunger. It has happened a number of times, but it still somehow never manages to feel familiar.

The lumberjack watches me, trying to read whether I am the right kind of drunk—loose and pliant but not messy or sick. There is, at times, a fine line between these states, and he knows this. I can see it—the knowledge of many sloppy, disorganized fumblings. He grabs my wrist, but not forcefully, and pulls me toward him in a way that might fool me into thinking he is asking permission. I fall against him awkwardly and he is trying to kiss me even while my mouth is laughing at my own clumsiness. The kiss doesn't really happen, a brush of hot faces—a near miss for both of us, my head turning away so that I can belch, as politely as possible, without his beard getting in the way.

"It was that cocktail onion," I say, and even my laughter seems to slur. "I ate it, you see."

I show him where one of the onions is missing from my earring. And what he does then surprises me. He turns my head a little roughly and puts his mouth to my ear, takes the remaining onion into his mouth, bites it free from the earring like a berry from a branch. He breathes hard into my ear, a shocking force of breath like the slap of air from an open car window, his wet mouth and the wet hair around his lips sucking at my earlobe. The heat of him makes me tired, and I know what it would mean to slump and surrender, but there is little to be gained from it other than the heat itself. I would rather be alone with my triad of sleeping pills, to sleep and sleep and wake in the privacy of sheets damp with my sweat and mine alone. I push against him then, but too hard, and fall back onto the stone of the courtyard. I laugh heartily because many of my best pratfalls occur when I'm drunk, and I am pleased with this one.

"You know," I tell him blearily from the ground, "every year a number of couples fall into the Grand Canyon while kissing."

"Is that true?" he asks, offering a hand to help me up. I ignore it, enjoying the view of his damp face better from this angle.

I shrug. "I don't know," I tell him truthfully. "But it seems likely, doesn't it?"

He lifts me off the ground and I feel almost grateful to him for how momentarily weightless he makes me feel. "Well," he says. "Lucky for you we weren't standing next to the Grand Canyon."

Is that luck? I wonder, while he puts his mouth on my neck like the images of Nosferatu we'd seen earlier projected on the living room wall. I even think for an instant he is going to bite me, but he keeps his mouth soft, like a hunting dog retrieving a bird. His beard smells of onion and salt and cheese that's been sitting out on a countertop during a long warm afternoon.

"Let's go somewhere we can be alone," he says, even though we are already alone in the courtyard, and despite the alcohol, that solitude begins to strike me as something frightening.

"Let's go back up to the party," I counter, but his hands are already finding the openings in my clothes, mapping buttons, beltloops. "Please stop," I say, my voice a small thing, a pebble, but he does not stop. My fear at the movement of his hands is more like a memory of fear, and I feel a flash of longing for full sobriety, as if all this could disappear if only the alcohol were flushed from my veins. He is saying something, the words blurred with his mouth that close to my ear, but I think I recognize: "You want it, you know you do." And I use my father's word then, nearly the last word he ever uttered in life. I say *"Enough,"* pushing hard against the lumberjack's chest. I break free of him, which does feel like luck, and, all woozy and fogged from the gin, I try to find the street with my eyes, the sidewalk, doing my best to trust my feet. There is already distance between us, I can feel it opening up, a little margin of safety, and I call back to him, from the far side of that canyon,

"Believe me, if I wanted to fuck you, I would fuck you."

It's a voice unlike my own—the voice of the gin speaking loudly and bluntly on my behalf, and I feel a rush of gratitude, as if the liquor were delivering me from this after all. *How can we even tell,* I am wondering hazily, *what will save us and what will push us further into danger?*

The lumberjack still could easily follow, I realize. It isn't yet a real escape. But he doesn't follow, and that is lucky too. "You're too drunk to know what you want," he calls to my back, and I wonder blearily on the way home how it is possible that, with all the risk—the climbs, the stumbles, the ledges—how is it that I continue, against the odds, to persist in safety?

Morena

BACK IN MY apartment, I drop a bottle of wine and, all at once, its shatter is everywhere, its smell. A little dark red river chases its way over the kitchen floor, and I move chairs out of its way rather than wipe it up, wanting to see how it follows the grooves of the tiles, keeping my feet away from it so I won't disturb its path. Such a slow, slow thing—a chase going at a snail's pace, the wine moving like a sleepwalker. I am drowsy looking at it, thinking sleepily of warm rooms in Prague, in winter, how the radiators pinged and rattled like undersized ships.

There was a part of the city, a little maze of cobbles and shops, where the streets seemed to clatter together at random, like bits of rock falling from the back of a truck. The streets were the color of honey drawn from a red flower. At Christmastime, the squares would offer themselves up to you even if you had no money to spend in the shops. In one of the squares there was a skating rink where a heavy man in a dark coat could always be seen struggling over the ice, the blades of his skates making jagged, punctuated lines, like dashes of Morse code. Sometimes the streets emptying into the squares would be blocked off with sawhorses, and people would clump up against them, watching a movie crew set up their cameras, watching the woman in her dark red dress move slowly, so slowly, across the square toward the cameras, pretending to look lost.

In open-air markets, there were rings of dough laced with cinnamon, baked slowly over a flame on rotating metal spindles. There were silty gold bottles of medovukha, a cheap kind of mead that tasted like old bread and nectar from honeysuckle blossoms. There were eggs, elaborately painted with minuscule nativity scenes. There were the black bodies of fish, live carp turning in their tanks like jointless elbows.

I used to walk there and think "I've been here before," realizing with a weird jolt of recognition that the streets in that neighborhood reminded me of the little winter village my father constructed each year inside the ring of train tracks that surrounded our Christmas tree—little market, little skating rink, little shops with snow on the windowsills. As if he knew that one day I would find the world he had made, find the life-size version of his handiwork, after he was gone.

It was on one of those bent streets near the market and skating rink that a woman named Morena lived on the fourth floor of an orange-roofed building. During that last winter before Nick and I went back to America, I went to Morena's apartment every week, sometimes twice a week: up the stairs, the elevator never working, the hallway always cold, though I'd be warm by the time I arrived, by the time she opened the door to let light out into the hall like fireflies escaping from a jar.

Morena was Italian. Her hair looped and curled and looked sometimes edible, like shavings of darkest chocolate framing her face. She was small—five feet tall, sliding over her floorboards in small stocking feet, her hands the size of a child's—but her voice boomed, operatic, rising up to the high ceilings like audible smoke. She was maybe a decade older than me, had lived in Prague just over a year. I didn't like the word "expat" in those days, but it was nice when she said it, the crisp waferiness of the *ex* pushed toward her teeth and then *pat* quickening like butter melting fast. Morena traveled a lot to see her boyfriend, a handsome thick-chested Scandinavian who was living temporarily in Amsterdam at the time, but she had a cat who needed a lot of looking after, a slick little seal-gray shorthair named Diego who, due to a spinal injury when he was young, was unable to urinate without assistance. His injury had affected the nerves controlling his bladder, and so he had to be "squeezed," as Morena put it, twice a day. Like a lemon.

Morena had put up a flier at a little British-owned café to advertise for a cat-sitter, and I'd called, trying in those days to make money wherever I could.

"It may take a while for you to get the knack of it," she told me over the phone. "The squeezing—it's tricky."

It was exactly that—this small mystery, my hands seeking through the cat's fur for that bulb of fullness. When I found it and gently pressed, the little balloon slipped and flitted away from my clumsy hands, and Diego began to squirm against me.

"Here," Morena said that first time, and many times after. "Let me show you."

Together we felt along the cat's belly, her hand over mine. I watched her fingers find that small sac so easily. She guided my hands to it. We moved slowly, and the cat began to purr a little, tentatively.

"There, you feel it?" Yes, a soft bulge full of liquid. I felt it.

But without her hand guiding mine, I could never seem to get it right, not even after weeks of trying, kneeling many more times with Morena beside the litterbox. Each time, she showed me again with infinite patience how to grip the cat, where to press. Then she'd take her hands away from mine, and I'd fail. The angle or the pressure would be wrong, maybe off by only the smallest increment, but still: nothing. I'd try to do just as she said, try to feel the weight of her fingers against mine, bringing my thumb and forefinger together, but always: nothing. I'd shake my head.

"You'll get it," Morena would say every time. "You'll get it soon."

After each of my failures, she'd take the cat from me, squeeze with the magic softness of her small hands, and a gentle stream would leave the cat where she held him above his litter. And then the relieved cat would wander off to resume his cat life, freshly emptied, and she would command me, "Stay and have a coffee with me," and I would.

She had a little silver Bialetti stovetop coffeepot, and the apartment would fill to the brim with the smell of good, strong, rich Italian espresso. We'd sit on her sofa and talk while it brewed. She'd play records, flitting across the room to lift the needle and start a favorite song over. She sang without fear, taught me the words and laughed at the knots the Italian would make in my mouth. When the coffee was ready, she'd open one of the tall, wide living room windows and the air with its rumors of snow would move against us. Then we'd sit on the sill and smoke her sharp, bold European cigarettes and blow smoke out over the peaks of rust-colored roofs. The smoke was spicy in our mouths, and the coffee made my blood seem visible in my veins, glowing faintly blue. We'd get gradually more wired, more chatty, more intense, Morena's hands moving, waving like a conductor's, forming the air into soft slopes, as if she was packing freshly fallen snow into round shapes.

We talked. A long, unbroken stream of talk coming from us like ticker tape. We talked about the foods from back home that we pined for the most—ranch dressing and pumpkin pie for me, zeppole and her grandmother's limoncello for her. We talked about the cartoons we grew up watching. She told me about a show called *La Linea* she loved when she was a kid. "So simple it was almost not anything at all," she said about it. In the cartoon, Mr. Linea exists as a plain silhouette, formed from a single endless white line that unspools from his feet. As he follows the line's path, he encounters a series of obstacles, turning always to the cartoonist, his creator, whose hand will appear holding a white grease pencil to trace a solution for him. Often, he'll reach an abrupt end of the line and start to fall forward into oblivion, and the cartoonist will draw a net to catch him, a pillow to land on, a ladder to climb back out of the hole. After his rescue, Mr. Linea is rarely grateful—he shakes his little fist at his creator and chatters on in a string of mock-Milanese gibberish.

I loved this. I told her about Keaton's obsession with cyclones, about Nick's and my obsession with Keaton. We watched the clip of the house falling down around him and she did not look away. Sometimes, we'd let Keaton films or episodes of *La Linea* play on Morena's computer while we talked, and I told her about the family superstition, about Jiří and the stonemason, about all the relations who'd died or hurt themselves falling, about a cousin of my mother's, a lawyer who worked in one of the big high-rises in downtown Toronto. He had a reputation as a prankster, fond of giving new employees a scare by throwing himself bodily against the shatterproof glass wall of the 24th-floor conference room. The thick, unbreakable glass wall always held his weight, and the victims of the prank would swallow their shrieks and he would chuckle at his desk for the rest of the day. But one day he performed his trick for a group of visiting law students, getting a running start and tossing himself against the glass like a stunt double in a movie. Just like all the other times, the glass did not break, but the outer metal framework bent and gave way, forcing the entire intact window from its frame with a tremendous creak, and he fell to his death.

Morena did not ask, "Why are you telling me this?" Instead, she nodded solemnly. Then she cleared her throat and started telling a story of her own:

"Once I was walking along with my brother, and—you know those metal doors you'll sometimes see in the sidewalk, they lead down into cellars below shops? Do those have a name in English?"

"A hatch, maybe?"

"Okay, sure, a hatch. Well, my brother walked right out onto the doors of the hatch, and I told him, 'Aren't you ever afraid that one day those doors might not hold you and you'll fall down into the basement?' And he stood there, stood right on the . . ."—she brought her hands together like doors meeting—". . . the seam? And he bounced on his feet and I yelled at him to stop. And right then, an old, a *very* old woman was passing by, and she said to him, to my brother, she said, 'I fell down through a pair of those doors once.' My brother stopped bouncing and looked at her. 'How far did you fall?' he asked. 'How deep was the hole?' And she looked at him right in the eyes and she said, 'Deeper than you can imagine.' And right then the doors made a creaking noise and he jumped about a meter into the air." Morena laughed. "I thought he was going to piss himself."

I laughed with her, looking at her with a kind of grateful wonder. I loved that her story seemed to match me, match my life and the stories I told, but was different too, a separate language for the things I loved. I felt then how easy it all was— easy to find places to belong in, spaces where I could be separate from Nick but wouldn't betray him by relishing that separateness—worlds that could be mine, but also just the slightest bit his *because* they were mine.

We laughed together, Morena and I, and for the first time I really felt I understood the ease of leaning forward, how simple it might feel to merely loosen your grip, let your footing slide and falter just a little, just enough—the ease of giving in. I felt how easy it had been for Nick to love Alex, for our father to love our mother, for the stonemason to love Jiří's daughter, for Keaton to love the cyclone, for Morena to love all the things that Morena loved.

We sat on the ledge of her window, four stories above the street, and she did not ask me, "Are you afraid?" She did not say, "Aren't you scared to sit here in the window with our legs dangling out against the side of the building, because of the ways that history can repeat itself, over and over?" I almost wanted her to ask me that, because I'd started to rehearse in my mind what I would do in response to her question. It was a stupid little plan: I had started to think that maybe, when she asked me if I was scared, I'd lean out from the windowsill, lean out as far as I could into the air above the orange rooftops and the street paved with stones the color of a creek bed. I'd have to find that moment before gravity could grab me, rip me free like a Band-Aid, but I'd have to lean out far enough that Morena would cry out, the way she had for her brother above the cellar doors. She'd grab my arm to pull me back into the warmth of the room, to the safety of the floors and ceilings and coffee cups, and right then, when she reached for me, in the moment when the danger had passed but the safety had not quite fully sunk in, it would be right then that I'd brush my lips against hers—just quick, just once, just to see.

But she never did ask me. And, much like the elusive knack of squeezing the cat correctly, it just never happened. Strange—how the near-falls are never mapped. The almosts. They add up, though. I know they do.

I thought about it a lot afterward. I knew that kissing Morena would've been the right kind of fall. Would've counted somehow, felt brave at least. But something in me still gripped the safety of the ledge. And I couldn't loosen my hold. Not even that night toward the end when we sat together in the window with the cold rising up from the street to push against the soles of our shoes, and she told me,

"I think my boyfriend is going to propose soon."

She dragged hard on her cigarette and I waited. "Probably at Christmas," she said, her voice drier, emptier than usual.

"If he proposes, I'm not sure what I'll say," she said, looking sharply at the side of my face, as if waiting for me to turn, to look at her, to make some sign or utter some word.

But I didn't turn. I couldn't. Instead, I kept very still, like an animal in sparse brush waiting for a hawk to pass over. She turned away, exhaled her smoke, and I knew it was over.

"Oh well," she said, sighing and laughing a little at herself. "He's a good man. Maybe that'll be enough in the long run."

I said nothing. I nodded, trying to make a show of listening to her while keeping as still and silent as possible. The smoke from our cigarettes drifted up in parallel streams that met and twisted above the sherbet-colored tile roofs. I realized then that I'd never really tried to grasp all this—the long talks, the coffee and cigarettes, the stories, songs, cartoons. It had all seemed so very simple and natural until now, as generosity so often does. I think a part of me had assumed that this was just Morena, this was just how she was with everyone, playing hostess, sometimes even inviting the young Czech mailman in for a coffee. But maybe she'd sensed how alone I felt in spite of having Nick, or *because* of having him. Maybe she knew what that loneliness was and how to share it.

But in the end, I was silent. In the end, the little girl who'd longed so much of her life for the high arcs of trapezes, the plunge and spiral of a biplane in free fall, the body knifing downward from the high-dive platform, had turned away, afraid.

It was almost Christmas. Morena was planning to go home to Italy over the holidays, and still my hands had not learned how to squeeze the cat's bladder. "It's okay," she told me. "Don't worry. There's a vet I know who can do it. You would just be cheaper," she said, winking at me. Maybe a part of me thought that if I *did* learn, all this would end, we would no longer see each other; that Morena would just leave the key under the mat for me, leave a tattered pile of bills in an envelope with my name on it when she went to visit her boyfriend. The apartment would be empty, but full of her smell. She would find a couple of my hairs afterward on her sofa cushions, the bottom of the coffee pot a little scorched. The idea saddened me.

But even so, I tried. I tried to hold my hands like hers. I felt my way through the cat's fur. Eventually the cat kept entirely still, used to me by then, but sometimes he'd protest very gently in his throat if I fumbled and squeezed too hard.

"Am I hurting him?" I'd ask Morena.

"No, no," she'd say. "He knows. He knows you are here to help him."

These bodies—such strange and foreign things—hers, the cat's, mine. We brushed together—the three of us. We learned our configurations, our silences, and then I guess something shifted, some window frame loosened as we flung ourselves against it, and all at once, we had nothing left to offer each other.

There was one night, separate from the rest because the hour got later than usual, because I'd gotten closer than I'd ever come to squeezing Diego's bladder correctly, when I told her that I was afraid for Nick, for his silences, for the dark threatening lines of poetry he was always tacking up in his room.

"My brother isn't happy," I finally said aloud, for the first time.

"Yes," she said, nodding, as she leaned forward to set her coffee cup down on an ottoman, her hands so certain of their movement, so wise. "Yes, that is worrying. But even more worrying is the possibility that you are making his unhappiness your own. That one is turning into the other. Do you know what I mean?"

I knew. I told her: yes. I knew. But I couldn't tell her: there was no other way. No other way that I could see. He was—he *is*—my twin.

That night—a shivery, moon-bright night in late December, when I walked home through the cold streets—I didn't once think: *Maybe that was the last time.* But then—it was.

It wasn't Nick's fault, my drift from her. I would never blame him. I blame only that I didn't seem to have room at the time to love and worry over my brother while giving whatever was left over to someone else. I was both too full and not full enough. Like the bladder waiting to be squeezed, without its own power to press the liquid free.

Blackout

SOME NIGHTS NICK came home at three in the morning, and the rattle and bang of the elevator door out in the hallway would pull me from sleep, fearful and sputtering.

It was an old-fashioned elevator. Prague was full of them. A narrow clouded glass door would open, frosted over like bathroom windows so you could see only a glow of light in there, the blurred outline of a human figure, but not much else. Sometimes the elevator would be elsewhere when you opened the door, an empty shaft stretching up and down, and you'd have to press the worn and oily button before it would send itself to you. If you weren't careful with the door, it could swing free and bang against the wall, and many nights this was how I knew Nick had come back to me.

We were on the top floor—the only apartment in the building with both east- and west-facing balconies. Some days Nick would be on one balcony while I was on the other, watching both horizons like a pair of sentries. Other days, we'd move together from one to the other as the sun moved, soaking up or avoiding the light depending on the season. We had no living room or common area—just a shallow entryway opening onto the two bedrooms on one side and the kitchen on the other with the bathroom in between. And so, when it became too cold or too hot for the balconies, we sat at the kitchen table and talked. We drank dark beers and made toddies with plum brandy and fruit tea. We drank cheap box wine you could buy in the markets for a mere 25 crowns—the cardboard containers looking like oversized juice boxes with bunches of grapes decorating the packaging so you knew what it was even if you didn't speak the language, like medieval signs hanging above inns and apothecaries. We drank syrupy liqueurs mixed with soda or tonic water. Drinking together felt right because it meant that, regardless of what that day or week had been like, we were, at that moment, sharing in the same grief or joy.

But I knew there was a lot of drinking that Nick did on his own—or with people I never met. Men he slept with, tourists he met in bars or bookshops. And I felt an odd jealousy, not that he spent his nights elsewhere, but that the booze wasn't something special or sacred to us, that it took on different patterns for him, granted different permissions.

I remember some mornings, after a late homecoming, we'd drink our coffee and his face would be turned slightly away, as if drawn toward heat. Some days my eyes would light on a bruise that I couldn't quite tell from shadow. I might let my hand hover there, not touching, above a band of faintly purple skin.

"Where did this come from?" I would ask, as if it had found him—an insect that rode home with him on the lapel of his jacket.

"I fell," he'd say flippantly, shaking me off although I hadn't touched him.

"You fell. Where?"

"Onto the side of my face," he'd quip, and if he didn't want to share his fall with me, I couldn't force it. At first I didn't bother to worry much, because he'd always been so good at falling. I'd seen his balance and pliancy so many times. But of course, when you've trained yourself to see only one kind of danger, you forget there are others.

"You should see the sidewalk, though," he might add. "I fucked it up good."

In winter, the patches of a beard began to appear. It covered swollen lips, scabbed chin—a map of all that was happening to him when I wasn't there to see it.

It was icy that year, and we skated whenever we moved. There were days, coming up from the metro and climbing a shallow hill, when I'd go down hard, roll over onto my side laughing, and passersby would keep their faces tight and secretive. I wanted them to laugh with me, to say something familiar and wholesome and Midwestern like, "Goodness, you really took a tumble, didn't you?" But slipping on ice-slick pavement is a private thing in Prague. No hand was ever offered to help me up, and sometimes, pretending the fall was invisible felt like the right response. Other times I rolled and cackled and flailed and would've done anything to have a single ragged soul ask, "Jesus, are you all right?"

So for a while I assumed this was what Nick was experiencing in his own comings and goings through the city—these slick topplings that Prague turned a blind eye toward.

But I knew there were men, even if he never brought anyone to our apartment. I could smell their cologne on his clothes, different shades of scent, of soap and sweat and sugar and salt, an inventory of all the ways a man could smell.

It was his world, closed off from mine, where his grief moved differently through him, where the drinking could act as a kind of bloodletting, where he could seek the easy collisions of knocking against others, or letting others knock against him. I couldn't picture it and he offered no descriptions. It was a blank space between us, and like the Czech passersby who chose not to acknowledge the icy flailings of others, I pretended not to see it.

Some mornings, his knuckles were raw and open. "What happened?" I might ask.

He'd look at me, eyes awash with a shamed panic. "I don't remember," he told me. And I had no way of reassuring him, of asking after nights that he'd let slip from him.

I could see that he was choosing a kind of erasure. He was pushing his mind toward a place where it could drift and descend. This is one of the many dark powers we hold over ourselves, I knew, but there was little I could do to intervene— except to keep finding the bruises, even beneath his beard, to keep asking him, "Nick, what happened?"

And for him to keep looking me square in the eyes, to tell me again that lie, "I fell."

Rise

IN MY DREAMS lately: the opposite of falling. I rise from the pavement so slowly I don't notice at first. Then I do notice, and, like a cartoon character who's become aware that the cliff's edge has dropped away beneath him, I start to sink again. I put a foot to the earth, and as soon as I touch it, up I go again.

The air is water I can part with my arms. I am so buoyant, lifted on the crest of a wave of wind. I start off down the road that leads from my parents' old house, the house where Nick and I grew up. I turn to follow the winding blacktop, on my way into town, and there are no other cars, no other bodies, just me, weightless. I am bouncing very slowly, setting a foot down on the road and then rising up high, higher than the trees, before softly floating back down like milkweed. I touch another foot down flat, and shove off like a swimmer in a pool. I move forward in huge sloping arcs. Rising, falling, rising, falling. All the way into town.

On the way, all the familiar landmarks are there—the boarded-up gas station, the bait shop, the storage shed, the blank field that floods every year; the weird squat house that has a slim curve of pond arced around it like a moat and is said to be haunted. It is all there, just as it has always been. The only difference, in the dream, is the slow rise of me, the drift.

The Bottle of Wine I Dropped Several Hours Ago

THE SPILLED WINE, in case you were wondering, has pooled beneath the stove. Its smell will return, heavy as a brick dropped through glass, whenever I turn the oven on.

Eutychus

MY MOTHER CALLS again while I'm home, and I let it go to voicemail. I leave the phone on the counter while I go out to get a bottle of wine to replace the one I broke. I drink two-thirds of the new bottle and then listen to the voicemail. Her voice is in my ear, reading from the Bible just as she's done so many times before. With no introduction or explanation, she launches into the following passage:

> Now on the first day of the week, when the disciples came together to break bread, Paul, ready to depart the next day, spoke to them and continued his message until midnight. There were many lamps in the upper room where they were gathered together. And in a window sat a certain young man named Eutychus, who was sinking into a deep sleep. He was overcome by sleep; and as Paul continued speaking, he fell down from the third story and was taken up dead. But Paul went down, fell on him, and embracing him said, "Do not trouble yourselves, for his life is in him." Now when he had come up, had broken bread and eaten, and talked a long while, even till daybreak, he departed. And they brought the young man in alive, and they were greatly comforted.

That's it. That's the whole message. It feels unsettling that she didn't offer anything else, no: "Hi, sweetie, I wanted to read you something . . ." I'd like to be reassured by it, I would. Because there is some beauty there, in Eutychus's fall—the drowse of him as he perches on the windowsill, his body opening to the preacher's words but opening simultaneously, like the winged helicopter seeds of maple trees, to dangerous flight. I know the sensation well, having felt it so many evenings with Morena, wanting to fall asleep or fall against her or fall in the very realest way of falling. But I listen to my mother's message, and I feel hollow as the recorded scripture buzzes against my ear like the rustle of very thin, gold-edged pages. When the bottle of wine is empty, I call her back.

"What was that all about?" I ask her, "What're you trying to say, Mom?"

I can hear in my words the voice of the men who often sit beside me at the bar: *Why are you telling me this?*

She's quick to reply, not skipping a single beat, breathless like someone who's made a great discovery, an inventor who's just stumbled upon a breakthrough:

"Don't you see?" she asks, a weird frantic holiness in her voice. "Don't you see what it means?"

I turn the bottle upside down above my glass to try to rescue the final drops. "No," I say. "No, why don't you tell me."

"It means," she says, reverent. "It means there's hope for him. For your brother. He's going to be all right."

And I know then, with a shiver of certainty, that sometimes a story can have a meaning for the teller that no one else, no matter how many times they hear it, can unearth.

The Falling Sickness

I TOLD NICK many times after it happened, "She only blames you so she doesn't have to blame herself." I told him, "You have to think about what Dad would've wanted. He would never want you to feel like this."

"You don't know what he wanted," Nick says. "You didn't know him. None of us really did."

He's not wrong. But my best guess: he would've wanted to make all this very small, far away, the way a painter adds a streak of blue to change the sense of distance between the viewer and the skyline.

We know our father's heart wasn't strong. It was in his blood, the way the fall was in ours. He was the sort of man who was always a little old, even when he was young. It was something we never considered because of how quiet he was, muffling even the daintiest cough in the crook of his sweatered elbow. In our minds, the danger was always elsewhere: outside, up high, not housed within like the rot surrounding a cherry pit.

He was well into his sixties by then, so maybe it wasn't as sudden as it seemed, easing into his own collapse. I told Nick, I told him, I did: it could've happened even if Nick hadn't come home that night, if he and our mother hadn't started shouting, circling each other like tigers in a cage. It would've happened *sometime*. But I guess we can't know that.

Afterward, I tried to make Nick go over the facts with me. "He was getting old," I said, holding up a finger, tallying. "He never really took great care of himself. All that Guinness. All those Twinkies." I held up a finger for the Guinness, another for the Twinkies. "It was in his genes, you know, from Grandpa Frank." Another finger. Then, just: "It wasn't in any way your fault, Nick. You can't blame yourself, you just can't." The last finger, a whole hand, a palm held up like a traffic cop signaling "Stop." Nick shook his head while saying, "I know, I know, I know." But still: it was there, splitting us apart little by little.

And it was undeniably an ending—our own collective fall reduced to this man, our father, dropping to his knees in the kitchen as if in violent imitation of our mother's praying, slumping sideways, still clutching one of his tiny trees like a sprig of parsley. The tree's leaves were still in the air after he collapsed, smaller than sequins, settling around him like green confetti. After his body met the linoleum, he seemed to spread out, stretching long, then crumpling up like a fist. We all saw it. There was nothing beautiful about it.

Afterward, I kept replaying it: my father going large, then small. It was the only way any of us were able to love: caught between offering ourselves up and tightening around the thing we thought we were losing.

According to my mother, her grandmother Agáta used to refer to the superstition, the curse, as *padající nemoc*, "the falling sickness." In the end, even our father—so calm and quiet and unencumbered by ancestry—was not immune. Although his fall, like much of his life, was very small.

I tried to free Nick from his feelings of blame. But our mother, we knew, held Nick responsible. There would have been no heart attack at all, she told me in that hideous stretch of days after the funeral, if Nick hadn't started "spouting his filth at them." And neither of us was willing to point a finger back at her, to say, "It was *you* he wanted to silence." To say, "Can't you spare a little blame for yourself?"

Maybe it was as simple as this: she couldn't forgive her son for Nick's name being the last word in her husband's mouth.

After our father's funeral, she wrote out a list of all the things in the house that were Nick's, then set these items out in the driveway for him to haul away. *"Not under my roof."* She had to stick to it. It was what her husband had died for.

We left all the things there—an old Sega Genesis, cords tangled and dusty; trophies from middle school track meets; paperbacks, their margins jittering with Nick's elated script; a ukulele missing one string; a Ziggy Stardust poster with the corners curling in the heat; chalk drawings I made for him of Keaton's serenely stoic face, his calm mouth the almost-lavender of a tornado's funnel; a large Ziploc bag full of loose-leaf herbal tea that Nick had purchased from a college friend who'd been studying ethnobotany. At the beginning of the summer, our mother had found that bag while tidying up my brother's room, and when Nick got home from work that day, our parents were both seated at the kitchen table with the bulging bag of green tea between them. Our mother looked as if she'd just solved a crime, solemn with a prim, pained nobility. Our father looked sheepish and wary. As soon as Nick entered the room, he recognized the confrontation and had to stifle his laughter behind his hand.

"That's not weed," my brother said, pointing at the bag. "It's tea."

I hadn't been there when it happened, but my brother described it so well, how my mother stiffened a little, uncertain, ruffling into embarrassment, and our father's face lifted into a benign smile. "I *told* you it wasn't drugs," he said to our mother, before dissolving into a heavy, shivering laughter—fluting like whale-song, out of control, contagious. Nick was laughing then too, bending in half, but graceful even in laughter, like an aspen tree in a windstorm. "That would be," he said, wiping his eyes, "quite a *lot* of weed." And our mother, watching her husband and son give themselves over to the humor of it, finally gave herself over too, and began to giggle. "I guess I'm just a little out of touch," she said, while the tides of laughter rose and fell around her like a pattering rainfall. For the rest of the day, and for days after, we'd catch our father pausing in the act of layering paint onto the roof of a tiny house; he'd chuckle, lean back, shake his head and say, "An intervention over a bag of *tea*," before returning to his work.

That bag of tea was among the things we left there. We left everything. So that, yes, after we were gone, our mother would have to haul it all back inside on her own. Or load it up in her car to drive to the Goodwill out on Route 13, then unload the boxes in the parking lot one by one, inhaling the Pine-Sol and hair gel smells of my brother's childhood bedroom. I could picture her lifting each box from the trunk, each one nearly as heavy to her, perhaps, as her husband's body had been when she tried to lift him from the linoleum, when she knelt and said to her children, "Help me," and we said, "Mom." We said with one voice, "Maybe it's better not to move him," and she lowered her face to his and I wanted to look away.

Our mother wrote a note to Nick. The ink of the pen she used was on the verge of running out so that spaces appeared in the shapes of the words, like the dotted lines of a sewing pattern. She wrote: *I feel I lost a husband and a son in the same day, and that is just too much for anyone. I will pray that we may yet forgive each other someday, Nickie. Until then, I think distance is the best thing.*

We had enough money saved that we could afford one-way tickets to Prague. We paid for our flights. We went. And so, I suppose, in a way, she lost me too.

"And a daughter," the note might as well have read.

We went. We found work in Prague that was small and insignificant. We taught language lessons. We walked dogs. We shoplifted bread rolls and foil-wrapped triangles of spreadable cheese from the bright multifloored supermarket in the city center. We made do. For a while, we stayed. Because staying was so much easier than going home.

And, put like that, it really does sound very easy and natural. Like spilled wine following the grooves of the kitchen floor, pooling up underneath the stove.

Interview

I REMEMBER THE exact moment when I was certain I didn't want to stay anymore.

In that last winter, the winter of Morena and that final drunken New Year's Eve, I took a tram, a metro, and two buses to get to a job interview at a language school in a distant suburb. When I arrived in my pencil skirt, I walked the sprawled-out streets from the bus stop, and the school behind its low stone wall was empty, its windows blank and dark. I circled the building, peering in the windows, seeing empty desks inside, scattered and thick with dust. I touched the locked front doors, pressed my face to the glass, saw a hallway dripping with Czech graffiti. I looked down at the scrap of paper where I'd scrawled the address, checked my phone for missed calls—no service that far out. On the window, a little smear of makeup where my nose had touched the glass. I turned away, moved down the walkway to the street, and began the long journey back home.

Word Games

DAYS AND DAYS—THE calendar stretching thin. The spilled wine is a smeared dark stripe across white tile, crusted to brown and burgundy, the color of blood in certain movies. My brother heals slow and steady in his hospital bed, and while we wait for his bones to mend, we play a game of Scrabble.

"I have more *d*'s over here than I know what to do with," Nick mutters, shuffling his tiles around.

He spells the word *puddled* out clumsily with his one good hand. I try to steer him, gently, away from talk of Prague, but he always steers me back. Every day he is a little stronger. Every day he names streets at random, as if playing a memory game with himself, building the city outward brick by brick.

He brings up that same corner of the city where Morena used to live, where it always seemed to be Christmas, even in summer. Winter waited in corners there, as if you could turn down an alley and find it had snowed in the middle of June, the lids of trashcans piled up with white, snow packed down beneath a delivery truck, ice coating the narrow secret windows, a man in a wool coat hurrying home with a live carp still wriggling in his woven shopping bag.

"Remember?" he asks, his voice taking on a mystical tone.

It's a kind of homesickness—trying to drown himself in the magic of that place, a place no longer ours. It's the same trick we used back then, like dangling a sparkly trinket before a baby's eyes, struggling to keep our heads above our grief.

"Remember when we tried to steal that giant pewter pitcher from the monastery?"

I don't want to remember anymore. But yes, climbing the hill behind the Christmas part of the city, a slow march up to the monastery where the air smelled like sunlit pavement after a heavy rain, and you could sit and they'd bring beer to your table by the pitcherful. The pitchers were gorgeous, well made, with lion's heads embossed on the side, and once it occurred to Nick that one of those pitchers should be ours. He ran his thumb over the lion's face and felt that it already belonged to him.

"Is your purse big enough?" he'd asked me. The pitcher was already empty. I humored him, as I always did. I opened the mouth of my bag and looked in: wallet, keys, cigarettes and tobacco dust, dirty notebook and used-up pen, a small blue Nokia phone with buttons that lit up when you touched them. Such a sad little world in there. I sighed.

"No," I said, looking at the tattered space. "No way."

Nick started trying to maneuver the heavy pitcher through the mouth of my bag, and I started to bristle at how reckless and entitled he could sometimes be.

"Nick, stop." I pulled the pitcher free, set it back on the table, looked around to see if anyone was watching us.

"No one's looking," he stage-whispered.

"Don't you think it could bring on some serious bad luck to steal from a *monastery*?"

We had gotten into the habit of shoplifting items that we deemed necessary but it felt unjust to pay for—like toilet paper or duct tape. Cartons of yogurt. A knit winter hat. We never stole items that were purely for pleasure. We paid for novels, decks of cards, black bottles of beer with gold foil caps. We never tried to sneak into a second showing at the movie theater. It was our unspoken rule. Only what was *needed*.

Nick's mouth went a bit slack. "You're kidding," he said. "You can't be serious."

I looked at him. He was a child—sad that the pitcher didn't belong to him, wanting to punish the people around us for belonging here in a way we never could. He laughed a cruel little laugh. "When did you get so superstitious?"

I said nothing. "You know," he continued, "you sounded just like Mom when you said that. *The Lord our father does not look fondly on those who would steal from a monastery*," he mimicked perfectly, bitterly.

It was the first time I ever walked away from him. I left him there sitting beside a moist gold ring around the base of the pitcher where the beer had pooled into a halo. I stumbled alone back down the hill, full of shame.

We were our whole world, Nick and I, and there was a kind of splendor in that—contained by each other, two yolks sharing an egg. But there was something in that doubling that made me feel all the more fragile—the two of us poised on a sweet precipice before falling blindly forward into the rest of our lives.

In the hospital, I shuffle my Scrabble tiles around, use one of the *d*'s from *puddled* to spell out *abide* on the board.

"You were too chicken to steal it," he says, taunting. And then, the edges of his mouth lowering: "You were right, though. It was stupid of me."

I look at him, really look. It's been difficult, his face half-wrapped in white around the small bud of his mouth, his lips dry, long slender cuts from the whipping of branches striping his neck.

"Nick, it really doesn't matter now, does it?" I say, not meaning to sound so dismissive. He stiffens a little, wanting to believe it *does* matter, and I slump guiltily.

"Your turn," I say, trying to work an apology into the words.

He spells out *wept*. Then says "Hold on" and puts an *s* in front of it: *swept*.

I keep coming close to reminding him: it wasn't all sweet. It wasn't all Christmas in July. But that's not what he needs to hear now.

He keeps returning, over and over, to that same New Year's Eve, the last before we went back home to the States. He remembers every detail—the wide blooms of fireworks, the crumbs of glass from the shattered green bottle, the frost slicking the soles of our shoes—while carefully avoiding the moment of sudden ugliness, never speaking of it, circling around the part of the night when I plunged away from him through the crowd. I cannot believe he's really forgotten; maybe it's what he's been reaching for in all this remembering—the moment when, both of us drunk, both dizzy, Nick had started making plans for the year ahead, falling forward into the future, saying, "Next year, we should spend New Year's Eve in Old Town Square, watch the clock strike," and something in me had reeled.

"No," I said. The word was small in my mouth, ugly in its smallness.

"What?" Nick reeled a little. "Why not?"

"I'm tired, Nick," I told him.

"We can start heading back," he said. "You wanna treat ourselves to a cab?"

"No." The word grew larger, almost a shout—my father saying before his heart attack, *That's enough!* "That's not what I mean. I mean: I'm tired of *this*." I gestured around me at the black water glinting like volcanic glass, the lantern light heavy behind frosted panes, lit bulbs like ripe fruit on the verge of dropping. I waved my arms toward the silhouettes of prayerful saints with their twisted brass halos, Saint John of Nepomuk's head bowed and the five stars ringed behind. It felt foolish and ungrateful to complain about all that generous beauty. But I'd had enough. Like too much sugar gumming up the inside of your mouth. "This place isn't *real*, Nick," I yelled at him.

It was what we'd loved about the city to begin with, its mythic glow. I was foggy with champagne, bending my mind this way and that, and staggering from the effort: When had it all started to turn? With Morena, maybe—wanting something that was mine alone. Greedy for it, and that greed mirrored by Nick's own brooding hunger for a world I couldn't quite reach, like my fumbling hands trying to find the right grip on the cat's bladder.

Nick looked like a person who'd been woken from a deep sleep with news of some catastrophe. I felt panicked, not knowing how to explain this seeping fear that had grown over the past three years, the fear that Nick and I could blur together like a chord of music until we could no longer tell one life from the other. There were days, seeing the bruises arrive on Nick's face like an overnight moss, when I thought I could almost feel them rising to the surface of my own skin, and it frightened me.

Nick's face was coming awake by the smallest degrees. He blinked, eyelids falling to meet his cheeks.

"I didn't realize you felt that way," he said.

I hadn't either. I hadn't realized how stifled I'd started to feel—by his grief, by how it seemed to outweigh my own, by the threats tacked up on his walls, the depressing lines of Hrabal's prose and morbid scraps of Yesenin's poetry. The way all of it anchored me to the unbeautiful ground, the loathsome eye-level world where the trash in gutters was plainly visible, where we once saw a dead swan's carcass beside the river, its neck flat and blackened by a bicycle tire, a man crouching near the bird's corpse to shit in a ditch.

"I'm sorry." I remember tears, just a few, a wetness that was in my throat more than in my eyes. "We can't stay here," I said, floundering, then amending: "*I* can't stay here."

It was right then that a little bride and groom, her gown sweeping frost from the stones of the bridge, moved past us, a small crowd of well-wishers trailing behind them like the train of her dress. They stood a few feet away beneath the statue of Saint John of Nepomuk, posing while a photographer snapped pictures and shouted directions in Czech.

"What do you mean 'We can't stay here?'" Nick asked. I was distracted by the couple—how, even though the bride wore no coat, and her arms beneath the lamps looked like lightly polished porcelain, she showed no sign of cold. None at all. I watched, waiting to see if she would shiver, but she did not.

"What are you talking about?" Nick said, prodding me. I felt so sorry for him. I wanted to lift all the words I'd just said back inside me, like gathering up the broken pieces of our smashed champagne bottle. I spoke gently.

"I need to go home," I told him. "I need to live my life."

I swallowed, then said, "And you do too."

The groom was lifting the bride, holding her by the waist, so that she balanced on the bridge's stone railing. It was strange to me that this was permissible, but not my drunken climbing of the plinth from earlier that night. I looked around to see if the cop would come, the one that had asked me, "Are you stupid?" But he was nowhere. Probably his shift had ended and he was washing down candlestick beef and bread dumplings with glimmering pilsners at some overheated pub. I wished faintly that

I was there with him, before shaking myself back to the present. *Jsi hloupá?* "Yes, sir. Stupid, yes. Definitely." While I watched, the bride's dress blew back, a white wisp of cirrus cloud behind her, like skywriting.

Nick looked around, wanting to see what I was staring at. He glanced at the couple, then up at the statue of Saint John of Nepomuk as if taking stock of where we were. The couple seemed to become aware of us, waving happily in our direction while I stared blankly and felt the cold bite down on me. The photographer snapped a picture of them waving. I could almost see the picture, developed and framed on a bedside table, and I felt the stupid sorrow of having shared this moment with them, of our hapless proximity.

"So," Nick said to me, his gaze falling back onto mine. "If we haven't been living our lives, what have we been doing all this time, I'd like to know."

"We've been," I paused, looking for the right words, "buying ourselves some time."

No, that wasn't quite right. The booze was doing me no favors. I shook my head. "We've been putting it off."

"Putting what off?"

I was getting frustrated. "*Everything*," I yelled. "You know?"

"No," Nick said. "I don't know what you mean."

The couple had become aware that we were fighting, and their smiles faltered, stiffened like icicles forming. The photographer didn't seem fazed, though. The camera kept whirring softly. These photos would seem more pensive, more solemn, but then marriage was a serious thing—two lives irreversibly intertwined—and the pictures would be no less alluring even with the mouths of the couple falling into straight lines, their eyes taking on some gravity.

I said nothing to Nick. The couple were moving off, their clasped hands swinging between them while the photographer clicked and snapped in their wake. I watched them go, feeling a wistful pang, like watching someone leave the bar whom you'd been hoping, all night, to talk to.

Nick waited a beat for me to answer, then made a small noise of exasperation and dipped away from me. The crowd had mostly thinned out after the fireworks, but there were still tourists, and he wove between them as they chatted loudly about the beautiful bride and groom, saying things like "Married on New Year's Eve, well, isn't that romantic?" and "I've heard a New Year's wedding is good luck." Nick brushed past the newlywed couple as they were nearing the end of the bridge, and there was a horrible moment when I gasped audibly, thinking that Nick was about to step on the train of the bride's dress—an image as hellish and shocking as seeing a dog pee inside a church—his beer-slick boot about to grab the fabric, about to pinch it between the filth of his heel and the grime of cobblestone until it ripped in a long, wrenching scream. And I could imagine the couple's unborn babies, the daughter who would inherit the dress, shrieking through the years, in anguish at the deafening noise of the tearing satin. But then Nick caught his footing at the last instant and spiraled away, apologizing. I called after him to stop, to wait. He stood on the bridge, turning to look just above my head at the empty plinth behind me where, hours before, I'd posed stupidly.

I caught up to him. I closed my eyes against the sight of his half-slumped shoulders and said, "Nick, it's not enough. All right? It's just not sustainable. Not forever. And not while I have to watch you just keep . . . sinking."

"Sinking?"

"You know what I mean."

"I don't, though."

His face looked cold. A small circle of red at the end of his nose. I was tired of being careful with him. People milled around us, turning an ear toward our argument, maybe recognizing the two drunk Americans who had burst into song earlier, belting their national anthem to drown out everything else. My eyes were tired, unable to take in any more, not even the sight of Nick's bewildered face. They seemed to lower on their own when I said, "Nick." When I said, "I think maybe you aren't doing very well." He didn't deny it. We both seemed scraped clean by my words, all our energy drained away.

"And I just think it's time we went home," I finished lamely. "I don't really know what else to do."

Nick turned away from me, dropping his eyes, those long lashes brushing the hard rise of his cheeks. "But," he said, lingering. "Home isn't there for me. Not anymore."

It broke something in me, hearing him say that. A snap. Like icicles breaking free from the roofline and cracking downward. Desperate, flushed, I shot back at him, throwing myself bodily against the words, "Well if you want to stay, you'll have to stay on your own."

It felt, after I'd said it, like a weak ultimatum. Nick said nothing in response, just started to move away. I wanted to stop him, to keep him there, on the bridge, in front of me.

"Please, Nick," I said, my voice thin and pleading. "You can't just disappear on me."

His voice was drained, nothing but grief. "But it's like you said: I already have." He walked slowly toward the western end of the bridge, the place where the couple seemed to have vanished like smoke, as though the darkness had wiped the night clean of them.

"You were right," he said, his steps measured and eerily soundless beneath the noise of the scattering crowd. "Been disappearing this whole fucking time."

Flower Bucket

OUTSIDE THE HOSPITAL, the air is dry but still inexplicably dense. This is the living I insisted I get back to: walking on streets cold enough to feel slippery even when there is no ice. I feel, walking, as if I'm kneading myself slowly into the city. The pockets of my coat are lined with pink satin, and I keep my hands in them, separating them like dogs who will fight if brought together. This is basically the kind of walking I did in Prague.

Everyone is beginning to feel cold and vulnerable, and it makes us do stupid things. There's an ambulance parked outside my usual bar, lights wheeling through the air like a carnival ride. As I walk up, some bystanders fill me in. A girl tried to vault herself over one of the parking meters, slipped, and went down hard. *Yes,* they echo one another, *she fell.* They seem certain that she was drunk, though there was really no evidence of her drunkenness before the accident occurred.

The ambulance pulls away, lights still going, the siren making small hoots like mechanized bird calls, and as soon as the spectacle is over, everyone pulls out cigarettes and lights them, as if this was what they'd intended all along.

There's a woman standing on the outer edges of the smokers who looks slightly like my mother—the same slimness of jaw, the same reddish tinge to her cheeks and hair—only this woman is more tattered and toothless. She's carrying long-stemmed flowers in a deep bucket that makes a sloshing noise when she moves. When she sees me watching her, she approaches and asks me if I saw the girl fall. I shake my head.

The woman says, pointing at me, "Now you and me, darling—we know how to hold our liquor."

"How can you tell?" I ask her.

"Because," she says, her voice husky and dry, "you're calm, level-headed. It's written all over you."

I deny nothing, thinking that the girl who fell could've so easily been me. I could've told the woman that yes, I could hold my liquor, but there were just as many nights when I felt it was holding me—as if I were a bug trapped in hardening amber. There have been times when the memory of the walk home from the bar has become irrecoverable, a blank space opening up where that journey should have been, a fissure in the mind that widens upon waking the next morning. I've woken bleary from the way the whiskey and sleeping pills met and mixed in me, taking stock of an unfamiliar litany of scrapes and bruises from a fall that I missed, a fall I could never return to—running my hands up and down my forearms and trying to read the story there, as if my body had been replaced, over-night, with a stranger's.

I lower my face to the mouth of the bucket and she tells me which blooms are the most fragrant—a white rose, a yellow rose, others. I name each blossom in turn, and the one I don't know she tells me is a Gerber daisy. It is brilliant orange, unnatural-looking. I can glimpse the woman's horrible teeth, the absence of them, and I remember Nick saying a few days back that he didn't want to have his teeth fixed. When I asked him why, he said: *Maybe I just like them better like this*, and it made me shiver.

The woman goes into the bar to try to sell her flowers, and I follow her in to watch. She circles the small patch of floor where a few older couples are swaying beside the jukebox. I stand at the bar watching her, her bucket tucked under her arm like a drum she might choose to play. The dancing couples sweep together in courtly, old-fashioned movements—waltz, two-step, foxtrot—and I am envious of them for knowing how to move that way. No one seems interested in the flowers, but the blooms glow at the edge of the room, as if they carry their own light beneath the petals. I want to eat one—or just put it in my mouth without swallowing. As a child, Nick once said this about a baby bird we found in a fallen nest—that he just wanted to feel its feathers on his tongue.

It occurs to me then that I could buy a flower from the woman, and I open my wallet, watching her watch the dancers. She lifts a long stem when a couple circles close and waves it at them like a conductor's baton.

But in the end, I turn away from her. I buy a whiskey instead, thinking: *What would I do with a flower?*

Country Roads

IN PRAGUE, THERE are songs in English that everyone knows. Sometimes, when you turn down a street, the night at its most purple, you'll hear a guitar clumsily played, glimpse a teenager with feet propped up on the railing of his balcony, singing in a heavy accent: *Where have you gone, Joe DiMaggio? Jesus loves you more than you will kno-oh-oh-ow.*

I believe that at any given moment, someone somewhere within the city limits of Prague is singing or listening to John Denver's "Country Roads." It is happening right now. Right now, a man in a black overcoat is standing on the Charles Bridge playing a weather-beaten accordion, an upturned hat full of coins at his feet. As he plays, chips of red paint shed themselves from the body of his instrument and take to the air like colorful dandruff.

It's easy enough to conjure all this. A circle forms around the man, and he is singing: *Take us home*, not quite getting all the words right. *Life is old there, older than a tree, younger is the mountain, growing like a sea.*

Nick never asks me what it is that I miss about those days. But if there is one single thing, it might be this: the moment of pausing to tilt an ear toward the song, feeling greeted by it, feeling a breath of ecstatic uncertainty as you ask yourself,

"Are the words really '*older than a tree*'?"

I don't know why that's the one thing that's so hard for me to let go of. Maybe because, easy as it is to picture the man with his accordion, it's easier still to picture Morena pausing to listen to him sing. She's on her way home to squeeze Diego's bladder, to make a strong dark coffee for herself, and she stops to watch the accordion collapse and expand like lungs, letting a twenty-crown coin fall from her hand into the darkness of his hat.

It is normal, I tell myself, to wonder about how things could have been different. If we had stayed in Prague, if I'd allowed myself to love Morena; if Nick and I had never left home, if my father had lived a little bit longer, if I could have prevented my brother from falling; if the stonemason, at the moment when

Jiří came up behind him, had turned just a second before, had later walked home at nightfall and crossed the bridge into Old Town, and, *dark and dusty, painted on the sky,* had seen the light drifting low, offering itself to his eyes, the sun shrinking down quickly like a coin dropped into a hat.

Casting

WHEN I LET the events play, like a reel of film, I always put myself in the role of the stonemason. I look out from the tower's familiar height. I feel a rough touch against my shoulder blades, and I stare down into the fall. The plunge is really no more fearsome than the high dive above the community pool when I was twelve. I feel the weight of my body, unwilling but resigned, as the air rushes against it.

All my life, I thought I could feel the stonemason's fall in my spine. I built my story, stacked like blocks of limestone, on top of his.

But now, ever since Nick's fall, I'm not able to cast myself so easily in the stonemason's role. I'm beginning to wonder if I've been getting it wrong.

This is something I might ask my mother if we still talked about such things: *How do we know what we know?*

Inside the tower's high room, there were only Jiří and the stonemason. The few witnesses squinted up toward that distant window from the stone courtyard below. They could only glimpse the faraway tininess of Jiří's head, the dark outline of his shoulders filling the space of the window afterward. And so, isn't it possible that Jiří's push was, in fact, an accident?

Perhaps he watched the stonemason's footing falter and reached out for him, his sweat-slick hand slipping against the fabric of his shirt.

Perhaps he looked down at the stonemason's lanky body twisted like driftwood on the cobbles below and fell to his knees, sensing the wreckage that could be made of a life simply because a man stumbles.

Perhaps we shouldn't have been so quick to cast him as a murderer.

I have dreamed it. Just once, a few days after Nick's fall, then never again. In the dream, we are in the high tower, Nick and I. I'm trying to get Nick to take in the view. "Look," I insist. *"Look."* He hides his face in his hands, not weeping or moving or making any sound. I try to pull his hands away, suddenly scared. He shakes me off. He takes a step back, away from my clenched fists, tripping over the open sill. I grab for him, but my hand closes around empty air, and the fall sweeps him away like a rushing current.

There are nights I lie awake, and it all pulses like neon. I sort and weave the lit threads. But still I keep returning, like a tongue that can't stay away from a sore tooth, to the same thought:

Even if it wasn't deliberate, Jiří still had to be there in order for the stonemason to fall.

Physics

I GOT A C- in my high school physics class. I think I put too much history behind the equations, substituting human bodies for hammers and feathers and bowling balls, extending the length of the fall, drawing it out like a still image from a film. I substituted the stonemason for every x and y, and Mr. Wecker, grading my exams, couldn't make allowances for that kind of hauntedness.

There are a few things I kept hold of, though, over the years.

First: I remember that the term "free fall" when applied to objects in motion does not necessarily mean that the objects are falling *downward* in the ordinary sense of the term. For example, any object moving upward wouldn't be considered by an observer to be falling, but if that object is being acted on solely by the force of gravity, then it is said to be in "free fall."

Therefore, the moon, *our* moon, is considered to be in free fall.

Second: On August 2, 1971, an astronaut named David Scott stood on the surface of the moon and simultaneously dropped a hammer and a feather from the same height. They fell at the same rate. They hit the ground at the same instant. This experiment was meant to prove that in the absence of air resistance, weight doesn't matter, has no bearing. In the absence of resistance, all objects might as well weigh the same.

Uncle Josef

AT TIMES, I envy the recklessness of my brother's fall. I do. I want something more reckless than walking the same tree-lined route homeward, over and over again, the ditch-bound creek blooming on one side of me, streetlights breaking apart in the water like soggy bread.

Outside the bar, the sidewalk is still a little dirty with blood from where the girl fell. Inside the bar, the flower woman hovers nearby while I take shots one at a time like a child holding tight to toy teacups. I melt onto the barstool like watercolor paint. The flower woman lays a single Gerber daisy on the bar next to me, as if placing it on a fresh grave. She keeps looking at me as though she's surprised to find that I'm still here. I keep looking at her half-convinced that she's an apparition only I can see. Suddenly she's telling me about a friend of hers who saw a UFO—a gorgeous blue disc hovering above a freshly shorn field, then plunging upward into the dark sky like a pebble falling down a well.

"Here's a good one," I reply, as if I'm about to tell a joke. I start to tell her about my great-grandmother's brother Josef, who lost his leg and decided to give his life to God in the same instant. The bartender is drying the inside of a glass with a white cloth, just like they do in the movies, and I'm fond of him for this. I can feel a low warmth coming off him as if he were a freshly baked loaf of bread. The flower woman listens beside me, but I speak to the side of the bartender's face, a half-smile planted there, making me think of the Gerber daisy's withered sunlight. I tell the side of the bartender's face about my great-uncle Josef, who, during the dustiest, skinniest years of the Great Depression, used to jump trains, ride the rails across huge swaths of the Midwest looking for work on farms and orchards. He got good at it—shinnying up the side of a boxcar like a spider. He knew how to gauge the speed of the train, to watch the spaces between the cars to understand how fast he'd need to run alongside before reaching out and pulling himself neatly up to safety.

Of course, there was a day it went wrong. The speed wasn't right, or his grip wasn't right. He slipped and fell beneath the train, and the turning wheels severed his left leg from his body just above the knee, tidy as a pizza cutter. Before passing out, he made a deal with God:

"If I live through this," he said to the darkness beneath the train, "I'll serve you until the end of my days."

It's probably the sort of bargain that occurs to you only while your blood leaves your body through the gap where your leg was moments ago. But he did live. And he did make good on his promise, still riding the rails to spread God's word to men in labor camps and shantytowns. Yes, even with one leg, he kept jumping trains. After his accident, a blacksmith fashioned a metal leg for him, and he got so that he was quite proud of it, pulling up his pants leg just enough to let the gleam show, giving packs of raucous little boys a thrill.

"But," I say, fingering the stem of the daisy, "here's the kicker: He fell a second time, same as the last. He fell trying to jump a train, and it ran over his metal leg, crushing it flat as a pancake. He lay there, shocked but not in any pain, and the railyard workers ran over in a panic, frantic and hollering: *This man needs a doctor!* And, cool as a cucumber, Josef called up to them, *Never mind the doctor, fellas. What I need is a good blacksmith.*"

The flower woman chuckles. The bartender stops drying the pint glass in his hands and looks at me. "Now that," he says, his voice is rusty and soft, "sounds to me like a tall tale."

I'm meeting my eyes in the mirror behind the bar, pleased with what I see, with the loose shirt that makes me feel smaller than I actually am.

"I swear to God," I say to my reflection. "Every word is true."

Wishing Cross

AT THE FEET of the statue of Saint John of Nepomuk, a bronze cross is embedded into the stone of the bridge's railing. It is a double-barred cross, its five upper points ending in five stars. These stars represent those five points of light that rose from the water's surface when the priest was thrown into the river in 1395. Tour guides and travel books inform visitors of the cross's magical properties: the pure-hearted are invited to place one finger on each star and make five wishes. Only five. According to legend, to ask for more means that none will be granted. To ask for more invites bad luck.

The cross is large. In placing your fingers, you have to stretch your hand wide, feel an ache in your palm. If you go during the day, you may have to wait in line, rehearsing in your mind what you want to ask for as you shuffle forward over the rounded cobblestones. Lovers titter and coo, stacking their hands, inter-twining their fingers. Tourists raise cameras to their faces, lower their voices to ask, "What'd you wish?"

I went at night. I went alone. It was toward the end—an act of desperation, maybe. It was in that dim, frigid spread of days between Christmas and New Year's, and nothing I'd ever touched in my life seemed as cold to my bare fingers as the metal of that cross. A film of frost coated it, pricking its way through my skin. The bridge glowed green and gold beneath the lanterns that night, and I looked out at the water arranging itself into sharp, light-rimmed shapes, like stained glass fragments all one color. All black.

Touching the stars as if they were piano keys, I went blank. I bent that blankness toward Nick. It would be easier to ask on his behalf. It would make the wishes more powerful, more certain. So I gave all five wishes to Nick. I was careful, counting them off. One: I wished for his despair to end. Two: I wished that he'd be able to build a life that he could love. Three: I wished for someone he could share that life with, who could nourish and value him. Four: I wished that any sense of guilt about our father's death would disappear. Five: I wished that our mother would make amends, would give back the remnant of family that he'd lost.

I felt a little foolish, standing alone with my fingers spread, throbbing and cold, against the bronze of the cross. I glanced sideways to see if I was alone. I wasn't. A small, dark-haired woman was there, looking out at the light checkering the river's surface, her eyes seeking the farthest point of darkness, and I thought for an instant that it was Morena—her hair loose and blurring the edges of her face. I almost said her name. And the thought of the two of us, side by side on her windowsill, filled me. I brimmed and sloshed with it. Her hand over mine as we groped together through the cat's fur, searching. *See? Your fingers know more than you think,* she said to me once. Her hair falling forward around her face. I'd wanted to wrap one of the curls around the length of a finger, dress my pinky up in the dark-ness of her hair.

And, for a brief flash, I almost believed in all of it. Here was proof. The cross had granted me this thing I hadn't been brave enough to ask for.

I leaned out over the water to catch a fuller glimpse of her, this prayer in me, and just like that, I made a sixth wish: *Let it be her.*

I didn't mean to. It just happened. It wasn't even a fully formed thought, more like a flush spreading from my chest down into my wrist to my fingers, still lightly touching the cold bronze. I lifted my hand away from the five stars, and the woman at the railing turned a face toward me that wasn't Morena's. She smiled, lightly. She said words to me in Czech, but I knew what she was asking. She was asking me, "What did you wish for?"

Last Call

THE WOMAN WITH the flower bucket has left the bar, and I have been absently pulling all the leaves off the bloom she left me—now a knobbed and naked stem that I twirl between two fingers like a miniature baton. There is something here I still want that hasn't yet found me—located, perhaps, in the proximity between the bartender and me even with the nicked surface of the bar dividing us. There remains the slender hope that his fingers might brush mine when he hands me my drink and I'll feel my rigid edges blur slightly—that layer of skin that marks where I begin and end, separate from the air around me, getting mixed up with his. I'm waiting for this, for some confirmation that lingering will be worth it, but the bartender eyes me as if I might become a problem, and I suppose I might. There is nothing but color in me—neon, loops of lighted letters that spell the names of things.

"We're about to close," the bartender says offhandedly. "Care to settle up?"

Settle. It is everything I don't want just then, but I tell him, "Give me a couple more for the road," no longer bothering to add a note of charm to my voice.

He is slow to respond, reluctant. "I don't think you need any more," he says.

I feel myself bristle, lifting up a little off the barstool and gauging its precarity.

"And what the fuck does *need* have to do with it?" I ask him. I become aware that if I were to shift my weight just right on the stool, it might topple beautifully. I might spread myself out in strange and elegant shapes like a medieval painting of a martyrdom. But I keep steady. That is: even though I'm swaying, the stool remains solid beneath me.

The bartender levels his eyes at me. "In my experience, there's a point when need starts to have everything to do with it. And that's what you wanna stay away from." But I cannot really keep track anymore of what we're talking about. In frustration, I put some money on the bar and move very carefully to the door so that if I do happen to fall, the fall won't be wasted on him.

Eyes on a Plate

IN PRAGUE, I worried about having so much beauty before us and being unable to really let it in. But maybe it's wrong to say "us." Maybe Nick was letting it in all along. For me, all that sun on colored glass, following the turn of streets like riding the back of a giant snake, the songs that fell through upper story windows and seemed to dust my hair like pollen—none of it was able to fully reach me, smooth me out. I felt I had little to offer Nick anymore except a kind of tired attention. I never dared to ask the question "What would it even *look* like if we were happy?"

It might feel, I tended to think, the way three or four glasses of hard liquor felt—indoor light coming up in you like a slow sun, outdoor light building a web of shadows you could pass through easily without getting caught. I kept trying for this same outcome once we got back to the States, returning to what had begun to feel like the one faithful thing.

I saw the ways the city took shape in Nick, watching the liquor reach his veins and spread along them like running a highlighter over the correct route on a road map. I didn't always recognize what I saw in him, but I clung to a sort of weary faith that if we just looked long enough, *hard* enough, at the way the world rested on each other's shoulders, we would figure out a way to be.

Perhaps the idea that a life is knowable, mappable, is the real myth. Perhaps Nick's drift from me was the only way the world could begin to show its true shape. But, my god, it wipes me out. A weariness so thorough it seems to reach even the ends of my hair. Is it any wonder that, in this state, I've come to believe that sleep is the thing that will save me? That the only thing capable of even touching the surface of that exhaustion is a night of drinking and a couple of sleeping pills in my palm, looking up at me like eyes on a plate?

I remember, in Prague, a time Nick and I pooled a week's pay to take ourselves out to a fancy rooftop restaurant that had just opened in Smíchov. The waiter brought out a plate of carp—the whole fish lying across the dish, head to tail, as if it had fallen asleep there. Nick poked it with a fork.

"I don't want to eat something while it's looking at me," he said, frowning.

This is what it feels like to swallow the pills: once they are gone, the gaze is gone too.

Lilies

IN THE HOSPITAL, I'm hung over. Nick is pale behind his scabs and wrappings, and I'm beginning to lose track of the face he had before the fall. I stand beside his bed, wriggling out of my coat, and he nods toward the windowsill, jerking his chin toward a clump of white lilies in a vase.

"From Mom," he says, the words clipped. I stare at the gaps in his mouth, the teeth he lost, the ones that held on.

"Was she here?" I ask.

He shakes his head, matter-of-fact. "No, she had them delivered."

"Is there a card?" I ask, and he waves a hand toward the flowers. I pick up the small rectangle of white cardstock, and the words are printed in a script-like font: *Take care of yourself, Nickie. Love, Mom.*

"Aren't lilies funeral flowers?" Nick asks me.

"Weddings, funerals, Easter Sunday," I say, picking one up and spinning it between thumb and forefinger. "They're multipurpose." The flower has a creamy, clove-like smell, and underneath that, a bite of oak moss that hints at urine.

I picture it: her quick untidy sweep into the room, leaves clinging to the soles of her shoes and making her slip a little over the clean tile floors. *Well, Nickie, you've really done it now.* Setting down her purse with the loud slap of leather, roughly brushing Nick's hair back from his forehead to examine the scabbed-over cut above his eyebrow.

"Would you even want to see her if she came?" The words are out of my mouth before I can weigh them.

Nick shrugs. "The damage is already done," he says, and a part of me wants to tell him he's wrong—that he's not invulnerable just because he fell and survived.

As a kid, I assumed that if we were going to fall, we'd fall together. Twinned. Even though I was the one who took the risks, longing for height, for the path toward grace that a body can build on its way through the air—the path, I have begun to realize, we each must follow separately.

And when I demanded we leave Prague, I was the one who'd insisted on our separateness, forced us to learn our edges, to tally the things we couldn't seem to share.

"I think it'd be okay if you were here," Nick is saying, but something about the thought of the three of us in this small room together makes me shrink. He looks frightened suddenly, and it's not a look I'm used to. "Will you stay?" he asks, as if afraid that she'll appear that instant, her scant shape in the doorway, leaning over Nick's bed, counting the toothless spaces in his mouth, tallying his injuries, each one evidence of some failure. Those failures mine more than his.

I stay. I don't want to face the walk home alone anyway. The night goes long and thin, and we're both awake with the smell of the lilies. I click through to the classic film channel around midnight and there's a Keaton movie on—the one where he's stranded alone on an ocean liner.

Nick nods up at the TV. "He's been following me around," he says of Keaton.

"Following you?" I laugh. "Nick, you haven't moved in two weeks."

"You know what I mean," he says. And I do.

We watch together, and I have this feeling that we are thinking the same thoughts in unison, that we've fallen in sync once again, but I find out I am wrong when he says, "You think you could sneak me downstairs? I would kill for a cigarette."

Maybe I should be less willing. Maybe I should wheedle and reason with him. But I don't. I angle his wheelchair toward the bed. He sits on the edge, one leg straight in its hard cast, the other almost completely unharmed; side by side they do not look as if they are part of the same body. I position myself to keep him steady. I lean toward him, offering my shoulder, and he stands on his good leg, wincing a little.

"Is this a good idea?" I ask, too late. He's already in motion, pivoting toward the wheelchair, settling into it with a quick intake of breath, a grimace.

"What does it being a good idea have to do with anything?" he asks. "Most of our ideas are bad."

I wheel him to the elevators and they ding lightly, as if muffled behind a curtain, and we feel the measured descent in our stomachs as the elevator moves downward through the building's layers. Outside the glass doors, we face the mostly empty parking lot where the streetlights buzz on their long stems. It's a crisp early November night, no snow but the smell of it, a possibility tucked up in lowering clouds.

I light two cigarettes and pass one to him. This is how it's always been. In Prague, we each carried packs of cigarettes—a cheap, scratchy Polish brand called Route 66: American Blend or smoother, pricier Chesterfields, for a treat, on the weekends—and we never extracted a single cigarette, always two, always alternating whose turn it was. Back and forth, this rhythm that arose from being near each other day after day.

We exhale, the smoke rising in parallel. Up and up—blue twisting into gray when backed by the streetlights. We are silent, and it feels like the right way to be. But then all at once, I speak, and words and smoke both leave me simultaneously.

I ask my brother, "Do you think you might fall again?"

Nick lowers his cigarette and jerks his head away so that his face is in shadow. "Now how can I know that?" he says. "Am I some sort of fortune-teller?"

My head dips, and I know he is feeling the lingering bite of his own sharpness. He takes my hand, and I feel how warm he is beneath the wrappings of gauze. His hand is hot.

"Look," he says, and I look at him. "I promise . . ." He pauses, as if he had no idea of what he planned to say when he started speaking. "I promise to try." He swallows loudly. "To try to be careful," he finishes.

I want to tell him how sorry I am, for every single weakness or failure, for every fall that led to his, but that seems like too much for right now. Too much, and not enough.

October 4, 1895

I REALIZE MORE and more how lonely it must be for our mother. How alone she was in her fear when we were kids, and how she tried to shape that fear into love, praying the beads of her rosary with our names interspersed. Nick's, mine—clicking together. She kept herself busy with worry, with the shadow of care and devotion that the worry cast. She kept herself nearby, sweetly hovering from a close distance, offering us warm shade.

My brother and I would pile into our father's lap, climbing him like a sweet, motionless almond tree. He smelled like almonds, also a little like molasses, like some kind of old-fashioned hair oil he must've inherited from the generation before him.

It's easier to think about my mother when I think about my father—to think of her bustling quietly at the edges of the living room, picking objects up from bookshelves and end tables, dusting underneath with a cloth. We sat close to the trunk of our father, and she kept busy; she brought us deep glasses of milk, brought us hard little gingersnaps on a plate, brought us blankets, brought us the cat that she settled among us, its purr buoying up beneath the baritone tremor of our father's storytelling voice.

Our father was telling us a story about Buster Keaton. Our father was one of us, and we thought of him that way. Our mother, on the other hand, was this firm fact of otherness, always nearby but always a little removed. We didn't think about the fact that she heard the stories too, that she was listening while she fluttered and swept and dusted.

Our father cleared his throat, immensely. The only time his voice seemed large was when he told us these stories.

"The night Keaton was born," he began, "the world went wild and still."

He was good with words. They were easy for him. He let himself get swept up in them. He told us what it would've been like on that night. He told us how Keaton was born in one of those moments of greenish silence that precedes a cyclone, the air a web of something electric, lifting the strands of your hair to warn of the coming gust that could lift you.

The year was 1895. The Mohawk Indian Medicine Company had come to Piqua, Kansas, had pitched their great canvas tent in the fading remains of afternoon light. Joe Keaton worked beside Harry Houdini to hammer stakes deep into a fresh-harvested field. There was a new-haircut smell in the air, dust taking to the wind in upward-spinning whiskey-colored lines. They waited for night, counting on the flyers tacked up in the general store and dance hall to bring in the crowds. And they came: coal miners and sharecroppers, coated in dusts of different colors.

The scene my father described was, I thought, not unlike the world that Jiří would fall into once he crossed the ocean with his wife and seven children, once the stonemason hit the stones of the church courtyard and everything was altered for us. There were miles and worlds between them—Keaton's birth, the stonemason's death—but they very well could've taken place on the same day, even, it's tempting to think, at the very same moment. I tried to make the events match up in my mind, thinking of Jiří climbing the steps of the church tower while the farmers and laborers began to arrive with their families, filling the seats, waiting for the curtains to part. I thought of the stonemason kneeling to carve my great-grandmother's initials into the stone of the windowsill at the same moment that Myra Keaton appeared onstage, lifting the hem of her skirt to show ankles as delicate as the lace of her petticoat.

She danced, pregnant and uncorseted, in slow circles, and Buster leapt like a fish within her, silently. She played an unwieldy bull fiddle, twirling it comically while the red-cheeked men of the front row cock-crowed up to her, "Why, that thing is bigger than you, little mite." She was a miniature one-woman band, balancing fiddle and cornet. The depthless full moon over farm flats showed her round silhouette. The burning aurora of the spotlight gripped her. They loved her, minuscule and with child; they loved the little mother and the quiet, spinning danger of her slapdash dancing.

She danced. Jiří climbed. The stonemason carved.

The night pressed bodily against the canvas of the tent, nosing beneath the awning to hear the scattered notes of her whirling fiddle. The audience was half-drunk by then. They held brown bottles roughly around the necks, syrupy "medicine" that sloshed with an ancient sound and clung in their throats. They watched Joe Keaton do his bit—a drunkard character stumbling and slurring—and the medicine did its work in their cider-warm bellies, making them feel like they were watching a mirror that reflected their image as something rapturous. Joe neatly kicked the hat from Myra's head, and she turned with a mock scowl. He pranced and cursed and fell, while his wife continued her song, the crickets crescendoing to drown her wilting soprano. The audience shook the dust free from their sleeves and hair with their laughter. They laughed together as if they shared one body; they laughed the way my brother and mother and father laughed when they discovered the puzzling relief of misunderstanding, the bag of tea leaves on the table rustling from the gusts of their breath.

And while the audience quaked, a storm was gathering along the fawn-stippled horizon. The world had narrowed, and Myra felt her womb stiffen, then loosen, wink-quick, just as a cyclone drew near, a spire of fury. It snatched the tent, leaving the rough wooden stage naked, the audience dashing for cover, and the canvas pinwheeling in the wind. Joe and Harry chased after it, taking off across the fields at a dead run, the night slivering around them as their feet creased the soil. Myra crumpled to the stage and was helped back to the boarding-house, the arm of some kind stranger supporting her, brushing the lump where Buster fidgeted beneath the flesh, stretching and struggling now with all his might.

Meanwhile, across the ocean, Jiří reached the top of the tower. The stonemason turned at the sound of his footsteps. There was a moment when they both must have felt what was about to occur. It itched in Jiří's hands, in the stonemason's shoulder blades.

As Joe and Harry ran, chasing the tent, the cyclone suddenly turned, shifting back toward the far-off sound of Baby Buster's first cry, and the stonemason's body traced a path through the air.

That is the way it was, the Kansas plains opening to offer cyclones, Prague's spired skyline pointing out the path between sky and street. Things moving, whirling—the air crackling with the luck of birth, a man peering down from the tower's height at the body wrecked against the cobblestones.

"And how could you not become the master of the fall with an origin story like that?" our father concluded his story reverently. Our eyes were as wide as they could go. We felt a small tide of magic run through us like being in love.

From across the room, our mother spoke quietly, as if to herself:

"Personally, I've always preferred Chaplin," she said.

Care Packages

IT MIGHT BE strange to try to get to know her again now, to make her more than a voice on the phone, a hurried lunch in a

garishly lit IHOP. I picture her alone, filling all her private soli-
tudes with scripture until her dreams brim with wings and
bright light, the soft-edged apocalypse she lives through each
day. I wonder what all the living she's been doing has looked
like without us—hardening around her like a chrysalis.

When we were in Prague, she sent us cardboard boxes
wrapped in overlapping transparent packing tape so that every
inch was covered, shimmering. I remember finding the boxes
on our stoop and being embarrassed that she had written
"Czechoslovakia" instead of *"Czech Republic"* in the address.

"Czechoslovakia doesn't exist anymore," I told her once
when she called, but it never seemed to sink in for her—this
idea that these faraway places could still be changing their
names, changing their shapes.

She filled the boxes with things she knew we'd be missing
from home: ranch dressing, peanut butter, Hostess snack cakes.
Canned pumpkin at Thanksgiving. She addressed the packages
to me, but often the box would be full of things that only Nick
liked: gas station jerky and Pringles, Easy Cheese and Fruit
Loops and SpaghettiOs. There were always notes inside—Bible
verses written out in her loose, scraggly handwriting, though
none of them were damning: *For I know the plans I have for you,*
declares the Lord, plans to prosper you and not to harm you, plans to
give you hope and a future. Sometimes there was even a note that
might say, "Take care of each other." This was perhaps her way
of offering a measure of her old love to my brother, passing it
through me like water through a sieve.

When we returned to the States, Nick and I settled in a city
that was a two-hour drive from our hometown. It was a city we
knew. It made sense. We could begin again here; we could
belong. Nick and I found apartments six blocks apart, and that

seemed to make sense too. It could be better, this life. Cleaner—as if sharing an apartment had begun to feel like clutter, our untidy collisions as we crossed back and forth from bedroom to kitchen to balcony.

Everything felt familiar on our return—the short stacks of diner pancakes, packets of hot sauce so readily available, the backroad driving with grease from fried chicken dripping down our wrists, the careless act of punching in numbers on juke-boxes that we had memorized.

Everywhere I went, I could understand overheard bits of conversation. So many words, jokes. The world felt full and noisy.

I saw her maybe two or three times a year, but never at home. I wouldn't go home, as if I was afraid that the pile of Nick's things might still be sitting in the driveway, bleached and musty from the weather. And so I'd meet her at a café or a park or even, once, a winery. She'd sit stiffly, twisting her paper napkin in her lap, the same way she used to worry the pages of the church bulletin into a limp helix, and she'd find ways to ask about her son without directly asking about him.

"You always were so close," she'd say. "Ever since the beginning."

She said, once, "I wonder what you'd do without one another."

Sister

IT'S NOT ACTUALLY uncommon for twins to be born grasping their sibling's heel. Fairy tales and Bible stories would have us believe it's something rare and strange and indicative of a lifetime of conflict when the babies grow up. Jacob and Esau, for example. Jacob, who stole his brother's birthright through trickery. Jacob, who was nonetheless chosen by God.

Nick held on to me during our birth. He kept his grip around my ankle. Even after, the doctor oh so tenderly had to loosen his fingers from me.

Any similarity to the biblical twins ends there. Nick is not Jacob. I am not Esau. Esau, the simple-minded lug who traded away his inheritance for a bowl of stew. Esau, who simply paved the way for his brother's entrance into the world.

Jacob, whose name means *He who supplants, usurps. He who takes by the heel.*

The doctor made a fuss about the strength of Nick's tiny grip, his small red hand already so strong and hungry. The doctor called him a "little warrior," and our parents were proud. The name Nicolas, meaning a "victory for the people," speaks of military-like triumphs, the world curled at his fierce infantile feet.

About me, the doctor said nothing. I was oddly quiet, making no noise while the doctor pried my brother's grip from my leg. In the end, they decided to name me Marta, meaning simply "sister."

Hard Weather

IN PRAGUE, TOWARD the end, there was a night of hard weather followed by a morning wash of gray that erased the steeples of cathedrals. Nick had gone out the night before and not yet returned at nine, ten. I watched the digital numbers change on my cellphone screen and didn't know what to do. I went to the west-facing balcony, then the east, as if the city would show me my brother in its midst, a point of brightness moving toward me or away. I looked up the number for the police station, and thought of the shuffling on the other end that would occur as they tried to locate someone present who spoke decent English. I thought of how I might describe him—tall, slim, dark-haired. It seemed like a description of anyone.

Finally he came. I heard the elevator door creak and shudder. I stood in the entryway of our apartment, and when the door opened, he stumbled inside. His face was not the one I knew. All cracked creases of blood. And how strange it was that I said not "What happened?" but instead: "What is happening?"

I soaked a washcloth in warm water, and we sat at the kitchen table. He was silent as I dabbed at his cuts with the cloth and began to find his face again.

"Nick," I said, "what are you doing to yourself?"

He swallowed. "I'm doing," he began, faltering. "I'm doing my best."

I didn't know quite what to picture—his feet carrying him into bars where he knew men gathered who would be willing to hurt him, a Czech word shouted after him in the street that he recognized as ugly. Or maybe there were embraces that began as urgent, furtive, before unwinding into a plea made for hurt, for punishment. I don't know whether he thought there was any kind of romance or redemption in the pain he gave or received. I don't know whether he sought it, planned for it, or simply allowed it. I only knew his face slowly reappearing from beneath the blood.

I could remember his old rages, white and red and hard to look at, like a lit road flare. Once, he broke a small bone in his hand from beating it against the steering wheel of our mother's car while he was learning to drive. I remember watching him rip pages from books he said were full of lies. Was this what he was trying to do to himself?

"Nick," I told him, dipping the cloth into a cereal bowl full of hot water. "It doesn't have to be like this. It can be better. It can."

Nick wiped at his eyes with the back of his hand. He had wrapped a handkerchief around his knuckles, spots of red dotting the fabric like watercolor poppies.

"What if I don't want it to be better?" he asked then, stubborn, childish. I was silent. His words had frightened me more than almost anything else he could've said. I remembered our mother's fear and how she never seemed to bother to hide it, how naked it always was, the fear that we would one day fall. I hid mine then.

Airport

IN THE PRAGUE International Airport, while Nick and I waited for our flight home, the word that seemed to follow us around was "overseas." *Overseas flight.* As if we were a pair of those birds that fly for days, fall asleep on an updraft of air, wings open and eyes closed.

It was weird to think about the solid gleam of ocean between us and the life we'd been used to for so long.

Nick and I left Prague the same year that a Boeing 777 flying between Kuala Lumpur and Beijing disappeared without a trace. Two hundred twenty-seven passengers and twelve crewmembers gone, presumably swallowed up by a patch of water in the southern Indian Ocean. After three years of searching, the debris still has not been located. So strange that so much can be misplaced so easily. So strange that the path of the fall went unnoticed by any but the 239 people on board.

In the airport, Nick and I sat close together but didn't speak. I could hear, in the rattle of Nick's cheap headphones, the song he played over and over again: "Trapeze Swinger." The sappy moan of guitar and a voice that somehow made me think of animals. I'd started to hate the song months ago, the leak of it through Nick's door, like the stink of the incense our mother used to burn when she prayed her endless prayers of protection. I hated thinking about Nick listening to the song and feeling understood by it, the way I'd felt understood by Morena's story about the cellar doors. I hated the orderly words of the song, making a display of something that felt private. I hated this stranger, standing in the gap between my brother and me, filling it with the cloying crackle of his soft growly voice:

Please, remember me—mistakenly,
In the window of the tallest tower.

I tapped his shoulder. He moved one of the headphones so his ear was free.

"Turn your music down," I said. "The whole goddamn airport can hear it."

He smiled wryly. "Fuck off," he said, his voice bright, and it felt somehow comradely. It felt like I'd been forgiven. He moved the headphone back, muted me. I saw a single hair growing from the corner of my brother's mouth that begged to be plucked. Or kissed. I watched it, thinking I might see it grow before my eyes.

"Love you too," I said to the hair. Nick wasn't looking at me, and likely couldn't hear anything over the sentimental lullaby he was putting himself through for the thousandth time. But the people sitting around us heard. The man with his briefcase in his lap, the girl sleepily braiding her own hair.

I hadn't slept, and my mind was so beautifully hollow with exhaustion that it seemed new, like an infant's. Waiting for our flight, I was so strangely embarrassed and eager and weary that it felt like love.

I had told him he could stay behind alone. But neither of us knew what that would look like. It didn't make sense to us. Like an entire airplane somehow falling out of the world. I knew that, underneath it all, I wanted him to believe that things could be all right as long as we were a pair, as long as we maintained our proximity—even though we'd seemed to have already abandoned that when I lost my will to stay.

Separate Rooms

THERE WAS A day, a couple of months after our ninth birthday, when Nick and I came home from school to find that our mother had moved all the filing cabinets and piles of books and boxes of paints and modeling clay out of the small spare room she and my father used as an office. She had dragged one of our twin beds down the hall and into the room and it was pushed up against the far wall, looking minuscule and lonely.

She had painted my name on the door with one of those ribbony swirls underneath that looks like half of an infinity sign. The name had a hurried look to it, slanting somewhat frantically. I don't think either Nick or I put up too much of a fuss. She did a good job of making it seem exciting, having our own rooms. She took us to a poster store where we could pick out whatever we wanted to cover the walls. We filled our separate rooms up with things we liked.

But at night, a new sound came down the hall from Nick's bedroom: the soft thud of my brother kicking a foot against his wall. It was something he did in his sleep. Sometimes I crept into his room and stood over him, watching his feet move like a dog chasing rabbits in its sleep. I'd stand there and wonder if I should wake him, before finally turning back down the hall to my own room.

I fell asleep to that noise many times. It went on for years—the sound of my brother kicking his way to me, like the scrape of a tunnel being dug, spoonful by spoonful.

Apartment 510

I FISH THE spare key to Nick's apartment out of my kitchen junk drawer, and it looks somehow puny in my hand, like the key to a young girl's diary.

The weather has changed, and it's an unseasonably warm morning, golden and fresh like an apple cut in half. I woke up wanting to feel useful, busy, so I walk myself over to Nick's place to get things ready for his release from the hospital.

His building is chocolate-brown brick and lumpily stacked stone, and as I walk up to it, I recognize the spot in the large elm tree out front where a thick branch snapped beneath Nick's fall, dangling now like a dislocated arm in a sleeve.

Inside, the stairwell smells like store-bought cinnamon rolls and unwashed hair, like burnt resin and boiled cabbage. There's a rickety elevator with lights that flicker in a quaky strobe, but I want to take the four flights up on foot, want to feel in my heels the height Nick traveled on his way to the ground. I climb slowly. I count the steps. The heel of my boot finds a wad of gum, and I carry it with me up two more flights, where it finally unsticks with a noise like a bad kiss.

Outside Nick's door, the hallway seems to narrow. I have the nonsensical urge to knock. But instead, I put his spare key in the lock, duck inside as though I'm plunging underwater.

The air is stale and dim, and I stand for a full minute just breathing. It smells like him—a smell he's lost in the hospital: the fresh pungency of Irish Spring soap, the bright twang of ink and clean sweat, and a lower wheaty note like sun-warm ale. It's a good smell. I always thought so.

A few beetles have come into his apartment through cracks around the windows, but they stay up high, milling around where the ceiling meets the wall, once in a while taking flight with a noise like a piece of candy being unwrapped. On the walls are pictures Nick likes to look at: a lithograph showing domes and spires half-draped in fog so that the city looks like it was built on a floor of cloud; a pen and ink drawing of a waif-like girl that I did in college. The girl is creeping down a twisting spiral staircase, feeling her way with her hands on the steps behind her—the night visible, a dense blob of ink, through the window behind her. I shudder looking at it; it feels like seeing a picture of an old injury.

There are a couple of dishes left undone. I wash them and feel restless. I shut the faucet off and enter the living room. I pick up his books and flip through them. I don't know what I want from this—probably a closeness to him that I can't feel anymore in the hospital—crumbs falling out of the spine of a novel, a smudge of mustard in the margins of a page.

Some of the books I recognize from our Prague apartment, but it feels strange to find them here. I open the familiar bleached and tattered copy of Hrabal's *Too Loud a Solitude* and something slips from between the pages into my lap. It's an envelope, unsealed, the unglued flap lifting like a paper tongue. I turn it over in my hands, feel an odd lurch at the sight of Nick's even handwriting, our mother's name printed solidly, our home address underneath. When Nick and I were four or five, our mother set our address to music so that we'd remember it, a ridiculous jingle that drifts through me even now: *One-one-seven Peach Tree Road, a little piece of heaven, our sweet abode.*

Inside the envelope: a single sheet of paper folded twice, covered all over on both sides with writing. The air in the apartment grows stifling even before I unfold the letter, even before I read the date that he's scrawled at the top of the page: *October 4, 2017.* The day before his fall.

I feel that same weird, squinty vertigo I used to get sometimes as a kid when I'd loom above my father's model train layout, staring with blurry vision down at the lumps of hills, soft tumors stitched with railroad tracks. I'd try to fool myself, make myself believe that I was in an airplane passing high above, the whir of engines in my ears. The letter in my hands shrinks and telescopes sickeningly, the words careening teenily into rows of corn miles beneath me, into sagging powerlines almost too small to be seen from this height.

I stagger out onto the balcony, the letter still in my hand, half-crumpled. I stand there, trembling, and force myself to read the whole thing through. When I look up from the page, I'm looking into the tree that my brother passed through on his way to the ground, staring at the place where the thick broken branch still dangles. My breathing isn't quite right, and an old urge flickers through me to climb, to pull myself up into the branches where maybe I'll feel buoyant with all that air beneath me, suspended, where surely I'll be able to breathe properly and look through the empty limbs at the world's soft heft, the way it was meant to be seen, the dark grass smooth and distant from up there. I'm half-reaching, wanting the lines of bark to leave a soft stamp on the skin of my palm, when I see a small flash of green, a flutter of wings, a little emerald-bodied bird perched near the trunk, an arm's length away. I stand unmoving at the railing of the balcony for a long time, the light beginning to shift while I watch the bird—a parakeet, I'd guess, likely escaped from someone's back porch and still somehow surviving.

It cocks its head at me, its eye a crumb of black glass.

Specificity

I REMEMBER READING a poem once about a philosopher getting thrown out a window and thinking, on his way to the ground, about why the word for what was happening to him—the word *defenestration*—even existed.

There's no special word, he muses, for being bludgeoned by a golf club, for being tossed off a bridge, for getting run over by a train. So why should this act have been given such a specific name?

In the end of the poem, he lands. He survives. He concludes that *defenestration* is not, in fact, limited to people being flung through windows. Its definition is not as narrow as its original inventors first intended. According to the philosopher, the word speaks, rather, to the specificity of all human experience, of each act being private and particular to the individual experiencing it. His own particular experience being, specifically, that he was hurled through an upstairs window, and fell, and survived.

Six Blocks

I STUMBLE HOME from Nick's place, and the air feels like a syrup hardening as it cools. I move like a fly caught in sap.

It used to be easier to move, the air in Prague parting around me like a curtain held open. I remember how, in Prague, there was always the smell of bread, always the sound of my own feet on stone. I remember walking to the metro, stopping at a cart selling waffles and feeling very sick afterward, but continuing to go back to that waffle cart anyway, giving them more chances. It was so rare for someone to say "Good morning," even in Czech, that when they did I felt I belonged to them. I walked and walked until my feet felt raw inside my shoes, always holding on to this desire to kneel by the riverbank, by the vendor selling almonds in pink paper cones, so hot they seemed dangerous in my mouth.

We used to stand, Nick and I, in the high gray air of cathedrals, looking up until our necks ached. All I could hear the tour guide saying, over and over, was: "See? See what they built?"

Nick doesn't remember the city the way I remember it: red and strange, curling in on itself like a dead centipede.

"What is it you want from going home?" Nick asked me, days after New Year's, when I'd already started to pack. I didn't know what to tell him. Now, I'm aware that it was the same thing I've always wanted: to locate the life that always seemed to drift from me, to feel touched by the world I was moving through.

As I span the six blocks between Nick's apartment and my own, sleep is already heavy in me, the familiar longing to shut my eyes to all the world's living parts that can never belong to me.

I remember the cathedral, the air full of living dust, the light splintering into color. I remember the almonds shredding the roof of my mouth into ribbons. And I realize that none of it, not then, not now, will ever be enough to make me feel that I've begun to live.

Arrival

WHEN I ARRIVE outside my apartment building, I see her car parked crookedly against the curb, the Virgin Mary air freshener dangling from the rearview mirror, unmistakable. I peer in through the driver's side window, a small bubble of fear in my chest. But the car is empty, and then I see her just outside the double glass doors of my building. Her phone is pressed to her ear, and my phone rings in my pocket. The buzz against my hip goes through me like the time, as a kid, I reached across an electric fence to stroke a horse's chest and the current was in my face at the same moment it was in my hands. She turns, sees me, and the buzzing stops. She crosses the yard toward me, and I shove the letter deep into my pocket, slipping against the pink satin lining.

"I'm sorry," she says. "I should have called. I was in the city for the orchid festival at the botanical gardens, and I thought I'd come by."

She hugs me, and the hug is real enough. "How is he?" she asks. "I wanted to go by the hospital but thought it might be better if we went together."

"Yes." It's all I have. Limp little assent. I clear my throat. "They're gonna release him soon."

"Oh, good," she says. "That's good."

We stand, gently swaying, not knowing how to touch or talk. There's this clogged feeling all through my skin, as if each one of my pores has gone blind. We wait at the margins of the sidewalk, wait for something to shift, and finally she says, "Are you going to invite me up?"

"It's a mess," I say.

"I've seen messes," she says. "Quite a few messes in my day. I doubt I'll be shocked."

"You might," I say, crossing toward the front doors with her alongside, putting my key in the lock.

Vocabulary Lesson

TO GO, GOING, *went*. Upon arriving in Prague, I shoplifted a slim paperback volume on English grammar from the big three-floored bookstore in Wenceslas Square. I brought it to the English lessons I taught. I made lists of useful vocabulary. I thought hard about words, the slipperiness of them. *Window*, I would say, looking across the café where my students and I met at the rain-slick panes—the glass and its seams and the things that could be seen through it: a flock of black birds blurring the dark ledge of a bulky high-rise, an umbrella blowing wrong side out while a man stumbled behind it. *Win-dow*, my students said after me. I tried to zero in stubbornly on the word itself. Instead, I thought of an unreal blue. *Windex*. I thought of a commercial of cartoon birds splatting up against glass so clean it was invisible. I thought of my mother's cousin, taking a running leap toward the freshly washed sparkle of a wall of windows, feeling a slight give, a huge creak, and then suddenly his body out in the air, falling as freely as a meteor. *Window*, I said again, trying to bring it back. But the word had already become something else. I'd lost it.

I remember reading somewhere: "A window is a weapon of opportunity."

I remember reading that and thinking, *"Now, who but me could've written something like that?"*

A Turn

SHE DOESN'T SAY anything when she sees the streak of wine across my kitchen floor, the dead bodies of stink bugs on the windowsills. She sits, prim. She takes things out of her purse and arranges them on the sofa cushion beside her as if she's about to do surgery: lipstick, Kleenex packet, hand sanitizer. She squeezes the gel into the center of her palm, looks at me.

"Want some?" she asks, as if she's offering part of a treat—a bite of cupcake.

"I'm fine." I'm leaning against the doorframe, watching her settle in.

"How's work been?" she asks me, shaping her voice into a "small talk" voice. "Do you like your students?"

"Yeah, they've been fine." I cough lightly into my hand. "I took a little time off, though, after Nick fell."

"Oh?" She raises both eyebrows. "And the school was okay with that?"

"I'm a substitute teacher, Mom. I'm not exactly 'essential personnel.'"

"Okay, okay. You don't have to bite my head off. What about Nick? How's his work been?"

"He's pretty much doing all freelancing now, so he can work from home once he's released."

She nods, frowning approvingly, businesslike, and I am still standing in the doorway, as if waiting for her to invite me to sit down in my own apartment.

"How were the orchids?" I ask her.

"Well, they were lovely," she says as if this should be obvious.

She used to rotate hobbies every year or so, a constant cycle, as if she were trying to find one that would finally convince her to dedicate herself to it permanently. I supposed orchids were her most recent fixation, soon to be shelved along with all her other solitary pursuits—photography, calligraphy, Chinese brush painting, crocheting, bonsai trees—to name just a few. One year, I remember, the house was suddenly full of flowers she'd made from delicate layers of tissue paper, as if she'd stayed up all night making them like an imprisoned maiden in a fairy tale. The next year it was potholders, filling drawers in the kitchen to the brim. If she was particularly proud of a painting or photograph she'd made, she'd buy a frame for it at the local Salvation Army and hang it up in one of the bathrooms. And so, when Nick and I were kids, the bathrooms were always full of her, of the parts of the world she thought worth capturing.

I move a stack of books and papers off a chair for myself and sit.

"I want you to know," she says. "I've been praying and praying." This is how she always used to introduce information we might find unpleasant, a decision we'd disagree with. In high school, for example: *I've been praying about this, and I just don't think you and Nick should be staying out so late on the weekends.*

"Okay," I say shortly. I am nearly desperate to open a bottle, to lick the stripe of spilled red wine up from the floor.

She sighs again. "Look," she says, drawing out the word. "You've been looking after your brother for a long time now." She pauses, counting. "And I'm worried about you, about both of you."

I have a difficult time focusing on her words. Nick's letter pulses in my pocket. My eyes wander around the walls of my apartment, and it feels very odd that I own these things, that I chose to buy this sofa and, on the shelf behind my mother's head, the figurine of a bearded man seated in a chair that I got at a yard sale in a northern suburb.

"I just think it's time I took a turn," she is saying.

"A *turn*?" I ask, confused.

Behind my mother's voice, I think I can hear, soft and distant, a very small repeating thud, knocking against the wall, like the noise of my brother's foot in childhood, the small muted kick of his foot. She squeezes more hand sanitizer into her palm, rubs it around.

"I'm going to take care of Nick," she says. "Give you a break. And when he's ready, when he's well enough, I'm going to ask if he wants to move home with me for a little while."

Buster

WHEN WE WERE very small, my father used to balance Nick on one knee, me on the other. He bounced his knees up and down, chanting a rhyme that went:

> *Ride the horsey down to town*
> *To buy some sugar by the pound*
> *On the way, horsey fell down*
> *Dumped my sugar on the ground.*

At the end, we slid together, Nick and I. Bucked free, gripping the sides of our father's legs. It was meant to give only the slightest hint of danger. We knew, through and through, that we were safe, falling in the midst of being held.

When we were a little older, we still sat one on each knee. Our father told us the story of how Buster Keaton was given his name. He told us how, in a boardinghouse where Keaton's parents and the rest of their vaudeville troop had rented rooms, baby Keaton toddled toward a long flight of stairs. He moved, unsteady, closer to the brink, taking some of his earliest steps, trying out his legs. He raised a foot above open space. He'd seen his parents, his uncle Harry, coming and going up and down stairs just like these so often, their legs long and bent like trees. He let his foot reach for the step and missed it. He tumbled down, end over end, and there was his godfather, Harry Houdini, waiting at the bottom. He lifted the toddler, filled with awe that Keaton did not even cry, did not bleed, and said with reverence, "That was quite a buster." This was what everyone called him afterward—a name that recognized all the beatings the world would throw at him. A spell of protection, of memory—a name that would remind him, all his life, of that very first fall.

And why, my father seemed to ask in telling us this story, *why are we not all named Buster?*

Water into Wine

I CAN FEEL around me the smell of the last cigarette I smoked, almost visible in the air, the color of tobacco streaked across skin. Neither of us has moved or spoken and the silence is tight, firm—all muscle.

"Can I get you something to drink?" I have chosen to ignore what my mother has said, about taking care of Nick, and she seems willing to pretend for the moment that it hasn't been said.

"I suppose I'd take some spring water," she says, looking out the window. I follow her gaze, and for a moment we both watch a ragged cardinal gripping a black wire, the edges of its feathers brown rather than red, like a leaf getting old.

"There's only tap," I say, and she shakes her head without looking at me. "There might be some orange juice, though. Or Canada Dry. Coffee, tea. Beer, wine." I try to say these last two words flippantly and fail.

She looks at me then with a twitch in her nostril, her eyebrows pulling together. "Marty," she says. "Honey. It's two in the afternoon."

"I'm just telling you what I have."

She sighs, and the room seems to creak, listing a little as if we were in the cargo hold of a ship. "Oh, well, with circumstances being what they are, I suppose a little drop wouldn't hurt anything. Is it red or white?"

"Red." Already it's moving through me—cherries, rubies, poppies, holly, maple leaves in fall, the few remaining bright feathers on the cardinal outside my window, the pinprick glow of Mars rising from an eastern lip of sky.

She shrugs. "Christ *did* turn the water into wine," she says, wavering.

"He sure did!" Much too perky, she's suspicious now.

"But that was a wedding," she continues to reason.

"And this is a reunion," I say, countering.

"Just half a glass for me," she says, waving a hand toward the kitchen as if I were a waiter. "Just a swallow, really."

I nod, revising. "A gulp," I say. She blinks slow like a cat and looks away.

In the kitchen, the cork makes a good noise pulling free, and it will be all right, it will surely, surely be all right. The sound of the pour, also good. I can hear my mother in the other room flipping noisily through a stack of my record albums.

"I want the one with 'Here Comes the Sun' on it," she says when I come back into the room holding the two glasses.

"*Abbey Road?* I don't have *Abbey Road*."

She's kneeling with her back to me. "No, no. You know, the one with that cute ditty about the octopus's garden."

"Yes, Mom. *Abbey Road*."

I don't know when it happens, or how, but suddenly she is crying. I drink my wine.

"I knew he was going to fall," she is saying. "I just knew he would be the one—of the two of you—to end up hurting himself like that."

My wine is gone already. I set the empty glass on the table. "How could you know that?"

Her face is beautifully streaked with mascara—lovely charcoal stripes across her cheeks and eyelids, as though a chimney sweep has touched her there with dirty fingers. "A mother knows things," she says to me.

"Is that so?" My voice lifts. I raise the other glass of wine to my mouth, my mother's glass. "Tell me, please." She is looking at me now as if she cannot quite place me, like running into your bank teller at the grocery store, seeing someone who's familiar to you out of context.

"Tell me," I say, sipping now from her glass. "What things does a mother know?"

Night Flight

WHAT IS THERE even left to tell that you don't already know?

Perhaps you already know, for example, that falling is the second leading cause of accidental death worldwide.

Yes. That common.

During the same year that Nick and I returned from Prague, more than 556,000 people died as a result of unintentional falls.

And see? That doesn't even include the intentional ones.

Perhaps you already know that studies have been made, and the studies suggest that, across all age groups, women are more prone to falling than men.

And perhaps someone has already told you about Juliane Koepcke, who, in 1971, fell from a commercial airliner that was struck by lightning during a severe thunderstorm over the Peruvian rainforest.

The airplane, a LANSA Lockheed L-188 Electra OB-R-941, disintegrated entirely upon being struck a full two miles above the forest floor. It took her nearly thirty seconds to fall to earth. She was conscious for most of that time and said afterward that she could see the jungle rising to meet her: "a deep green," she said, "like broccoli."

As she fell, she remained strapped into her seat. It was suggested afterward that perhaps updrafts of air from the thunderheads slackened her fall, like the slowed descent of a coin dropped into water. Another hypothesis was that the row of three seats that held together during the fall (the two passengers beside her were thrown free) spiraled like the helicopter seeds that drop from maple trees, reducing the speed of her fall just enough to make survival possible. Another possibility was that the close-knit canopy of thick foliage buoyed her when she hit, functioning as a dragline—similar to how my brother survived his drop from the balcony, the tree limbs grabbing him like hands on his way to the ground.

In any case, Juliane Koepcke landed in the Peruvian rainforest on the night of December 24, 1971. Her only injuries were a broken collarbone, small gashes in her left leg and right arm, and an eye that had swollen shut. She was seventeen years old.

It was Christmas Eve, and she and her mother were flying home from the German-language high school Juliane had been attending in Lima. Her graduation ceremony had taken place the day before the crash, and Juliane and her mother were among the ninety-two passengers granted seats on the last crowded flight out of Lima that Christmas Eve. The search and rescue crew, upon finding the crash site several days later, said that the trees where the plane broke through were all strewn with Christmas gifts, torn strips of wrapping paper, red and green and gold ribbons hanging from the branches like decorations.

Juliane's parents were both German biologists who lived and worked at a research station deep in the Amazon rainforest. They had taught their daughter what it meant to live in the jungle, and so she knew the danger of storms and nightfall and injury, miles from anywhere. She knew that survival depended on finding water, that upon finding it she must follow the current downstream toward the small, lucky spaces that men and women had carved out to live in.

Juliane woke up hours after the crash with the row of seats covering her like a small tent. She called for her mother, who had been seated beside her when the lightning hit, but there was no one. She was entirely alone. It wasn't until two days later that she found any other trace of wreckage: another row of seats, like hers, but these seats were driven deep into the soil, with only the feet of a passenger still visible, wearing a pair of black high-heeled shoes. She had a thought—nonsensically, she realized later—that this passenger could be her mother, and so she took a long stick and touched one of the feet with it. When the shoe fell away, she saw that the toenails were painted a pale pink, and she knew, without question, that this woman was not her mother, because her mother had never painted her toenails, not once in her life.

Not far from this row of seats, she found a bag of candy, chocolates wrapped in colorful foil, and a Christmas fruitcake still in its tin. These she ate. She heard the cries of waterfowl, and she followed their calls. Her luck held: she came upon a muddy creek. She stood knee-deep in the flow and felt the current on the backs of her legs. She waded downstream, just as her parents had taught her. Eventually, the creek became a tributary. The tributary became a river. Ten days after the crash, she found a boat moored to the bank. She took gasoline from the boat and poured it over the gash in her arm to clear it of maggots. Then she waited. Later, when asked why she didn't just take the boat and continue downstream, she replied, "I didn't want to steal it." In the morning, a group of three local fishermen found her sleeping in the boat and took her to their village. They sent word to a pilot, who flew her to the nearest hospital, and it was there, not long after, that she was reunited with her father.

I was very young, maybe six or seven, when I wrote to Juliane. I was careful in shaping the letters with a blunt pencil tip. I carefully copied down the address of the zoological library in Munich where she worked. In the letter I remember that I wrote, bizarrely, "Are you one of us?" She never wrote back.

Perhaps more than those patron saints of sudden death or lost causes, more than Rita of Cascia or Jude Thaddeus or Saint

Andrew Avellino, who all failed to survive, my mother should've prayed to Juliane Koepcke who, at the age of sixty-four, is still living.

Her mother's body was discovered on January 12, 1972, nearly three weeks after the initial crash. An autopsy made clear that her mother was still alive upon impact, though badly injured, the only other survivor of the crash. It took her nearly four days to die.

"Tell me," I said to my own mother, looking at her across my dusty living room. "What things does a mother know?"

After Juliane had fully recovered from her injuries, she followed in her parents' footsteps and enrolled in biology courses at a German university. She returned to Peru in 1980 to study bats. Seven years later she published her doctoral thesis, which was titled *Night Flight: An Ecological Study of a Bat Colony in the Tropical Rain Forest of Peru.*

The Things a Mother Knows

"I KNOW THAT you need help, Marty," my mother says. "I know that you can't do everything on your own."

The Longest Journey Home

IF YOU WERE to remove the trees, erase the low-hanging vines, the whispered sideways tiptoe of tarantulas, the freshwater stingrays covered with soft inches of silt, the ferns curling with brown circles of spores like ancient writing underneath—if you got rid of all the things that make a jungle a jungle and replaced them with reddish cobblestones and narrow curved streets with tall archways of stone, lampposts, wires above tram tracks, shops with bells on the doors from a century ago, old church bells, old doors—then I think that I've almost known her journey. Juliane's. A miniature version, maybe. I know that must sound insane, that comparison. I never risked my own survival. But I did move that desperately. Mapless. A mad dash, blind from too much light. I threw myself forward as if to break through invisible underbrush. I stumbled, some nights, forward onto the heels of my hands. The city: my wilderness; Nick: my downstream destination, the river always following alongside, neck and neck.

Once, in winter, I stopped at the Kentucky Fried Chicken on Radlická and ordered a bucket to take home to Nick. He'd mentioned a craving a few days before. I cradled the cardboard bucket in my arms and waited at the tram stop while snow fell so thickly that I could feel its weight across my shoulders like an arm. Inside the tram, the passengers looked like Arctic explorers that had just been rescued. We stamped our feet. We breathed heavily and leaned our heads back against the frosted windows. The tram had made it about halfway across the Palackého bridge when it slowed, stopped. The surface of the bridge was a clean, unbroken sheet of white, the tram floating above all that snow like a boat. The driver stepped onto the tracks, looked underneath the tram, and shook his head. I trudged home through snow that was above each knee, climbing my thighs like a white rash. I held the bucket of fried chicken to my breast as if it was the only thing keeping me alive. It was a two-mile journey, the same distance that Juliane fell when the plane broke apart. I fell forward through white air so slowly that time seemed to go into hiding. I moved through that snow like clouds, like blank thunderheads. I couldn't tell the street from the sidewalk. The snow was still falling, throwing itself headlong against my eyelids. I followed the river as Juliane had done, kept it beside me—hip to hip with the stone parapet above the bank. I passed abandoned trams, empty and still lit up inside as if the world had ended very quietly, no noise except the hush of my legs moving the drifts aside.

At home, I set the bucket of chicken on the table. Some of the pieces had frozen together. The snow that fell from my coat and hair made its own smaller storm in the doorway of the kitchen. Nick looked at me and laughed. He clinked two pieces of chicken together like ice cubes and laughed harder.

"You just never make it easy for yourself, do you, sis?" he said to me. And I laughed then too.

Denial

THE WINE HAS loosened nothing in me, except maybe that soft red color behind my eyes. I look at my mother, the long-stemmed glass stuttering in my hand as I lower it onto the coffee table.

"I'm not the one—" I begin. I see no path through the words. "I mean. It's not me that needs—"

"Yes," she says, standing up. "You are." We look at one another—mother, daughter, and Nick a ghost too small to see. Like a germ. "You can't always be your brother's keeper," she says, her voice jerking. "I know it's hard for you, Marta. It's always been hard for you to get close to people. To anyone other than Nick, really. But maybe it's time to try. You know," she gestures, faltering, flapping her hands a little as if seeking to gain momentum. "To try to live your own life."

I feel for the letter in my pocket, as if the envelope with the folded paper inside is the only thing that could confirm or deny her words. But the letter isn't there. It must have slipped out, maybe in the stairwell. But no, I'm wrong. I see it—a pale island between my mother's feet and mine. Our gazes fall to it at the same instant. She bends down first to pick it up. She holds it in her hands, and it seems absurdly small—a letter a doll might send to another doll. The air crackles with the noise of the envelope turning over in her hands, the flap lifting, her eyes beginning to flit over Nick's words, and I remember—so strange—the love I had for her when I was eight, when she stood at the base of our backyard sycamore, fluttering anxiously and lifting her arms to me as if she could shorten my fall that way, calling up in a frantic little stream: "*No higher no higher, that's high enough, Marta.*" This is how she loved us, that tired reaching. And she is reaching now, her arm extended to its full length above and behind her like a birch branch as she holds the letter away from my grasp.

"Marty," she says, her voice hardening. "He wrote it to me, not to you." My teeth make a hiss in reply while I grab for the letter again, and this time snatch it up like a bug I've caught. The paper crinkles against my palm.

"Get a grip on yourself," she croaks at me. "You're not a child anymore."

There was a song we used to sing in children's church. It was the only song that seemed to make my mother nervous, a retelling of a Bible story set to rhyme that I would belt out from the very highest backyard branches:

> *Zacchaeus was a wee little man,*
>   *And a wee little man was he.*
> *He climbed up in a sycamore tree*
>   *For the Lord he wanted to see.*

In our own sycamore, I waited for him. I looked up and around me to catch a glimpse of God. Though he was never anywhere that I could see, I went on waiting, thinking, "Why doesn't he come?" And when my mother came out to the yard, making herself as large as she could with her arms high above her head, I always had an urge to drop down to her, but to do so, I thought, might be to abandon the hope of holiness itself.

"No, you listen to me," I am telling my mother. I'm winded, panting a little. "You already gave up your right to know him, okay?"

She is shaking her head. There's a look on her face that I wish I hadn't seen.

"He's my son," she says, laying claim to him belatedly.

"Go home," I hear myself yelling at her. "We don't need you here, okay? We're doing fine, just fine without your fucking care packages, all right? Just go back home."

I move away from her. I don't know where to go, so I go out to the stairwell. I float down the steps, feeling like some sort of leakage, like water seeping beneath a bathroom door. I keep moving and I can tell she is at the top of the stairs behind me like a long shadow. I stumble a little. I knock the arch of my foot against a stairstep so that it throbs faintly, but I catch myself, regain my balance, and I can hear, beneath the beats of my move-ments, the lofty words of scripture she used to write out on Post-it notes:

> For he will command his angels concerning you
>> to guard you in all your ways;
> they will lift you up in their hands,
>> so that you will not strike your foot against a stone.

I push through the glass doors out into the yard, the sidewalk, the street, and then I'm running. It's been a long time since I've run and it feels a little ugly, gawky, but then my legs find a rhythm and I can hear my feet and it's a good noise. Good like wine being poured. I don't know where I'm running to, until I do. The bar. The only holy place left. *My refuge and my fortress.* I'm running to the bar and the letter is a small, a very small heat in my hand.

Homecoming

THERE ARE TIMES I've wanted to ask Nick if his fall felt like a homecoming.

I want to ask him: Was it a relief? Do you breathe a little easier now, in spite of all your cracked ribs?

Not every break is a clean break. I know this.

I dream some nights that I try to mail a letter. To Juliane. To Keaton. To Hrabal. To my brother. And they keep coming back, those letters, *Return to Sender* stamped in blue ink. I don't know what the letters contain. In the dream, I never open them to see what I've written. I am asking them, maybe: "What should I expect?"

But I believe I am telling them—my dumb squarish handwriting still a little childish, a little plaintive—that I'm still waiting, have been waiting for years.

And the waiting, I want to tell them, is a sort of fall in and of itself.

Bar Talk

WHAT WE ASK of holiness, what it asks of us—a gathering of breath or the slow adjustment of the eye to a new light. The light inside the bar softens the day into a bluish dimness, the hour we all want, the hour we wait for. The neon whispers something to us like: *no clocks, no windows, no worries.* Tells us: *it's that easy*, that easy to erase the day by shutting it out. At one end of the room, the jukebox and the pinball machine hoard all the colors. The bar is gorgeous and filthy, vinyl curling from the stools like rubble from a ruined city, the floor carpeted and muted and rich with stains. There is a feeling in me of slow ripening, of gaining shape in the darkness while a trio of weathered-looking women over by the jukebox all talk at once like birds. They are the only other customers. The darkness makes their voices cool and sleek, like ice melting at the bottom of a glass.

"What can I get you?" The bartender is my age, maybe a little older, wearing a T-shirt that says *Thanks but no thanks.* I am immediately grateful for him.

"Well, what have you got?" Easing into a playful role.

"You name it." He has a dirty towel slung over one shoulder, like someone in a boxing ring.

"An Aperol spritz, *s'il vous plaît*," I say, putting on my best country club drawl.

He laughs, a bassoon kind of laugh—all brass and spit. "We're fresh out of spritz, *madame*."

"I'm gonna pretend that you called me *mademoiselle* so that your tip won't be in jeopardy."

"*Pardonnez-moi*," he says, bowing a little. I like this game made of words. It's like Scrabble, or a crossword puzzle; I want to make something fit. I name my drink and he pours it for me, and I take it down. Not all at once, but not gradually either. Three swallows. I count them like pills knocked into a waiting palm.

There's a silence between us after our banter, as if we're both a bit embarrassed, and I know I don't need to fill the silence, but I do.

"I have a twin," I tell the bartender.

"Is this the start of a joke?" he asks, grinning.

"I wish it were," I say, mirroring his grin. The empty glass throbs dully like the slight pain in my foot. "Have you got any siblings?" I ask him, genially.

"Sure," he says. "One or two."

I lift the empty glass like I'm toasting him, and he makes me another, holding down the button on the soda gun like a painter carefully mixing colors. I let the gold liquid cast a glow onto my face, like children holding buttercups against their chins to ask, "Do you like butter?"

I keep the glass near my mouth, can smell the heat of the liquor coming up in waves, like lines of shimmer over a highway in summer. *This one*, I tell myself, *I will take my time with*. But I am wrong. Two swallows, and gone.

"Any twins in the family?" I ask him.

"Is that a normal thing to ask?" he shoots back.

I shrug. "There is only one other set of twins in my family as far back as anyone can remember. My great-aunt, when she was well into her forties, got pregnant with twins: a boy and a girl. Just like me and my brother. But the boy, he went ahead and killed himself when he was nineteen."

"Is this true?" he asks skeptically.

I set the glass down. I raise my right hand like a Girl Scout. "I swear to God. Why would I be making this up?" I feel strange, entirely sober—the two drinks I just finished feel like a memory from weeks ago. The letter remains in my purse, like a used Kleenex you are waiting for a discreet moment to throw away. I can feel the eyes of its looping ink words on me, passing judgment, and I set the drink down again.

"The funny thing was, there was no real indication that the brother was unhappy, except that he became obsessed with horror movies. Monsters, aliens. He went to the movies all the time. Like, every day. And then, one day he took a whole bunch of pills. And that was that."

"Okay," he says, in an *I'll-take-the-bait* kind of way. "So what happened to the girl? After her brother died."

We're talking, I tell myself. *We're just talking, like people do.*

"The girl started wearing her brother's clothes. This was in the fifties, mind you. And she went around town in his suits dressed up like a man. Drinking, gambling."

He leans forward a little at that, as if he's about to tell me a secret. But instead, he asks me a question, his voice winking: "Was she into the ladies?"

"I have no knowledge of her sexual preferences. It was before my time, you know."

"Well, did she ever get married?"

"What would that prove?"

He gives me a look that I can't really read. Or that maybe I don't want to.

"You know what I don't get?" I say. "I don't get how you can come into this world with someone, I mean inseparably linked to someone—sharing a *womb* for god's sake—and then, all at once, they can just leave you alone in it. Can you imagine that?"

He doesn't say anything, but I can tell he is listening. I can tell. I tilt my empty glass toward him and he starts to make me another, scooping ice into the glass, counting the seconds of his pour. He places the new drink in front of me, and we both seem to eye it suspiciously, as if it is an unwelcome stranger. And I suppose it is strange, how my words seem to blur and the drink gleams up at us both like a single unblinking eye, and this new drink in my fist refuses to enter me, and I am alone.

"I wouldn't do that to my brother," I tell him. "Would you?"

The bartender says nothing, and I relish his silence. I rejoice in the fact that I've silenced him. This is my trick, and I'm good at it.

"But it's really not uncommon," I continue. "People in my family are always trying to leave. They're always saying, 'That's it for me. I'm done being alive.'"

I want to shock him, but he is not shocked. Not at all. He meets my eyes, and I shudder. It feels like something shifting beneath me, the frozen surface of a lake, and my body's on the other side of the crack.

"Look," he says. "It seems like you're going through some-thing right now, so why don't you drop the act and just tell me what it is."

And here I am—the one that's silenced. And there he is—the one filling that silence.

"You know," he says, sighing. "There's a history of mental illness in my family, too. It's more common than you'd think. And my brothers and I were always scared growing up that it might get passed down to one of us or all of us. And we were never taught by our parents how to deal with that. It's a really scary burden to have to bear."

I stiffen. My body is a corridor with panic moving up and down it. I know that I cannot stay. I know that in moments I will have to be back on the garish street. This is the hard part of the day to get through—the long, wobbly hours of afternoon. The faces on the street will all be the slightest bit monstrous, the sidewalk's glare showing everyone to everybody. It isn't that I want to hide. No. It's only that I want the light to soften, to go blue at its edges. And that bluing is such a long way off. I had tried to wait, to remove myself to a holy place, a sanctuary where I could spend a few hours waiting, let just enough time pass for the air to go blue and soft.

But I couldn't. I can't. I stand up from my stool and dig through my purse, avoiding the letter with my hands. I pull out a few bills that I leave on the counter in a neat stack, next to the untouched whiskey soda.

"Hey," the bartender says as I move toward the door. "Was something wrong with your drink?"

I pause with a hand on the knob. "I doubt it," I say, knowing that if anything is wrong, it's with me.

I take a deep breath, as if I'll have to spend a long time underwater. I fill my lungs, I open the door, and I plunge out into the blaze of the day.

What Is Inevitable

NICK ONCE SAID to me, "I think one of the reasons you love Keaton is because he's always silent. You can give him any voice you want."

It's true. The first time I heard Keaton's actual voice in a screwball talkie from the thirties, I actually started to cry. It was in many ways the right voice, but it was wrong also—all chest and gravel, such a deep resonant rasp for such a small man. It was the voice of someone who'd spent weeks in isolation, trapped in a mine shaft maybe—someone who hadn't spoken in a long while.

Nick was right, I'd already assigned Keaton a voice in my head. I'd even given him things to say to me and I recited them like prayers at night while I waited for the sleeping pills to kick in. Sometimes I still do. Little fortune-cookie-like aphorisms, things like: *"What is inevitable happens all at once, in its own time."*

In all those years of stunts and falls, Keaton was injured on set only once. It involved a flight of stairs. He was working on a short film called "The Electric House," which featured an old mansion filled with eccentric mechanical gadgetry. In one gag, a long, steep flight of ordinary-looking stairs would start moving, escalator-like, upward or downward without warning whenever

Buster stepped onto it. Then a series of comedic falters and falls would ensue as Buster tried to find his footing again.

Keaton had practiced the falls many times, but one of the crewmembers had accidentally recalibrated the speed of the escalator. As a result, Keaton's timing was off just enough that his foot caught at the top of the stairs, trapped in the rubber lip of the escalator. The bone snapped audibly.

Later, he watched with keen interest as the doctor set the bone. "I just wanted to see how it was done," he said afterward, his voice as jagged and raw as the bone's spiked edges had been.

The Landing

YES, THERE HAVE been times I've stood on the landing above the stairwell outside my apartment, and I've felt an urge in my limbs like a full-body itch, like the madness of a sunburn across the soles of your feet. The urge to let everything loosen and lurch forward, to uncoil the tight spring of your body and set all your parts in motion. Free fall.

That urge isn't about living or dying, giving up or giving in. It's about *possibility*. It's about standing at the top of the stairs and counting the steps and imagining where the body would land, then trying to map it out like a physics equation, drawing nonsense numbers in the air with quivering fingertips.

It's a way of meeting the thing that's already moving toward you, greeting it bluntly, with bones that can bend, unfold like blossoms, and begin to heal as soon as you hit the far-off floor. You can stand there above all these right angles, this height that's been spanned with wood and stone, made climbable. You can stand with your toes up against that height and look down and picture the untidy sight you would make against the linoleum of the entryway, should you choose to hurry all this waiting to its end.

From Now On

I GO TO the hospital. It feels as if there is nowhere else to go.

But inside everything is white, and I wish I'd stayed in the bar. I have a brief moment of peace in the solitude of the elevator, all the polished privacy of a chrome confessional. But then the doors scream open with a ding as if I'd been trapped inside a microwave and I stumble out into the fluorescence of the hallway.

In Nick's hospital room, the light coming in through the window by his bed looks solid, thick, something you could slice with a knife and serve on a plate. He is doing a crossword puzzle and throws it aside when I come in.

"Perfect timing," he greets me. "I was just getting a serious hankering for a cigarette."

Nick looks more frail than the last time I was here, so pale among white bed linens. I root in my purse again. I toss the sweaty, crumpled-up envelope onto his lap, another scrap of white. "I was over at your place earlier," I tell him. "I found this."

He smooths the wrinkled paper. I can't read his expression beneath his bandages. "And you read it?"

I nod.

"Mar," he says. "I'm sorry."

"Mom is here," I tell him. "She wants to get you back home where she can keep an eye on you."

"She's here *here*? Like, in the hospital?"

"I left her back at my apartment, but I wouldn't be surprised if she's heading over here right about now."

"She saw the letter too?"

I don't answer. I'm looking out the window without looking, seeing only that slanting yellow light, lemon curd and buttercream.

"Is that for real?" I ask. "What you wrote?"

There seems to be the very faintest tremble to his hands, an insect-like quiver, the jerky whirring of june bugs maybe. He swallows, his Adam's apple moving softly inside his throat.

"She wanted to know . . ." He speaks very slowly, with notes of weary dignity, like a politician making a speech in the aftermath of some major disaster. "She wanted to know how you were doing."

"And this is what you told her?"

"Well," he says, his eyes filmy behind the clean bandages. "I didn't mail the letter."

I think about reading parts of the letter out loud to him, forcing him to be accountable for his words, but that would require so much effort, and I'm suddenly so tired.

I sit down on the edge of his bed. It feels like the last time it will ever be like this—just us two, with the heavy cumbersome world on the other side of a wall, its light coming in through a window like frosting we could lick off a spoon.

I go ahead and tell him this, tell him the precise texture of my thought, because this thought, it seems, is already common knowledge anyway:

"It's going to be different from now on," I say.

Countenance

STRANGE THAT WE refer to original sin as "the Fall" when the motion itself is absent. We can find it, though, if we look for it. Indeed, it is difficult to separate the entrance of sin into the world from the physical drop of the bitten apple from Eve's hand into Adam's, then from Adam's hand to the ground.

Strange that so many people have agreed on this. So many people have said, again and again, "Yes, this is how it all began. This is the path forward: away from God, then back toward him again." My mother believes that this *happened*, that there was a man and a woman in a garden, their flesh the same flesh and so, in a way: twins. My mother sees, in the fall of the apple from the mouths of the first of us, a great need opening up through centuries until Christ reversed the arc of the fall with his body. The Bible tells us that Christ fell, too, stumbled beneath the weight of the cross he carried on the way through the city up to the hill of his death. Fell again when his body was taken down, dropping into the arms of his grieving mother as I had wanted to do in childhood, perched on the limb of my sycamore tree, feeling the long reach of her fear.

It is strange to see this everywhere. It is surely strange to be my mother, praying her way from one fall to another with this image of one man's death in her mind, its effigy gripped in her fist or tacked to the wall.

It is strange that we try to keep ourselves safe in light of all this, to dare survival when even God could not keep himself alive in our midst. I know, I know—one fall requires another. This is what our mother believes. The apple needed the body. Story can only open a need for more story, falling backward and forward across time, trying to map these histories that never quite reach a final understanding. She's right to be solemn, I suppose. The religion she's chosen does seem to carry a collective mourning for the state of the world. Perhaps this serves to lighten her own grief by comparison.

But I know that the same things that separate you from another can also bring you together. As children, when my brother and I still shared a room, my mother used to put out the light before bed, and the last thing she would do, even after she'd said goodnight, was to crouch between our twin beds and offer one hand to each of us. We turned our faces toward her, and she put a cool palm to each of our foreheads, linking us. Her hand was cool at its center, like a night-blooming orchid. Then she would speak a blessing, her voice so tender that the tenderness was almost troubling, unearthly. *The Lord bless you and keep you,* she said. *The Lord make his face to shine upon you, and be gracious to you. The Lord lift up his countenance upon you, and give you peace.*

As a child, I thought often of that word "countenance," believing I knew what it meant, even if I wasn't sure I'd be able to explain its meaning if someone asked me to. I felt the meaning, rather, in the glassy coolness of my mother's skin.

It was a word that always made me think of windows.

The Letter

October 4, 2017

Mom—

I'm sorry it's taken me a couple of weeks to reply to your last letter. One thing I love and hate about the city is it makes me feel busy even when I'm not.

To answer your question, I'm not sure I feel ready just yet to talk on the phone. This seems easier somehow. It's more natural after all the silence. Writing was always an easy thing for me anyway, and this way I get to admire my handwriting. All those Bible verses you made us copy out by hand to practice our penmanship—I guess I'm grateful now.

About Marta, I wish I could say that you're wrong to worry. But there is no one else to worry about her if not us. It hasn't been easy—maybe it's never easy being a twin, or a brother, or a son. I don't know anything else because this is all I've ever been. So much of what I know about anything at all is Marta, is filtered through her, and so, I think: the two of us can keep each other at a certain remove from reality. For good and for ill. It isn't always healthy (how much of living is good for one's health anyway?)—but it is what it is. Or was. I don't think I really know what's different now, but there was a day not long after I received your last letter when the two of us were walking together downtown. We'd just gone to the market, and we were crossing the sidewalk to move around a small crowd that was gathered there. There'd been an accident—someone had been knocked off their feet by a passing bicycle and had hit their head on the pavement. People were grouped around this man in his mid-forties who was lying down with a bloody handkerchief pressed against his head. The sidewalk narrowed there, and we had to slip around the scene in single file to keep out of the street, and Marta went ahead of me. I don't really know what it was that gave me pause. I mean, she didn't say anything, but I watched the back of her, her shoulders, and she turned to look at the hurt man, and I saw the side of her face, and there was something there, something in her face, this look, and I just knew that she wasn't okay. And maybe hasn't been okay for a while, and I've been missing it.

And yes, there is the drinking. There's always been the drinking, but I believe it's even worse now, has taken on a form I don't recognize, or maybe recognize too well. It was a means of escape once, for both of us. And now? I don't know. Now she seems to drink to bring danger out in her, bring destruction closer if that makes any sense. I know it might seem absurd to see the side of her face as we move past a crowd and in that moment to say, with certainty, "something is definitely wrong." But I know Marta. It might be all I really do know. She is, as one of my Czech students used to say, "in hurt." She looked at that injured man like she wanted what he had. Like she not only envied him his injuries, but longed for them.

I know she's always thought of herself as "the strong one" of the two of us, and I think casting me in the role of the unstable brother has helped her to feel stable through the years. But I'm realizing this isn't a pattern that's really sustainable in the long run. Cracks are already beginning to show. One thing I do know about being a twin: your twin can serve as a kind of mirror for you. And this mirroring can be deceptive; you can give to your reflection the parts of yourself that you do not want. You can see, in your twin, all that you never wanted to see in your own self. I'm guilty of it too. Mostly, since getting back from

Prague, I've been doing all right, and I've wanted to believe the same of her. I really don't know what she needs. And it scares me, this not knowing.

I also wanted to thank you for "coming clean" about Jiří and the falling story. I've had my suspicions, but I understand how and why families choose to sweep certain truths under the rug. Our family always seemed to have a special talent for it. I can read your concern "between the lines," but I would definitely hold off on sharing any of this with Marta—she's always been very attached to the narrative as she knows it, and her edges are thin just now.

Your Devoted Son,
Nicolas

Bad Blood

EVEN BEFORE I read Nick's letter, I thought that the story of Jiří and the stonemason couldn't bear any more alterations. It was like a torn shirt that has been patched and mended so many times that it is now made up entirely of scraps of other fabric. The age-old question: *Is it still the same shirt?*

I try to see every possible arrangement of events. I try to follow each narrative in turn. Maybe, like Nick wrote in his letter, it is better not to know which one is true.

Maybe it's better not to uncover those lives, the hungry days whittling the stonemason down almost to nothing, the orphanage where he grew up and the cruelty there that began to make him wary and mistrustful. Maybe it's better not to see the labor that went mostly to putting bread in the mouths of men he hated, men who called him a "lazy gyp" while he worked to gain an apprenticeship with a gruff, elderly mason who showed him no kindness but taught him everything about sawyering—smoothing cuts of quarried granite, marble, gorgeously dark slate, and honeyed sandstone, then fixing the even blocks with mortars and grouts so the chamfers were straight and tight. He was good at his work. For a long time, it was the only pleasure he had.

The story will keep fraying the more you handle it. But I can't quite leave it alone.

Perhaps, as he grew older, he began to learn that he could wield his beauty like a weapon, his dark eyes shaded by the brush of hair across his forehead. And perhaps, after many slurs from the sharp-tongued overseer of the renovations to the cathedral that the stonemason was spilling his sweat to make strong and sturdy and lovely, the stonemason caught sight of the overseer's daughter bringing bread and apples to her father at the worksite one day, and he saw how very young and shy and lonely she seemed, how easily he could ruin her, and perhaps he saw a means of getting even with the overseer.

He bided his time. He continued to tally Jiří's insults, his stubborn refusals to offer fair wages. Until eventually the stonemason stopped Jiří's daughter as she was hurrying home from the market with her arms full of wrapped parcels of butchered meat and packets of spices and sugar. He saw the laces of her little boot dragging through the muck below the hem of her skirt, and he knelt and delicately tied her shoe for her with his rough-palmed sawyer's hands, looking up at her meanwhile through the glossy sweep of his bangs.

Maybe it started that way, as a plan of revenge, a way to get back at the man who was profiting from the stonemason's hands, who made at least ten times the stonemason's daily wage to do less, to stand in the shade with his back to the cool stones that the stonemason had smoothed and polished himself, to call him a sluggard and a lazy clod and *cikánský flákač;* yes, maybe the stonemason's plans had started from hatred. But maybe the girl loved so easily, so willingly, and maybe her hunger to know even the very quietest parts of him began to stir something in the stonemason—something dormant and contained that all the cruelty hadn't been able to reach. Maybe, after they made love, he'd remain inside her while she stroked his hair and he wept into the nape of her neck. It was the most he'd ever felt—too much, but also not enough. Each longing fed another, and he felt rage for all he'd never felt before, all the lack opening up in him. And these moments with her were all that gave him any hope of filling that lack, though still, it was never filled.

And maybe when, months later, she told him about her pregnancy, he became terrified. He could think of no life he'd ever be able to offer her. And so, he told himself, he'd disappear. He would find a way to get his wages to her and leave the city once the job he'd been hired to do was finished. But in the meantime, he returned to his work without another word to her.

The daughter was beside herself. Distraught, weeping, not knowing what else to do, she finally revealed all to her parents, and Jiří, in a blind rage, went to confront the stonemason. It's quite likely that Jiří never meant to kill him, that he only wanted to accost him in the privacy of the tower. But maybe Jiří's anger was uncontrollable. Maybe, because of the stonemason's Roma blood, Jiří referred to the love between the stonemason and his daughter as an "abomination," referred to the unborn child in his daughter's belly as tainted, as "just another gypsy brat," and maybe it was then that something in the stonemason snapped. Maybe he started shouting into Jiří's face a vivid list of all that he and Jiří's daughter had done together in the quiet attic garret above the daughter's room, in the stable loft with the hushed bodies of horses stirring gently beneath them. Maybe he told Jiří about how they'd place their hands over each other's mouths to keep their moans from being heard, how she'd bite his shoulder hard enough to draw blood, to keep from crying out while her body bucked and heaved with pleasure. Maybe he spat it all out, biting the words into pieces: all the ways they touched each other. And then, unable to hear any more, maybe Jiří grabbed the young man by his frayed collar. He shook him until the stonemason bit his own tongue and there was blood at the corners of his mouth, just like the blood that ringed Jiří's daughter's mouth after their hungry lovemaking. Jiří couldn't stand the sight of the blood. He shook the stonemason hard, to silence him, to blur the red trickle, to make all the frenzied words cease, but that was the moment when the stonemason took a step back, away from Jiří's clenched fists, his frothing lips. That was the moment, with the taste of blood fresh in his mouth, the stonemason tripped over the open sill, the fall pulling him free from Jiří's grasp as easily as plucking ripe fruit from a branch.

I feel like a witness to all this, outside it but also contained. The earliest seeds of me present. Nick too. We are there. Curled up in Jiří, unknown, unborn, unthought of. It is a lonely place to be. But still, it is ours.

These days, the phrase *"bad blood"* keeps coming back to me. Like a smell clinging to the inside of your nose. Sometimes the phrase grows into *"bad blood between them,"* and I think about a literal rift, as if Nick and my mother were separated by an actual ditch, and at the bottom there was a gaudy trickle of that sugary fake blood from the backseat of Alex's car. *Bad blood between* . . . I stared too long into that ditch perhaps, and when I looked up, they were both on the same side, my mother and brother together, looking across at me.

What happens when we can no longer move toward or away from the things we fear? Is that what the fall becomes—both an escape and an arrival?

In another version: the stonemason's seduction of Jiří's daughter was not a seduction at all but something much, much darker. Maybe his death was no great sorrow to anyone.

I'm not saying that's how it was; I'm just trying to follow every possible track, to take my turn trying on the masks of each player in the scene.

In still another version: the shove to the back of the stonemason was just the senseless act of a madman.

There are things that could so easily be ugly and end up being beautiful instead. And so the reverse must also be true.

Mess

MAYBE I'VE BEEN getting it wrong all along. How did he phrase it in his letter? . . . *Keeping each other at a certain remove from reality.* Maybe Nick has chosen one method for measuring us and I another, and the two can no longer reconcile.

I sit on the edge of his hospital bed, and he's pulled up his good leg to make room for me. I'm sitting on my hands to warm them and to hide their tremble.

"I feel like you've rewritten history," I say.

"Look," he says. "I know I was a mess in Prague, and I'm sorry. I put a lot on you back then."

"A mess," I repeat.

"Yes," he says. "And you took care of me. You did. But now," he pauses, licks his lips. "Now, you need to take care of yourself."

I look up at the little television in the corner of the room, bolted to the wall, and I'm grateful for the blank screen at the moment. It would feel wrong for there to be some cheerful commercial for fabric softener there just now. It would feel wrong for Keaton to see us like this.

"You know—" I swallow and try again. "You know, I thought maybe that you'd tried to kill yourself when you fell. I thought," I continue, faltering, "that when I found the letter, maybe what I was finding was your suicide note."

He startles at this, as if the thought has never occurred to him until now. He reaches for me with his good hand. "Oh my god, Marta. No. I would never do that, okay?"

"But the story." I feel dangerously close to losing my voice entirely. "The bird, the doughnut. I thought you'd made all that up."

"Marta." He is as gentle as he knows how to be. "Maybe I embellished it a little. Everything was beginning to seem so, so"—he grapples for a word—"so *stark* between us. I just wanted us to be able to laugh a little about it."

Like Keaton, I thought. How all his falls were comedy but also something else. In his short film "Hard Luck," Buster's character repeatedly tries to kill himself, but all his attempts are comically thwarted. In the end he leaps from a high platform and hits the ground so hard that his body makes a crater. The crater is so deep, the impact so intense, that it carves a tunnel through the center of the earth. And yet Buster still doesn't manage to die. From the tunnel that his body makes in its fall, he emerges on the far side of the globe, unscathed, immortal. Like Christ, I suppose.

Nick is watching me. I can feel the chill of his gaze on my forehead, the place where my mother's palm would rest to bless us before we slept each night.

"Look," he says. "I promise, okay? I *swear* it was an accident."

"I would never leave you alone like that," he adds then.

We are getting closer to something that's been unspoken until now. I can feel it in the room with us.

"Listen, Mar," he says, bringing his head closer to mine by an inch or two. "It's a lot, you know. Feeling like I'm everything to you. Don't you want the stuff other people want? Don't you want—I don't know—to fall in love? To make a life? To share yourself with other people?"

Suddenly I see myself the way he is seeing me—a closed door that is able to grant access only to my twin brother. I stare at it, this image, thinking: *Is that me?*

"Don't you want a day where you don't feel the need to drink your way through it?" he asks me now.

"I am trying," I tell him, weakly.

"Are you?" he asks. "Maybe it's time to try harder then, Mar."

I want us to get back to a place of jokes and cigarettes and Scrabble games, but those things all feel far away. And so I linger in Nick's words, his view of my life, the space I tried to carve at close remove from him. I try to find my way through all this, like the time in the mirror maze when, looking for a way out, all I kept running into was my own image.

"You know," he says, breaking in on my thoughts, "I'll always be here." Then he amends, "I'll always be your brother."

Flesh of my flesh, I think but don't say. I feel a surprising longing for Prague, sober and cold and bringing that bucket of fried chicken home for him. Those offerings felt so meaningless at the time, but when tallied, they added up to a life. This was how a life was made.

"Is this our curse?" I ask him. "That one or the other of us is perpetually on the verge of a nervous breakdown?"

"I doubt it," he says. "I think our twenties have just been sorta rough."

"What if it is, though?" I persist. "What if this is forever?"

"You believe too hard in curses, Mar," he rebukes me gently. "But if we go through life with one of us always struggling, then we'll bear it as best we can." He pauses, checking to see if I'm reassured. "That's why there are two of us. So we won't be alone."

Sitting on Nick's bed, I want very badly to cry. I cannot recall the last time Nick has seen me cry—after our father's death maybe. But it was both of us then, wiping our faces on each other's sleeves. I want to give myself over to the grief, but Nick is still watching me worriedly with strips of gauze framing his eyes above and below. I want to cry because I feel unable to know him anymore, and so—unable to know myself.

I want to cry because: Is it really only each other that's keeping us both in the world?

I remember that New Year's Eve on the Charles Bridge, how he kept dipping away from me through the scattered crowd, how I kept watching his shoulders recede, his foot nearing the train of the bride's gown, and how I called out to him, "Don't you disappear on me." The memory is like a cramp in my gut.

"Oh, Nick," I say. "Don't you get it?"

He blinks, waiting.

"I've been alone this whole time."

Nick opens his mouth to speak, but a nurse comes into the room. She looks at us, hovering, uncertain, her posture curved like a question mark.

"I can come back," she says, and her voice is all apology.

"Oh no, it's fine," I say, giving Nick's good hand a pat and standing to leave. "Perfect timing."

Hooch

MORENA AND I got drunk together only once. It was the only time we ever left the dusty warmth of her little apartment, the only time we ever went out into the world together. It felt strange to see her on the narrow streets outside her building, a wool cap over her hair. The trams sent up a high keening as they moved past us, all lit up inside like party barges, the cables throwing sparks.

She had just had a fight with her boyfriend during their last phone call, and she told me it had made her feel like she "couldn't sit still." She seemed jittery and reckless, her hair unwashed. She kept saying things under her breath like "Couples break up over less all the time."

On the sidewalk outside her apartment building, she grabbed my hand and we ran, full speed, to catch the number 3 tram toward Vyšehrad, the tram's bell ringing busily to hurry us. I don't know what our urgency meant, only that it felt cleansing to be sitting there breathless in the tram's warmth, Morena's laugh as high and wild as the tram's bell.

We stopped at a corner store for bottles of the very cheapest slivovice, the kind with the red label that tastes like prunes soaked in kerosene. And, for a treat, a glinting green bottle of clove-scented Becherovka to wash the prune flavor clean again. She said, "Tonight I want to feel very Czech," and I knew what she meant: she wanted to feel like she belonged here.

We climbed up the city's second-highest hill to Vyšehrad, the old fort's thick cannon-pocked walls looming high above the river, the stone almost black, the crusted remains looking smug and ancient up there.

This was where, in times so old nothing was even written down, the very first settlement was built, the first seeds of Prague. Most of the fort was remodeled in Jiří's time, and now it's a clunky patchwork of Baroque rotundas, Empire-style gates, and Romanesque bastions. But there's still a ruined Gothic lookout tower and a few feet of east-facing wall, perched on a jutting chunk of raw cliff. These are the only fragments preserved from the Middle Ages.

We sat on that old bit of wall. We pressed our palms against the stones where moss was trying to grow. We watched the absent rim of sky beyond the city where airplanes and radio towers blinked red. On the river, long spires of yellow light moved like underwater plants. Morena told me about the fields outside her hometown in Italy: carrot-colored orchards, a lone donkey who got fat each year feeding on the fallen fruit.

We took turns listing for each other the things that we know. Morena knows how to shear a sheep. She knows a little about the history of baseball from dating an American once—she knows, for instance, that it was the Cleveland Indians who first decided to add numbers to their uniforms in 1916. She knows how to play the harmonica. She learned when she was twelve; once she carried her harmonica deep into the woods behind her grandfather's house and, when she played a bit of song, something answered back, an owl maybe, but maybe something stranger than an owl, she was never quite sure.

"We should go," she said. "We should go to Italy. To my grandfather's house."

I nodded. The slivovice burned all the way from mouth to stomach. I reached for the Becherovka, coughing a little. And then a thought occurred to her: "Tonight," she said. "We should go right now. We should drive to Italy."

The night seemed to wake up a little, becoming aware of itself, catching its own reflection in the glassy black of the river, admiring its shape. I felt my blood shift with the fresh current of the alcohol, catching the thrill of her words.

"Why not?" Morena kept saying. "I mean: why not? My car is parked in the garage over by the Palladium. If we start heading there now, we could be on the road by nine."

"How long is the drive?"

"Ten hours. It's nothing. Slice of cake."

There was a flash in which I could see the long drive south, unspooling from us like cloth: Morena behind the wheel, her hand flipping down the visor to shield her eyes because the moon was that stupidly bright. The plunging noise of air coming into the car. Colors along the roadside going from brown to green, as if we could make seasons turn just by moving through the world. The miles shrinking down, the languages on the signs of petrol stations switching as we passed through Pilsen and Munich and Verona.

"What's that phrase the American boy taught me?" Morena said then, giddy. *"What've we got to lose?"*

I shook my head, and I felt the magic of the drive already beginning to break apart. We sat on the wall smoking, and I knew that this little fissure into the future would close back up again if we didn't prop it open with more plans, more possibility. But the cold air rose off the river and shocked us back to ourselves. And just like that the drive passed back into fantasy.

"What other phrases did he teach you?" I asked her.

"*I get a kick outta you*," she said, delighted with herself. "But I think maybe it was Frank Sinatra that taught me that one first."

She started to sing: *Some get a kick in a plane, flying too high with some girl in the sky.* But I didn't want the song. I didn't know what I wanted. I thought of us sitting on a porch somewhere in cane-bottomed chairs, the night racing, purple, to cover over a wooded hillside, and her telling me the names of the trees as they each blinked out into shadow, like rows of candles being extinguished, reeking of juniper and spruce and laurel. I thought: *Not tonight, but someday.* Then I thought of Nick, and the porch, the chairs, the trees, all seemed to collapse inward, like sand sinking through an hourglass.

"We're all out of hooch," Morena said, turning the bottle upside down.

"*Hooch*?" I cracked up. "Was this American boyfriend of yours a bootlegger from the thirties?"

"What's a *bootlegger*?" She leaned hard into the word, made it beautiful somehow.

I took the empty slivovice bottle from her. "The guy that makes this stuff in his basement is a bootlegger."

"Like my nonno," she said, almost ecstatic.

"Your grandpa makes liquor?"

"He makes grappa. He'll put it in his coffee and say: 'Now this coffee has been corrected.'"

I could hear her voice beginning to grow drowsy. After a little while, we walked down the hill to the tram stop together and took separate trams home. I wondered if I'd believed just a bit too hard in the drive, believed it was more than a drunken dream we wanted to share, more than a fantasy we could build like the idle stacking of sugar cubes. But there was that slimmest sliver of a moment when it became real, when I lost track of Nick on the lengthy drive south, when I could imagine letting the words fall from me like a casting of dice, saying the words and meaning them: *Yes. Yes, let's go.*

The Hottest and Coldest Place

IN PRAGUE, NICK and I kept saying to each other, not recognizing the numbers on the Celsius thermometer that hung from the kitchen balcony, "Is it just me, or is this the coldest winter in the history of time?"

In summer, we asked, "Has it ever been this hot?"

Prague: the hottest and coldest place. It surprised us, these extremes.

One summer, I let the hair on my legs grow long. I didn't want to pay for razor blades and felt too tired and lazy to shoplift them. The hair grew dark on my calves, like the thin soil-sooted roots of potted plants—an outer coating that moved when I moved, like the slender legs of insects.

On the tram once, I watched a little Roma girl stare at my legs in wonder. She was alone, no older than nine, and everyone on the tram looked at her as if she were planning to rob every passenger blind—readjusting their purse straps, touching their money clips in back pockets.

She looked at me, and I looked back. She wore a limp, over-sized soccer jersey, and her face was clean and bright like a freshly minted coin. Her hair was loosely woven into a hurried braid, and she made me think of home—of the crisp, fragrant heat of small-town laundromats; of roller hockey games in parking lots as an endless summer day finally begins to fade, the streetlights turning speeding bodies into a purplish blur.

Finally, as the tram drew nearer to my stop, the girl reached over to touch the hair on my shin. It was the first time I'd been intentionally touched in months. She kept her hand there, soft but certain—the way you might touch a stray dog that you know will permit you to pet him. The girl looked up at me, curious, mesmerized by this animal growth on my long, femi-nine legs. But I was not embarrassed. I greeted her look, my eyes on the brink of laughter. She said a couple of words to me in Czech that I did not understand, and I said to her, pointing at my chest, *"Americký,"* as if that word alone explained every-thing. I shrugged an apology: *"Promiňte."*

She nodded wildly as if this made every kind of sense. *"Americký,"* she repeated gleefully. *"Jako* Chuck Norris."

I nodded. *"Přesně,"* I said. "Just like Chuck Norris."

In practiced English, she then said a very simple sentence: "The dark is afraid of Chuck Norris." I laughed. She tried another, shaping her mouth very carefully around the words: "Chuck Norris makes onions cry." I kept laughing, nodding wildly, encouraging her, and her little hand was still there, resting against my leg. She said something in Czech, then held up a finger as if to say, "One more," and then she told me,

"Chuck Norris can drown a fish." She grinned hugely, pleased with her own performance, and then finally, almost reluctantly, removed her hand from the hairs that her touch had somehow made beautiful. The tram slowed to a stop, its bell dinging, and she hopped quickly down the steps to the pavement below, waving at me through the glass from the street.

Without her there, the other passengers refused to look at me, and I felt a loneliness much heavier than if she'd never touched me at all.

The Hill

IN THE HOSPITAL parking lot, I shade my eyes with my hand just as I've seen Keaton do many times, just as I did myself on that icy plinth in Prague on New Year's Eve. But I see only the stark outline of my mother moving toward me across the light-bleached asphalt. I know her by her gait, the clop and hustle of her feet. I'd hoped to leave the hospital before she arrived, but I've timed it all wrong and now she's here, her hair lightly frizzed at her temples, pulling free from the clip at the back of her neck. We forget, sometimes, that the people in our lives are beautiful. I never thought about her beauty, only Nick's—perhaps because, as he said in the letter, his was a reflection of mine. A vanity of sorts. *Flesh of my flesh.*

She sees me standing outside the glass doors beneath the little overhang at the front of the building and approaches. When she stops with a few feet between us, she is winded, slightly ruffled. There is a long crease across the front of her skirt.

"Marta," she says. "Are you all right?"

I pretend that the moment of grappling over the letter never occurred. "I'm fine. What about you? How are you feeling?"

"I'm feeling like we should have a talk," she says, smoothing the stray hairs around her face with the flat of her palm.

"Yes, I'm sure you are." My voice is all shrug. "I was just up there, he's awake right now, seems chipper."

"I don't mean Nick. I mean—"

"Don't you want to see him?"

"Yes, of course, but—"

"But you haven't seen him in years, so what's the rush now?"

She shakes her head, flustered, just as she used to when Nick and I, at the age of nine or ten, went through our practical joke phase, when we used to loosen the tops of salt shakers, poke holes in our mother's umbrella so that the rain could leak through.

"Marta," she says then. "Why did you run off like that? Why did you take the letter?"

I feel a heaviness, a desire to plunge into sleep. I want to surrender completely, to get into bed and lie there for nine days without waking. But I can't let her see it, how tired I am.

"He has a right to his privacy, you know. I thought he wouldn't want you to see the letter," I say, speaking a little too quickly. "And he told me, just now, that he never meant to send it. He only wrote it to get some things off his chest. Anyway, I left the letter up there with him, so it's up to him now what he wants to do with it."

Her face is a dim pinkish blur with the light behind it. "All right then," she says slowly, suspiciously. She opens her mouth to say something more, but I break in, steering us elsewhere.

"Why now?" I ask her. "He fell weeks ago. What took you so long?"

"Well," she says, swallowing. "I wanted to tell you . . . To explain . . ."

There are some things that do not bear explaining, and she knows this. I wonder what it will be like now. I feel a tightening at the base of my throat, like a gentle noose, something closing in very gradually, and I know that it must be a form of dread, but its touch is almost a comfort. I'm realizing, watching my mother struggle to speak, that I've loved very little, really, through the years. I've loved Keaton and his work. I've loved the slow, reckless seep of booze—clouding you up inside so you can be a stranger to yourself again. I've loved the stories we keep close because we are afraid of ourselves, of our blood, of our own frailty. I've loved the tiny worlds my father made— treetops delicate as spun sugar and hills like an infant's knees beneath a blanket, and a town that he lit with LEDs smaller than dewdrops. He timed them so that when dusk came to the world he'd made, the lights would appear one at a time like fireflies coming out, and I used to stand above the layout, staring down, waiting for the lights to finish blinking on. I loved that—that waiting.

And I've loved Prague, I realize now. I've loved its tattered richness, its constant drizzle of good light—gold during the day, purple beneath the lampposts at night. I've loved, in a way, that it didn't want me—that it drove me back to the things I thought I knew, with its cold and relentless beauty.

I've always loved Nick too, of course. Perhaps all those other things were just a different form of the love I had for him. Perhaps there wasn't really room for much else besides him. Perhaps the world will always seem just a little too large or too small, once you've shared a womb with someone. Yes, I think that is what we're up against. That's our struggle.

My mother lowers her hands from her face. There aren't tears like I thought there might be.

"I've been praying . . ." She tries to begin again.

"You've always been praying, Mom," I tell her.

"I know I haven't been there," she says. "And I know it isn't right."

She looks at me, almost as if asking for help, but I give her nothing.

"I didn't know what to do. When your father died, it altered my whole world. It was like I couldn't recognize myself anymore, couldn't remember how to be a mother. It was all just foreign territory to me."

I am trying not to look at her, to look past her into the rows of parked cars. But my eyes keep returning to her face.

"I don't want to make excuses. I know that everything I did since Nick came home that night was pretty much the wrong thing."

"Pretty much," I mutter softly, but she ignores the interjection.

"I don't know how to make amends. Or if you'll let me. If Nick will. But I want to try. I want . . ."

She loses the thread, her list of wants. "I'm so sorry, Marty," she says then. "It's not right to be so alone."

I'm not sure whether the loneliness she's speaking of is hers or mine or even Nick's. But I recognize it, and the word gives me a tiny, prickling jolt, like static against my fingertips.

"I should've tried harder. To understand . . . And now it's just me. On my own . . ." She pauses and looks around as if suddenly aware of where she is. The hospital doors open and a very old man holding an umbrella across his lap is wheeled out by a woman in mint-colored scrubs. He clutches the umbrella tightly and looks around as if he's hoping for a chance to use it, but the air is bright, and a promise of rain couldn't be further off.

"I'm not asking you to feel sorry for me. I have God, of course," she goes on, her eyes leaving the old man and drifting upward. "I always have. But to have God and no one else is not what he intends. For anyone."

She is not looking at me. She is looking everywhere else. "I want to be better," she says, and the words sound so distant, as though they are spanning the tunnel that Buster's character made in his unlucky suicide attempt—the fall that pushed apart the earth and spat him out on the other side. "I want to help you and Nick be better. Stronger, I mean," she amends. "Happier." She shakes her head at herself, as if displeased with the word—knowing, I think, that she does not have the power to grant happiness where she wants to.

"Mom, the fact is, you don't know us anymore." I wanted to say *You're not a part of this anymore*, but it felt false. Even in her absence, she'd been an unspoken force, a ghost in the room, a string of noisy prayers still audible through the years.

"But we can know each other again," she says, wheedling. "You can fill me in. We can start fresh."

"No." I can feel myself stiffening. I do not know anymore who or what I am protecting. "No, this just isn't good enough. Too little, too late."

She looks weary. Things are not going as well as she expected, perhaps. The truth is: I don't feel I have much resistance to offer her. I'm just as tired as she is.

"Won't you at least let me try? It's all I'm asking," she says. And after a pause, in which a distant car alarm can be heard and then just as quickly falls silent, she adds, "Please."

She is finished. She has said her piece, and we both seem scraped out afterward. I don't know what I can offer her. I think of the years when she harbored and sheltered her grief, her prejudice, until one cracked open the other. I think of the empty space of the house with her moving through it, the swipe of a cloth sending sparks of dust into the air, the garbage bin full of used coffee filters as she sat forward on the edges of chairs and scoured the Bible for some sense. I know what it is to get lost inside a belief. I know the desire to grip tightly the lore and lessons that have been placed before you, longing to be told how to live.

I do not move. I do not offer my arms to her as she did to me so many times while I floated in our backyard tree branches. Her face is lit behind with the slanted sheen of a cloudless afternoon; each hair on her head is sharp and backlit, her silhouette this untidy arrangement of uncoiling lines, and a brief urge flickers through me—an urge to draw her, though I haven't sketched in ages.

The old man has dropped his umbrella and it is caught beneath one of the wheels on his chair. The woman in scrubs bends to pick it up, and the slight slope of the pavement carries him a few inches away from her. She spears the spokes of his wheel with the umbrella to hold him in place, pulls him back to her, and they move on.

"Listen," I say to my mother, my voice limp, buttery. "Let's not do this here. I know a place. Where we can talk. I'll drive us, okay?"

I hold out my hand for her car keys, and she hesitates, but then roots them out of her purse without saying another word and hands them over. I start walking to the car, and she follows behind like my shadow. I can hear the clip of her little pumps on the asphalt, and the sound makes me think of long afternoons at elementary school when I'd sit in the principal's office with a stomachache or a sprained ankle from playing kickball too wildly, and I'd watch through the blinds for my mother, and when she came, we'd cross the parking lot together, and I'd hear the clicking of her heels and feel the day all washed through with salvation, feel the unshakable gratitude of someone who has been lifted out of a dark dream.

But then the memory turns over to show its underside: as children, Nick and I being made to kneel, miming prayer, until our legs went stiff and prickly; waking us in the thick untampered-with predawn black to attend a sunrise mass and shouting at Nick for how sloppily he'd tied his tie with sleepy fingers, making me rub the scuffs from my white shoes long before any promise of daylight had arrived. And I remember the angry twist of my mother's mouth when she said stubbornly, "Not under my roof"—as if she'd built the house herself, laid the bricks, the shingles. I suppose it was always this way—there was bad, there was good. She wants nothing less than any of us want, I guess: to be loved for the good and forgiven for the bad.

When we get to her car, I open the driver's-side door, and it smells like it's always smelled in there—like makeup and old Earl Grey tea bags, the air freshener reeking of old aftershave. It reminds me of those mostly empty bottles you sometimes find in thrift stores, unscrewing the little silver cap to breathe in what some old man, now long gone, used to pat against his freshly smooth cheeks for a night out on the town. A man not unlike my father, come to think of it. I used to love the smell of that car, loved when I first learned to drive how I'd enter this mobile world where I could carry these familiar odors around with me everywhere—a portable piece of everything I knew.

She settles in, buckling her seatbelt fussily, and I put the car in gear. It's been a decade since I've touched a stick shift but my right hand and my left foot know what to do. Nothing is different. Somehow the car hasn't aged, shows no wear.

I drive her up to one of the only high places in the city. It's called "the Hill" because there's only one, and the unofficial story is that it was once an Osage burial mound, though it's never been excavated, and maybe people just want to invent a reason for this strange lump of earth that rises up from the flat, even ground beneath. The slope climbs steeply, then flattens at the top, and there's a small parking lot up there, a little outlook, a scraggly playground. You can park up there and sit in your car and feel separate from the back-and-forth of things, the hustle of the interstate down below. And so I park, and we sit in the car, and neither of us says anything for what seems like a long time. But then she starts to talk:

"You know you always, always wanted to be up high," my mother says, looking out through the windshield at the yellow-green hillside sloping toward the highway. "As a little girl, you used to climb up onto the top of your bookshelf, do you remember that? Sometimes we'd find you sleeping up there. Sometimes you'd climb up there with a blanket and a pillow, as if you needed to get up as high as you could in order to get any rest. It used to send me into panics, of course. I would give you hell about it, and you'd tell me you'd been sleepwalking, or 'sleep-climbing' I guess, and you'd cry and say it wasn't your fault, and you were right: I couldn't punish you for something you had no control over. At one point, I tried to get your father to build a sort of net beneath your bookshelf, just in case, but you never fell. Never once."

"I don't remember that," I say.

"Oh, you were really little. Couldn't've been older than four."

I roll my window down a little to get some air. It is nice to sit here in parallel, not to have to look at each other.

"Do you think you would've been as worried all the time, about me falling, if it weren't for the superstition?" I ask her.

"Maybe I still would've worried," she says. "Maybe it's just in my nature. But then, would you have become so obsessed with heights if it weren't for the superstition?"

I can feel a smile. It feels odd, my cheeks lifting unnaturally. "Maybe not. Do you wish you'd never told us?"

"Sometimes," she sighs. "But I suppose it's a part of you. Of us."

"Yes," I nod. It's strange to be talking to her like this. And I realize that maybe the strangest thing of all is that I've never asked her, in all these years, whether she has ever fallen. I guess I assumed that, like me, she's always been waiting. But I ask her now, and she is slow in answering.

"I was very young," she says. "I don't really remember it. I fell all the way down two steep flights of stairs. I broke eight bones. I was maybe four or five years old."

There's a flicker of fear in me, a chemical tang in my mouth, and I roll the window back up, thinking it's maybe just the reek of skidded rubber from the interstate below. My mother is still talking.

"I don't remember the fall itself, but I remember after. I remember my mother telling me to keep very still, that I'd heal faster that way. I remember her bringing me bowls of soup. I remember looking down into the bowls of broth and not wanting to see my reflection, because my face was all bruised and swollen. I remember lying there and wanting to move, to scratch an itch, but I was afraid that if I moved, the bones could break again, and I'd have to start healing all over again."

"I didn't know," I say lamely. "I didn't know any of this."

"Well, it was a very long time ago," she says.

I feel the urge to offer some incident of mine that is equivalent, but none occurs to me. I feel trapped inside the story she's just told.

"What happened?" I ask her. "When you fell. I mean, did you trip or what?"

It's the wrong thing to ask, I can already tell. She faces forward, blinking. "I told you, I don't remember that part. I just remember my mother," her voice wavers slightly, like a candleflame in a light breeze, "my mother bringing me soup."

"And your father? Was he still alive then?"

"Oh yes. He didn't die until I was twelve. But he, he—" she pauses, searching for something to do with her hands. She opens her purse, takes out her bottle of hand sanitizer, busies herself with that. "He didn't live with us anymore for a few years after that."

"Where did he go?"

"Well," she's still rubbing the hand sanitizer around, carefully coating the backs of both hands, catlike in her movements. "Well, he was sent away, you see. He wasn't well. In his mind. I suppose that was the main problem: his brain was just never quite right. He lived in his own world, you know. He had trouble being present. He would *obsess* over things: stories, ideas. He couldn't let things go, and they'd consume him. Fill him up. Sometimes he'd be *convinced* of things that just weren't true, and there was no arguing with him. And it started to cause a lot of problems. But on top of everything else, he was a heavy drinker, a terrible drinker, and of course that didn't help anything either."

She says this very naturally, very matter-of-fact. I work to make my voice come out the same way. "Sent away where?" I ask.

"It was a very nice place. We still visited him. Most of the people there weren't insane, you know—most were just very sad and confused. Like my father. It was a very progressive place for its time, and he was very content there, much happier than at home."

There's another pause, and suddenly it all feels so familiar, even though I'm hearing it for the first time. "An institution?" I ask.

"Well, yes. You could call it that. A hospital of sorts, yes. But I believe they called it a 'rest home.'"

I am picturing my mother's fall, lightly tinted like those early photographs that were hand-colored with unnatural-looking dyes. "Your father," I say cautiously. "Was he the reason you fell?"

She clears her throat carefully, all her motions very slow and measured. She drops the hand sanitizer back into her bag, zips it closed. "He was at the top of the stairs with me. My mother was calling me from downstairs, and I could hear her—this part I remember. He said, 'Go to your mother, girl,' but I knew that she wanted me for some chore, or a bath maybe. Something I didn't want to do. So I hesitated, and he told me again, but I wouldn't listen. I felt a push. A push against my back. It wasn't a *big* push, he didn't mean for me to fall like that, but you know, he wasn't quite right in the head; I mean, he wasn't 'crazy,' he was just terribly out of touch. What I mean is: he'd get certain ideas in his head and he'd fixate on them, you know, and he had a hard time engaging with what was right there in front of him, with what was real—and in that moment he was fixated on the idea that I needed to go down to my mother, to take my bath or finish my chores, and in the moment, he didn't have an understanding of his own strength, of what that push could do to me, and the drinking of course didn't help on top of everything else, he'd probably been drinking—so he gave me a push and I went down, all the way down. But I don't remember that part. And I don't remember after, not until the soup."

I feel a little as if I've fallen with her, and at the end of her story, I can't move or speak. The air in the car goes stale, and it's my mother rolling the window down a crack now, opening the glove compartment and feeling around inside for a plastic container of scented lotion. She rubs it around almost cheerfully, and I feel that I've been left behind, at the bottom of the stairs.

The interstate below us is far, very far—a dull ribbon with little red and silver and black-bodied bugs dashing along it. I watch them, trying to bring them close, to know their actual size, to measure them. I wonder if that's what vertigo is—the distances moving rapidly toward your eye, your mind trying to flatten and shrink the height, so that you'll be less afraid.

A Brief History of the Pratfall

AT FIVE FOOT five inches, Keaton never longed for height. His height, that small body he could keep close around him, tucked tight, gave him mastery over his art. His body never held a bruise for very long; the patchwork map of color would fade quickly from his skin, like lamplight spreading outward, shades of ink and violet and rust and egg yolk.

He always knew how to take a fall, even from the beginning. This was why we watched him, Nick and I—to be prepared. We saw how he held his legs and spine accountable, trained his body to tense and soften in perfect symmetry. He knew how to loosen, then sharpen, all the separate fibers of himself. He slowed time down with his body, made it bend to him. It was like memorizing a speech or a song, names and dates—that's how precise a fall could be.

At a very early age, he studied the shapes of falls by dropping things out of upper story windows—apples, coins, a hammer, a broom—watching the paths these objects followed on their way to the ground. And he made note of how certain things fell straight, how others tumbled and turned, end over end, the angles of their descent smoothing into loops and spirals, the objects collecting in a strange, angular pile on the patch of soil beneath his window.

He could learn any fall just by watching. He learned card tricks that way, too. He loved how quick some things were. Quicker than the eye. The eye, he knew, is slow. His body gathered speed on its own, spending enough time in the air to understand its own weight.

This is why he seemed indestructible.

He had to rehearse, then unrehearse, the falls to make them look natural. A mechanical-looking fall would ruin the illusion of accident, of happenstance. And so he'd let his body speak from the floor or the wall or against the stairwell or ladder propped up at that rakish angle that he loved so much. He tried. He worked so hard. He made do with nothing but his own body. One thing he used to say: "When you can only do a thing once, it had better be right that time. If it's not, you make the best of it."

Lunatic

"WHY DIDN'T YOU ever tell us any of this?" I ask my mother.

"It's just, it's pretty ugly. I didn't want you to think about your grandfather that way. No one wants to feel like they have some sort of, well, *lunatic*, to use an ugly word, for an ancestor. I mean, I never thought of him like that, but other people did. People are cruel. So we always kept it quiet. The family did."

Something clicks then, it might be the word "ancestor"—a window thrown open somewhere in me, the noise of a stiff latch and a gust blowing through.

She is still talking:

"And you know, the drinking—there was so much stigma there too. It just seemed easier, better, for you and Nick not to know. About any of it."

I try to focus on the interstate, that steady strip of movement, but it blurs. I open the car door, step out into the day.

"Where are you—" I hear her, but I close the door. The rest is muted.

The Fraudulent Alchemist

LIKE THE MAN clutching his umbrella in the hospital parking lot, I suddenly long for rain. Little tatters and fits of water, impossible to hold on to except in the dampening of my hair.

My mother used to tell us there was a legend, a rumor, that the fall went even further back than Jiří. Like the Osage burial mound, a thing hidden deep in time—unfindable now. Unprovable. The legend was that Jiří was in fact a descendant of a famous charlatan, a man who wheedled his way into the court of Rudolf II with phony displays of alchemy and alleged conversations with angelic beings.

In his home village, years before his rise to fame, the charlatan was convicted of forgery and counterfeiting. The sentence for this crime was the cropping of both his ears. After his punishment, he grew his hair long and wore a cap with flaps covering the jagged holes where his ears had been. He traveled to Prague, where no one knew him, and started fresh. It was 1585, and the emperor Rudolf had assembled an array of scholars and scientists, built elaborate alchemical workshops for them. This man, Jiří's supposed ancestor, offered to the emperor small bottles filled with a red powder that, he claimed, an angel had revealed only to him because he spoke the angelic language. He told the emperor that this holy powder, unearthed from the ruins of Glastonbury Abbey, could be made into a tincture that held the power to transmute base metals into gold.

It's strange to think that this was how some men made their living back then—with these bizarre and gorgeous lies. They invented a world for themselves, lined with magic powders and words from angels, and then they lived in it, that world of their own making—knowing that everything they offered was false, or else digging so deep inside their own fictions that they began to believe them.

The legend goes that, through sleight of hand, the charlatan performed a convincing test for the emperor Rudolf, and a speck of gold no larger than a breadcrumb appeared at the bottom of an iron cauldron. That is all it took. That is how loud hope spoke back then. Rudolf provided the charlatan with money, materials, wine, a workshop. Months passed, years, and no more gold appeared in any of the charlatan's cauldrons. Eventually his past began to catch up with him; rumors spread that years before, he had narrowly escaped a sentence of defenestration for peddling fraudulent necromancy in the outer territories, a punishment that had been approved, in writing, by the papal nuncio himself. It was a popular form of execution back then—defenestration.

Not wanting to appear weak, easily duped, the emperor Rudolf finally imprisoned the charlatan in a tower of the Křivoklát castle, just beyond the city's western borders. It was there that the charlatan waited, forgotten, for three years.

During those years, he stood at his one window and measured with his eyes the height of the tower. He counted stones. He memorized the curved wall all the way from his window to the ground below. Then, from the threads of his own clothes, from the linens of his bedroll, the charlatan began weaving a rope. When the rope was long enough, he waited for night, and then began lowering himself down the outer wall. But the rope was too frail to hold his weight, and it snapped, and the charlatan dropped through the darkness, perhaps calling on the angels he'd spoken with so many times before to lift him in their hands so that he would not strike his foot against a stone.

But the angels did not come. He flickered through the air like a coin, still clutching the rope he'd made from his clothing, and upon reaching the ground, he broke his leg so badly that it had to be amputated. The emperor, in his great mercy, provided the charlatan with a wooden leg and banished him from Prague. The charlatan wandered between the outer villages of Bohemia, translating messages from the angels for the farmers and weavers and shepherds in exchange for hunks of bread. The years went by like this, until perhaps an angelic message arrived that was too much for even the charlatan to bear. At last he brewed a poison from the red powders he still carried with him and then, lifting his cup toward heaven in a toast, he drank it all down.

This piece of family history always felt impossibly distant from me. I had trouble locating myself in it. Maybe I felt that it showed too nakedly our desire to place ourselves inside history. It was never much more than a story for me, one that my great-grandmother Agáta had liked to tell her grandchildren because, she told my mother, it was good to look back as far as we could, to try to look back past the thing that had shaped us, into those older worlds where everyone, even kings, were innocent enough to be easily fooled.

Whiskey Flight

KEATON'S FATHER STOOD six foot four, almost a foot taller than his son. Although Keaton inherited nothing of his father's stature, he did inherit his father's love of whiskey.

This is a love that can take hold in disturbing ways. We know this, of course. For Joe Keaton, the liquor would sometimes bloom and open, burning as brightly, as fiercely, as his love for his wife and son. He'd grab young Buster up from the floor and toss him high. Buster would skim his fingertips against the ceiling as if it could open up and he could keep rising until the world shrank to a small turquoise stone miles beneath him. The smell of his father's breath would brush against Buster's face as he fell back into those huge hands, a breath that had remnants of Kansas cornfields in it—sunlight, pears drizzled with butterscotch, a warm wheaty sourness. And any slight unsteadiness, any falter of grip, any time Buster almost slipped to the floor, the thrill would only increase, the promise of his body's weight would become so much more real and potent. The smell of his father's breath, he would come to recognize, was the same smell coming up from the bottom of a small tin-handled cup that his father often kept at hand. The cup sometimes brought on the sound of his mother's sweet, mouse-voiced protests as she stood in the doorway, chiming like a grandfather clock, her voice ringing at her husband, *"Don't you drop him!"* And his father's voice boomed back as Buster rose once more—closer, ever closer, to lifting right through the ceiling—loud enough to be heard from the stars, it seemed, *"Goddammit, woman, I know how to handle my own son!"* And the sounds of his parents' yelling, the smells of his father's breath—these were what he knew of love.

Danger, we know, is not real until it is.

Braid

I STAND AT the brink of the hill's steep slope, and there is no urge to fall now—it would only be an absurd slapstick tumble, a childish roll of the sort Nick and I used to do, crossing our arms over our chests like dead bodies in old movies and letting ourselves go, gathering with our clothes and hair all the stray grass cuttings and the weightless fluff from dandelions we passed through, taking their seed with us all the way to the bottom. The world would remain in motion as we stood up, wobbly, shaking ourselves clean of all that tried to cling.

My mother has followed me. She stands at my side, and I feel a weird gratitude that she's chosen not to say anything yet. The wind grabs a fistful of my hair and yanks it back. I have an urge to cut it, to watch the strands sail free like parakeets through the teeny door of their cage. It itches in me, so badly I almost ask my mother if she has scissors in her purse—the little brass ones she uses to clip her nails. But it's like she reads me, like I've written it out for her in the air; my mother moves to stand behind me as the wind dies down, and she gathers my hair in her two hands like bread dough and starts to braid. This is good; she will not see my face as I speak to her.

"It wasn't just your father, was it?" I ask. "It was Uncle Ivan and Aunt Petra and Jiří, too. All of them."

She says nothing at first, and a horn honks piercingly out on the highway. I startle, and her hands are steady gathering the strands, working them together. I close my eyes. "Not *all*," she says, her voice muted behind a slap of wind. I wait, but she doesn't say anything more.

"Nick mentioned in his letter, the one I wouldn't let you see—that you told him about Jiří, about what really happened."

I feel the braid pulling a little tighter, but it's not an unpleasant feeling. It feels, I imagine, the way reins might feel to a well-trained horse.

"He wrote to me—your brother did. He was asking me about a history of mental illness in our family. Or mental *problems*, I guess. And so—I told him. I mean, I told him what I knew."

"Tell me now." The words sound too commanding to my ears, rough—I wish they had sounded softer—but she doesn't seem to notice.

She tells me what I'd started to recognize while I was sitting in the car beside her moments before. She tells me what my great-grandmother Agáta did not want to bring out into the open—wanting, instead, to offer her children and her children's children something full of strangeness and splendor and super-stition, a piece of lore they could hold inside them to feel that their blood and bones were made differently from the rest of the world's. This is what she meant when she said "You cannot choose your blood"—the things built into you like the unsee-able inner spaces within a block of stone. But you can, yes, you can choose which lies to believe. If the story could be made beautiful, why not beautify it—she might've said as much to herself: *Why not try to lend magic to the thing beyond the reach of magic?*

When my mother finishes speaking, the braid is done, and I know that soon I will have to turn around, to look at her. But not just yet. I take a breath. I am breathing the smells of hand lotion and car exhaust, these two smells meeting in the air, tumbling together like tangled kite strings. She puts her hands on my shoulders, presses down gently, as if afraid I might lift upward without the weight of her hands, rise and keep rising. She keeps her hands there a long time.

"I told you," she says. "I told you all along that it was only a story."

The Names of Others

ONLY A STORY, yes, but the fall was real. Even if we do not know the stonemason's name, the name of the one who fell.

We know the names of others: Juliane Koepcke, who fell two miles from the husk of a lightning-shattered airplane and survived; Vesna Vulović, the Serbian flight attendant who fell nearly six and a half miles and still holds the world record for surviving the highest fall without a parachute.

We know the name of Frane Selak, who survived three falls in four years. In 1962, Selak was on a train from Sarajevo to Dubrovnik that derailed while crossing a canyon. The railcars plunged into an icy river below the tracks, and seventeen of the passengers were killed, but not Selak. The following year, he took his first and only flight. A faulty emergency exit door opened midflight and Selak was sucked out of the airplane. Nineteen people were killed in the incident, while Selak was found, unconscious but alive, sprawled out across a haybale, as if he'd fallen asleep there. In 1966, Selak was a passenger on a bus that skidded off a slick roadway into a steep ravine. Selak climbed out of the debris, scraped and bruised but otherwise unharmed, and jogged up the road to the nearest village to get help. In 2003, this same man won 900,000 euros in the Croatian lottery, money that he distributed evenly among his relations and closest friends. He is currently eighty-nine years old. You could write a letter to him now. You could stamp and send it. It would reach him.

Twenty-year-old elevator operator Betty Lou Oliver dropped seventy-five stories down an elevator shaft on July 28, 1945, when an American B-25 bomber crashed into the Empire State Building during a heavy fog. All of her elevator's cables were severed during the crash, and after the elevator finally reached the basement, Betty had to be dug free from the crumpled rubble. She lived to be seventy-four years old with no long-term physical or psychological damage. And here's something strange: Betty had given her notice two weeks before the crash, and July 28, the day the airplane hit, was scheduled to be her final day of work at the Empire State Building. She'd circled it in red ink on her calendar, and written below the date: LAST DAY.

For these people, the fall is not "only a story."

I met a man in a bar once—I wish I remembered his name—who told me about a friend of his who'd always wanted to learn to fly. When this friend finally received his pilot's license, he offered to take the man on a flight in the yellow Piper Super Cub that he co-owned with a few other recreational pilots. They went up, just the two of them. The weather was good that day, the takeoff smooth. The man was seated behind his friend in the plane, and he felt a deep fondness as he watched him work the controls, handle the plane's movements. He felt a shared grace, as if he were contributing, just by being up in the air with his friend, to the way that the plane pushed through the clouds—the dip of a wing, the wind lifting them as if they were a ship at sea.

He watched the back of his friend's head, his neck and shoulders so straight and firm, and the two of them didn't speak during the whole flight, but the man told me he felt a closeness with his friend that he hadn't felt with anyone in years. This sense of intimacy came on so strong that it nearly brought tears to the man's eyes, and he had to force himself to think of other things, to watch the farmland below unspooling like yards of wrinkled cloth, green and gold, the tracks through half-mown fields like stitches of embroidery. It was then that something went wrong. The engine began to stutter and stall, and things happened very quickly. The pilot pulled up on the controls but the plane was losing altitude rapidly. Before the plane hit the ground, the pilot turned in his seat to say to his friend, "I'm so very sorry, Gene" (that was his name: Gene), and he kept saying, "It's my fault this is happening. There's nothing I can do. I'm so sorry." And then they hit the ground and the plane broke apart, cracked right in half. Gene suffered a mild concussion and a couple of broken ribs, but his friend was killed.

"I thought about it every single day," Gene told me. "I thought about the fact that he turned around to look at me, to tell me he was sorry for the mess that we were in, and then I looked at him, looked right back in his eyes, and didn't say a word. There was time. There were whole seconds before we hit the ground when I could've said, 'It's all right, buddy. It's not your fault,' when I could've said, 'You've always been such a good friend to me, and I love you.' I could've said any number of things, but instead I said nothing at all."

Maybe it's this *nothing at all* that we fear most. Maybe survival is sometimes more terrifying than its alternative.

Simon Yates knew this. He was a young mountaineer who, in 1985, tackled a difficult peak in the Peruvian Andes with his climbing partner, Joe Simpson. It was just the two of them on the mountain that spring, and maybe they felt the way Gene had felt when he was in that plane: the blessing of two souls alone together at a great height. They'd reached the summit and were just beginning their descent back to base camp when Joe's line slipped and he shattered his right knee against the cliff face. Yates did his best. He roped himself to his injured partner with a few feet of line between them. He tried, over the course of many hours, to lower Simpson from the peak in small intervals, feeding the line out a few feet at a time. They had made nearly 3,000 feet of slow, painstaking progress when Yates's strength began to give out. Then a spring storm rose up—crystalline at its fringes and purple at its center like the inside of a geode. Yates hurried. He fed the line out until Simpson was dangling free, a deep gorge yawning thousands of feet below, and Yates started to slowly descend, trying to calculate for Simpson's weight as well as his own as he sought footholds. But Yates felt something shift—the snowy ridge that was bearing their weight was beginning to give way. From his pack, Yates took the Swiss Army knife that Simpson had lent him days before and began sawing at the rope connecting the two men. The rope frayed, broke, and Simpson disappeared into the gorge. With his load now lightened, Yates was able to scramble to safety.

After returning to base camp, Yates weighed his decision. If he hadn't cut the line, they both would have died. There was nothing else he could have done. *Yes*, he told himself, *if one life can be spared, if one can survive, then shouldn't the rope be cut?*

Because fuel was scarce at that altitude, Yates burned his dead partner's things: all his clothing, his pack, his spare harness, his washcloth.

Three days later, Joe Simpson crawled into base camp, dragging his mangled leg behind him. The first words that Joe spoke to his partner were, "Thank you, Simon. You did the right thing."

They sat close to remnants of the fire Yates had built from Simpson's possessions, and Simpson told Yates that he had been lucky enough to land on a narrow ledge 100 feet below them rather than spinning into the gorge. From that ledge, he was eventually able to struggle back to camp.

Afterward, the world hated Yates for cutting that rope. It didn't matter that Simpson firmly believed that had the rope not been severed, both men would have died. In interviews with reporters and daytime television talk show hosts, Simpson always claimed that the only foolhardy thing that Yates did during the entire operation was not leaving Simpson for dead when he shattered his knee.

"He should've left me up there," Simpson said. "It's a debt I can never begin to repay."

But Simpson's gratitude made no difference. None whatsoever. All anyone could talk about afterward was the cutting of the rope.

Sometimes interviewers asked Simpson whether Yates said anything to him when he was cutting the rope, whether he called down to his climbing partner, whether, like Gene's pilot friend, he had said, "I'm so very sorry, Joe. There's nothing I can do."

Joe told them, "There really wasn't time to say much of anything."

Nothing. *Nothing at all.*

It's that silence I can't conjure—the creak of the ice, the sound of the rope fraying beneath the knife's blade.

In one of Nick's favorite novels, the narrator, a man named Haňtá, has worked for thirty-five years as the sole operator of a machine that neatly compresses piles of discarded books and wastepaper into large bales. It's just him, alone, in a basement full of trash, and so Haňtá is able to rescue as many books from that sea of rubbish as his apartment can hold. He works very hard to make the wastepaper bales as beautiful as he can, arranging the newspapers and encyclopedias and old tattered Bibles in such a way that when they are compacted, they will be brought together in shapes and combinations that are miraculous and surprising. He does everything in his power to make these bundles of rubbish into objects of beauty, always placing, at the center of each pile, a single discarded book, a work of history or philosophy that he has read and dearly loves. He leaves these books open to his favorite page or sentence. Then he presses the button that sets the hydraulic press in motion.

In the end, Haňtá is forced into retirement when a more efficient method of waste management is introduced. In the novel's final scene, Haňtá climbs into his trash compactor, presses a button, and the walls of the machine start to move.

Yes, this novel was written by Nick's favorite author, Bohumil Hrabal, who fell to his death trying to feed the pigeons that were perched on the windowsill of his fifth-floor hospital room. And, yes, it was within the pages of this book, in Nick's apartment, that I found the letter he had written the day before his own fall. Yes, see—how stories can sometimes build toward what is real?

In the novel's final moments, Haňtá sits in his trash compactor and waits for death, for the walls of the machine to crush him. He says then, says something like, "I refuse to be driven from my Paradise, and so here in my cellar I will choose my own fall."

Nick and I used to argue about this. Back and forth. I'd say, "Okay, so, he 'chooses his own fall,' but then what? If he doesn't survive, then how are we receiving the narration of his suicide as it's happening? How are we hearing his story?"

He'd say, "We have access to his mind, his thoughts. But that's not the point . . ."

I'd say, "He calls his death a 'fall' in one breath and an 'ascension' in the next. How can it be both?"

He'd say, "Why are you getting so worked up over this?"

And I didn't know what to tell him. I didn't know then why it bothered me so much. But now I know:

I couldn't understand how a narrator could abandon us so easily right in the middle of his own fall.

Free Fall

I KNOW WHAT I now know: that my mother's telling is itself a fall and we are surviving it. The hearing of history is a descent we must weather and manage—my mother already having fallen through it long ago and landed at the foot of the stairs. I am looking down at her from that height, measuring the gap between us with my eyes. Her gaze waits for the swipe of me in the air, saying with her eyes, "I know it is survivable because I am here, alive. But you? We'll have to see." I cast myself down alongside all the others: Juliane Koepcke and Vesna Vulović and Betty Lou Oliver and Joe Simpson and Gene and Keaton too. They keep me company in the air. After the plunge, there is silence. *Nothing at all.* But I know the silence isn't permanent, isn't irreversible. At any moment I can speak, can say what my brother said in his letter: *Thank you for setting the record straight.* Yes. That is what I'll say. But not yet. They are still waiting for me down below. I am not through falling, you see. I have not yet landed.

The View from Up Here

LIKE BITING DOWN on an apple and catching a bit of your own cheek in your teeth—that moment of startling at the ease with which you can do yourself small harm—that's what it feels like, to stand with my mother behind me, her hands still on my shoulders, not wanting to turn around.

A part of me wants to say, very calmly, the way Joe said to Simon after limping into camp, *"Thank you. You did the right thing."*

A part of me wants to screech at her: *"Don't you get it? Don't you know what it means to have to live with all this?"*

But that doesn't seem fair, when I don't really know either.

I suppose all it really means is: it doesn't end with the fall.

A Magician's Trick

KEATON ALSO KNEW this. He moved through seasons, touched by the world's motions like a windmill. He, too, had to choose to believe in his own stories: the fields that the cyclone crossed at his birth, and the storm that pulled him through an upper story window as a three-year-old, setting him down on an empty patch of ground to find his own way back home.

He chose to believe in his first fall down the stairs, Joe Keaton swaying at the top of that long flight, the legendary Harry Houdini poised at the bottom, waiting to lift him back up like a magic trick.

Recently, a magician who calls himself Mandrake drowned while attempting a Harry Houdini stunt. He was lowered from a boat into a river shackled with heavy iron locks and chains and never reappeared. Moments before attempting the trick, a reporter asked Mandrake, "Why risk your life for magic?"

The magician replied, "If I do it right, it's magic. If I make a mistake, it's tragic."

These things, we know, are so very close to each other—a mere hair's breadth away.

And this is why Keaton chose to believe the stories that his father told him, why he chose to embrace his own invincibility. He had to. He had to choose the magic over the tragic. He had to believe these stories were proof that he was built for the fall. Otherwise the stories were only the drunken ramblings of a tired old vaudeville performer struggling to draw crowds to their show. COME SEE THE KID, the posters screamed. KEEP YOUR EYE ON THE KID. Keep your eye on the miracle child who did battle with storms and survived, who withstood the world's worst beatings, its rampant bad luck.

Yes, all his life Keaton was asked about these stories—by reporters and fans and co-stars and by his first wife and then by his second and eventually by his own sons. And always, any hint of skepticism was met with his wide, watery stare, the thin grim marbled line of his mouth opening to give his sturdy, unceasing reply:

"Oh yes," he'd say. "Every word is true."

Spell

MAYBE TELLING THE story will loosen something, like the breaking of a spell.

The year was 1895. Jiří was overseeing the renovation of one of Prague's most famous cathedrals. Years before, his wife had started to note odd behaviors. Any attempts to confront or correct these behaviors would humiliate Jiří to a point of rage. These rages started to come more and more frequently. He drank, and the rages became worse, sometimes resulting in violence toward his wife or their seven children. He should not have been at work that day in early October of 1895. He'd already been fired from his job for "mental instability," which had come to light after a series of incidents reported by his workers. At the time, the renovation committee was interviewing candidates for the position of new foreman. But Jiří went to the worksite anyway. He climbed the unfinished tower, and one of the stonemasons was up there, taking measurements for the windows. The stonemason knew Jiří, knew that he wasn't well, knew that he wasn't supposed to be at work, and so the stonemason tried to persuade Jiří to come down with him, tried to encourage him to return home. But Jiří would not be persuaded. There was a struggle.

Another defenestration for the city of Prague to add to its list.

After that, the family had Jiří committed to an institution just beyond the western periphery of Prague, and his wife took the children to America. She wanted to find a cure for Jiří, and she'd read about a mental hospital near Chicago that had treated cases like his with great success. She planned to work and raise money and send for him when she could. But Jiří died in the Czech institution two years later from a bad case of pneumonia.

Eventually, Jiří's wife remarried. He was a simple, hardworking man—a mule driver in a coal mine. His name was George.

Said and Unsaid

I TURN AROUND. My back is to the slope of Easter green that reaches all the way down to the ditches beside the road, crowded with empty Mountain Dew bottles and silver Pop-Tart wrappers. I thought my mother would be crying, but she isn't.

How we got here: the story sideways then upright, small then not quite so small, like a ship going into a bottle, unfolding its little canvas sails.

I try to see what it was she wanted for us—withholding a narrative that would force us to always mistrust our own minds, trading it for one that sought to imbue a degree of caution but would still allow for something magical.

I do not think I can really blame her for that.

The light is dropping, the day rearing back. Lavender rises toward us from the base of the hill like a lifting curtain. She is right there in front of me, and it's time now to begin to forgive ourselves. But I can't give myself over to speaking. I hear in my mind how the conversation might unfold:

> "But you, you always seemed to believe so firmly in it—in the superstition—even though you knew it wasn't true."
>
> "It isn't always as simple as belief. You do what you can with what you have."
>
> "But. Didn't you ever think, with all these people—Jiří and your father and Aunt Petra and Uncle Ivan—didn't you ever think that maybe Nick and I—or you yourself—that we might be unwell? Didn't you ever question?"
>
> "Yes, but that is why I turned to God. That is why I turned my mind over to Him. And I prayed and I trusted that you and Nick would one day do the same. And then you'd be safe."
>
> "But what if that day never comes?"
>
> "It will. Maybe not in the way I imagined, but I know that, one way or another, grace will surely come. For you both. For all of us."

"How do you know?"
"A mother knows things."

It wouldn't have to be God, I realize now. That's only what my mother chooses to call it: this faith you can have in your own life, in the unseen shapes the world sometimes takes, in the stories you tell yourself to gain back trust in your own understanding, in your mind's cliffs and valleys—the stories you tell yourself to prove that you aren't so fragile that you can't continue.

It's my mother who speaks first:

"Marta, I'm sorry."

"What are you sorry for?"

"Oh, just . . ." She is very tired, I can tell. Even more than I am. "Just all of it."

I want to believe that this will do for now. But, dissatisfied, she offers more:

"Marta, you know I worry about you. You've seemed so, I don't know—*adrift*, ever since you got back from Prague. Can't you—can't you promise me, if you're not all right, that you'll tell me? Or tell Nick? That you'll try to let us help you?"

Trying to fall asleep one night a month or so before Nick fell, I recklessly knocked an inadvisable quantity of sleeping pills into my dry little palm and swallowed them down with gin. It wasn't intentional. "Stupid," I told myself when I woke the following afternoon, sluggish and aching. *"Hloupá"*—the same word that Czech policeman had thrown up at me as I knelt on the frost-coated plinth.

"No, no, no," I said, shaking myself free from sleep, slapping myself awake.

It was so strange, coming through the murk of pills and liquor, the milky light of afternoon hitting my windows all at once, beating wildly against my eyelids. See, I hadn't wanted to fall asleep and stay asleep, but I also hadn't *not* wanted it. I had both longed to wake and resisted it, letting myself drift, perhaps, into the pulse of fate, the tide of history.

When Nick fell, I thought his fall was what mine would've been—not something willed, but something dared. How roughly we sometimes handle our own mortality. I thought maybe, like our uncle Ivan, it was a way to test the touch of warm-palmed angels against your back, holding you in place—to see how badly you might want to climb back in through the window and keep living.

Sometimes we dare a little too much.

"Look," I say to my mother. I remember what Nick said in the hospital parking lot when I asked him if he was going to fall again. "I promise to try . . . To try to be careful."

It seems like the only real promise any of us can make to each other.

Aftermath

I TRY TO ground myself with this:

When I think back on this time years from now, I will think of my street. I will think of coming home at the end of the day, just like that day on the hilltop, my mother driving us back to my apartment. And when I picture my street, I will see its houses rise up behind my eyes—the night-smeared bulk of them, purple and crimson—the yards all full of growth, some so dense you can almost hear the soil whirring. I'll picture these nights, stacked up like bricks, as though I was building something out of them.

I will think about how well, how thoroughly, the houses always held on to their own light after nightfall, those liquid golden rooms with the curtains pulled up high or folded back like the collar of a shirt.

Some things change, reconfigure. If we still love, we love differently. If we still live, we live more carefully, hopefully.

There will always be a lot to fear: the mind straining against itself, the grip of things loosening. Today, one of my neighbors' kids lost a tooth, running across the concrete of her driveway holding out this minuscule bead of bone, grinning and streaming blood. I almost envied her, envied the proud grip on the tooth, the body losing itself with joy.

Already I can feel the glow that time will give to all this—the vines growing up over the porch rails, coming home after stopping by Nick's apartment to bring him food in white paper sacks, staying indoors with light coming in, steady, on one side of the room. At night, I can sometimes hear a single high note, a tremble in the air like the audible hum of electricity, the braking of city buses making a noise like whalesong. If I cannot sleep, I eat whatever is in the fridge—cupcakes left over from our birthday, clumps of cottage cheese with bright rings of canned pineapple, pickles crisp and briny straight from the jar. The wine in its bottle on the countertop has somehow been made innocent again, because I no longer allow myself to need it.

I know that these are the things that will remain. I know that after all this, I will still walk at night between lavender buildings, listen to the noises of a party gliding downward from a high balcony—bodies, voices, a fizzling radio—all up high, while I am down below. A beer bottle might fall from the railing and shatter, and the silence afterward as I continue up the street will be like the sound of water moving beneath a thin sheet of ice.

Recovery

MY MOTHER DRIVES us down from the hilltop, and on the way to the hospital we go through a Wendy's drive-thru because "Nickie must be sick to death of hospital food."

It's so strange how normal it has begun to seem.

In the hospital, I try not to see how fragile we are—how fragile I am. I try to radiate something that will say, *"We do not need to forgive each other just yet, but maybe we can position ourselves toward forgiveness."*

We sit with our hands folded and keep our eyes away from one another's faces. I believe that soon Nick will begin to look healthy, no longer the same color as his wrappings. While he spoons bites of his Frosty into his mouth, my mother and I sit beside the window, waiting for him to finish. For the moment, nothing is said. My mother has fallen silent again after her initial chirpings and whirrings, her voice getting small as an insect's to ask him, as if he were four years old, "Where—where does it hurt the worst, Nickie?"

In reply, he shakes an orange plastic bottle of pills at her, saying, "It doesn't hurt right now." And she nods, eyeing the bottle warily, eyeing the vase of the flowers that she ordered and had delivered here with that same kind of wariness, as if she's decided, after all, to disapprove of them.

There will be time, I suppose, for more to be said—for my mother to suggest to Nick that he come home with her and for him to refuse, as politely as he can. There will be time for her to admit her wrongs, to try again, to try harder. Time for Nick to be himself. Time for me to tell them it can be better than this. It can. I can.

We can almost hear one another's breathing. We are trying to get used to the idea of all being in the same room together.

Finally, my mother slaps her hands against her thighs.

"Well," she says, and the silence splinters into lovely spidery lines. "What do we do now?"

Return to Sender

THERE IS SO much choice in what to tell and how to tell it. Some nights, though not often, I still feel myself leaning a little too hard into sleep, and, even without the aid of the pills, the sleep will haunt my limbs the whole next day. It will stay with me like a private illness that makes me move around inside my apartment as carefully as a hermit crab. I will float through the day, suspended like a kite above whatever I'm doing.

In the midst of this, I think about Morena. I write things down on a pad of paper, things I think she might like to know—the time I thought she'd appeared beside me in the cold air, the time I placed my fingers on the wishing cross and believed I'd conjured her just by thinking hard enough about what could be.

It is difficult keeping track of myself this way, but I know it has to be done. I know that one day the letter I write to her will be finished and will need to be sent. Even if it never reaches her. Even if she no longer lives in that same Prague apartment with the cathedral-high windows where we'd pretend our lives didn't matter as much as we feared they might, that our days could be tossed up and laughed over and caught again like handfuls of snow. Even if she's married and happy, and the Italian summers are what she waits for all year—the homecoming when the fields brighten into a bittersweet apricot fire—even if she makes that drive each summer with someone who isn't me.

Even if this letter comes back to me, stamped across with ink so starkly red it makes my eyes tired. Even if I read beside her name *Return to Sender*, in a language I still don't know. Even then I will be glad, knowing I gave what I could give, letting my hand rest for an instant against the hope of her.

Yes. Even if I don't reach you, perhaps it will be enough to have tried.

The Tower

WHAT NOW, I do not know. Some days seem to be entirely outside any season. The other day, for instance, right in the frost-crusted middle of November, I could swear I smelled pear blossoms for a moment, like a heavy-bodied insect moving, all pollen-drenched, toward my face. And then: gone.

I think often of Prague, and sometimes the thought itches—a gorgeous rash. Sometimes I even tell myself: *maybe in the spring.*

In Prague, the stone itself seems to bloom in early June, blushing pink like dogwood blossoms. And it was in June, yes, early June—one of only two times that Nick and I went to the tower. *Jiří's tower*—we still call it that, that hasn't changed.

It was the same summer of the stifling heat when I let the hair grow long on my legs and Nick and I would walk all day through the city, following each other wordlessly, until we ended up wherever we ended up. It's been years now since that June day in the tower, but the view from up there is still printed on me.

The view from the tower is like all views: like breathing through your eyes. On that far-off day, Nick and I could see the rooftops sloped like sand dunes. A few streets away, there was a dark-haired boy on a balcony holding a ukulele—our vision inexplicably sharp enough to see the strings vibrating as he strummed, though we could not hear his song.

We tried to imagine what he might be singing: *Take us home* . . . And felt that, yes, maybe we *could* begin to feel at home here after all. The city spread out beneath us like the thick shag carpet Nick and I used to sprawl across to listen to our father tell his stories, to watch the TV screen where Keaton rose and tumbled like the slow easy rhythm of planets.

In the tower, I looked around for the stone where my great-grandmother Agáta's name had been carved in, deep as years, but I found nothing. We decided nonetheless on the precise window by closing our eyes and trailing our fingers over the sill.

"This one," I said, opening my eyes again. "This is where he fell."

We stood there, framed, looking out, a photograph that could move and speak. The courtyard below was the colors of fall back home—gold and brown and rust. We were sing-ing—the song doesn't matter now, it only matters that we were not solemn or silent. Nick took a flask from his pocket, unscrewed the cap. He held the flask out above the naked air and his wrist moved so that a thin stream, the coppery-nut color of dust motes caught in a sunbeam, poured out. The liquid made a bright line in the air between the lip of his flask and the ground.

"There's one for my man Hrabal," he said. "You weren't family but you should've been." He held the flask aloft, then put it to his mouth and drank long and slow. He passed the flask to me.

"And here's one for Aunt Petra," I said, letting the liquor splash all the way down. "For making us all terrified of pianos."

"For making us terrified, also, of little goblin men. And hallucinogens," Nick added. And we laughed and we drank.

"Here's to Uncle Ivan, beloved of the angels," Nick said, lifting the flask to toast the air, then letting fall another generous pour.

"To whatshisname—our cousin in Toronto," and we both drank to whatshisname.

Others were named—our great-uncle Josef, our great-aunt Flóra. We left no one out.

"To Keaton!" I said, triumphantly. "Our little lord and savior."

"Oh yes," Nick said. "We can't forget about him."

The liquor fell through us, fell from mouth to stomach like a pebble dropped from the railing of a bridge. The golden air was in us, and we were in it—you couldn't tell one from the other.

"And here's one for the Devil himself," Nick called out, getting grandiose, "who had to fall a long, long way just to get to hell."

We laughed, we laughed for them all. Hands on knees, we gave ourselves up to it, unholy, unhinged, unrepentant.

"To Juliane Koepcke! May you live forever!" We kissed our hands to the air.

"Just a small one for Dad," Nick said, drunk now, tilting the flask so only a few drops came out. "Who hated whiskey almost as much as he hated raised voices. Sorry for shouting, Dad."

We drank to our father.

We saved Jiří for last. We turned our faces upward, and the sun drank from our cheeks. We called down to the cobble-stones, the corners of the courtyard ripening into shadow.

"Jiří, you bastard," we called out, but still it felt fond.

"Yeah, thanks for nothing!"

We stood for a long time after all the liquor was gone. The light was beginning to narrow along the outer perimeter of the city, slanting so that the rooftops sharpened, like sunlight striking the blade of a knife. From up there, we felt we could see all the things we'd ever loved, spread out in a lovely tangle.

We stood until we could hear the shuffling steps of the security guard on the stairs below us, his keys jingling from his belt.

"It's time now," we knew he would say. "The cathedral is closing for the day."

We waited for him to come. The evening bells had started and were already drowning us out. But the day still felt very young—we had the sense that something was about to begin out there, something that we could see only from this height. We shielded our eyes with our hands, and we gazed so hard our inner lids were stamped, even when we closed them, with the angles of rooftops. We stayed like that as long as we could. We waited until the guard came. We waited to be told it was time to leave. And even afterward, there was still a lot of good light left.

ACKNOWLEDGMENTS

A very hearty thank you to my agent, Frances Coady for believing in my work since first laying eyes on it and for being my champion and cheerleader through the process of bringing this book to publication. Profuse thanks to the whole team at Bloomsbury, especially to my editor, Daniel Loedel, for an abundance of patience and precision, and for humoring my obsession with similes and with the word "tiny." Thank you to Akshaya Iyer and the copyediting team for their hard work and for acquainting me with the difference between biplanes, monoplanes, jets, and prop planes, among other things. Thank you to the art department for putting together a truly stunning cover. Thank you also to the folks at Jonathan Cape: Michal Shavit and Robin Robertson especially, for taking good care of me and my novel. Thank you to the National Endowment for the Arts and to everyone on the 2020 prose fellowship selection committee for throwing some immense good fortune my way during a very unfortunate year.

I want to thank Charles Baxter for modeling what the very highest standard of both teacher and writer look like, and for providing vast encouragement while I first started figuring out how to write about Keaton. Thanks to Dina Nayeri for writing me a really generous blurb. Thanks to the rest of my teachers and fellow workshoppers during my time in the Iowa Writers' Workshop, especially Jessie Gaynor, Ruth Joffre, Thomas Gebremedhin, and Jonathan Gharraie for providing me with food and friendship. Thanks to all my friends and faculty at the University of Montana for being excellent readers and supporters both in and out of the classroom, especially David Gates, Kevin Canty, Debra Earling, Judy Blunt (thanks, Judy, for all the soup), Eve Kenneally, Rachel Richardson Jepsen, and Lisbet Portman. Thank you to KJ Kern for being there for me while I struggled to piece together the difficult puzzle of balancing life and writing. Thank you to Chris Bachelder and Michael Griffith who have both been amazing advocates of my work and have provided me with a wealth of gracious feedback while putting eyes on early drafts of this book. Thanks to Jenn Glaser and the rest of the English Department for making the process of taking a semester off super painless. Thanks also to Leah Stewart and to everyone at the University of Cincinnati who was in workshop with me for exhibiting admirable kindness and fortitude while I submitted some pretty hefty drafts. Thank you to Alyssa Konermann for teaching me how to "smize" and to Claire Kortyna for gifting me the dress in my author photo and for being a quality friend in general. An essential thanks to Maggie Su for keeping me sane with karaoke and to Dr. John Henning for keeping me sane with therapy.

Thank you to Art Omi for all the good meals, good company, and for a beautiful space to scribble in during my residency. Thank you to the owners and staff of Sitwell's Coffee House in Cincinnati for keeping me caffeinated while I wrote this book. Thank you to Liana Quill Camper-Barry for putting up with me during our Prague year and for being the very truest and bluest of companions before and after—this book would not exist without you. Thank you to Nathan Staley for providing support and encouragement back when the seeds for this book were first being planted. Thank you to the people of Prague for introducing me to fried cheese and for letting me call your city home even for a short time. Thank you to Diana Kazandjian, who I'm sure never suspected would serve as the inspiration for a character in a novel while offering me so much delicious coffee and conversation. Thank you to Leigh Werrell for inspiring me with your talent and spirit, for letting me eat all the hummus, and for doing the crossword puzzle with me even when I was grumpy. Endless thanks to Richard Dillard for feeding and nourishing the seeds of my love for Buster and for being an essential mentor and friend. Thank you to Michael Keenan for our trips up to the mountain, for many a late-night meal at IHOP, and for introducing us to Prague in the first place. Thank you to Hollins University, to all my teachers and classmates, for a wealth of enriching friendships, memories, and learning. Thanks to Raphael Peterson for turning your apartment into a movie theater, and thanks to Cortney Phillips Meriwether and Stephanie Lohmann Fallon for continuing to restore my faith in the good of humanity. Thank you to Jenny Christie for showing me what the heart of a writer looks like back when I hardly knew what that meant. Thanks to all the Martins for treating me like a family member, and to Brenda and Dave Locher for the use of the beach house during the editing process. Thanks to Neil Thompson and Percy Thompson-Martin for having gorgeous souls.

The biggest thanks of all to my family—to my mother, Rhonda, for a lifetime of patience, support, and inspiration, and to my father, Joe, for modeling kindness, devotion, and grace. You both showed me what it means to look at the world with keen attention, gratitude, and wonder, and always fanned the flames of my love for books and words. To my sister, Faye, thank you for being the most ideal big sister I could ever fathom and an incredible companion on many an adventure. You have made my life vastly richer and more joyous from the very beginning. All three of you have always celebrated the good times with me and weathered the bad. You are the reason that I write. Thank you for being such a huge component of my work. Thanks also to my grand-mother, Wanda, for so many years of laughter and comfort. Thanks to all the animals and their owners for the snugs provided during the writing of this book: Sky Boy, Bonzy, Penny, Percy, and Egg the Cat. Thank you to my dearest friend, Sara Martin, for constantly fueling my awe and curiosity, for always being a perfect audience for my work, for shaping my writing ceaselessly with your spirit, and for showing me what true friendship is. Thanks also, Sara, for giving me the final scene of this novel one unsuspecting morning over breakfast.

The following works were incredibly helpful in the writing of this book: Rudi Blesh's biography of Buster Keaton, Werner Herzog's documentary on Juliane Koepcke, Bohumil Hrabal's *Total Fears* and *Too Loud a Solitude*, Alena Ježková's *22 Czech Legends* (a gift from a student—thanks, Renata!), Kino's *The Art of Buster Keaton* DVD set, Tom Dardis' *Keaton: The Man Who Wouldn't Lie Down*, Buster Keaton's autobiography *My Wonderful World of Slapstick*, and Richard Burton's *Prague: A Cultural History*. Thanks to Toni Judnitch for calling the "Most Beautiful Suicide" to my attention. Thanks are also due to Joanna Newsom and Sam Beam for providing the soundtrack to my time in Prague and during the writing of this book.

KING RICHARD THE SECOND

When Henry Bolingbroke, son of John of Gaunt, accuses Thomas Mowbray, Duke of Norfolk, of treason and of the death of the Duke of Gloucester, Mowbray rebuts the charge and challenges Bolingbroke to fight. At the lists at Coventry King Richard stops the fight and condemns them both for endangering the peace, banishing Bolingbroke for ten years (reduced to six) and Mowbray for life. Richard fears Bolingbroke's ambition to be king and the people's affection for him.

Visited by King Richard, the dying John of Gaunt paints an eloquent picture of England and denounces the King for leasing out the land. Despite the Duke of York's protest the King seizes Gaunt's estates to pay for wars in Ireland, leaving York behind as Regent. Defying banishment Bolingbroke returns to claim his father's estates and title. Northumberland and other nobles join him, leaving York little power to defend the realm. At Berkeley Bolingbroke persuades York to join him.

On his return from Ireland King Richard learns that his supporters Bushy and Green are dead, that twenty thousand Welshmen and even the Duke of York have abandoned him. With his spirits and fortune at a low ebb he reaches Flint Castle, where Bolingbroke asks pardon for returning to England while banished. Richard gives his pardon, aware that his authority has passed to Bolingbroke. In Parliament Richard bitterly yields Bolingbroke the throne: unable to read out a confession of his crimes because his eyes are blinded with tears. He breaks a mirror into pieces to show how brittle is the glory a king enjoys. Taken first to the Tower, Richard is then sent to Pomfret and the Queen to France. She pleads to go with him, but in vain, and they part in sorrow.

Finding his son Aumerle involved in a plot to depose the new King Henry, York hastens to tell the King, despite the Duchess's pleading. She urges her son to ride post haste and throw himself on the King's mercy. Aumerle reaches the King first, tells him of his guilt and remorse, and asks pardon. York arrives, calling for his son's execution. The Duchess enters, pleads on her knees before the King and will not rise until he pardons Aumerle.

At Pomfret, as Richard's jailor brings his food he lets in murderers, led by Sir Piers of Exton. Richard grabs a weapon and kills two before being struck down by Exton. When Exton brings in Richard's body King Henry denounces him, saying he wished Richard

dead but hates his murderer. Exton must live with his guilt and the King will travel to the Holy Land to wash away his own guilt.

WILLIAM SHAKESPEARE

KING RICHARD THE SECOND

Complete and Unabridged

CHARNWOOD
Leicester

First Charnwood Edition
published September 1992

British Library CIP Data

Shakespeare, William *1564 – 1616*
Richard II.—Large print ed.—
Charnwood library series
I. Title
822.33

ISBN 0–7089–4513–9

Published by
F. A. Thorpe (Publishing) Ltd.
Anstey, Leicestershire
Set by Words & Graphics Ltd.
Anstey, Leicestershire
Printed and bound in Great Britain by
T. J. Press (Padstow) Ltd., Padstow, Cornwall

Preface

William Shakespeare

William Shakespeare, born in Stratford-upon-Avon, was the son of John Shakespeare, a native of Snitterfield in Warwickshire, who settled in Henley Street in Stratford, where he traded as glover and merchant. He was elected to the Common Council, rising to hold office as Chamberlain. He became alderman in 1565 and Bailiff in 1568. In 1557 John Shakespeare married Mary Arden, daughter of Robert Arden, a yeoman farmer who had died leaving Mary a house and land at Wilmcote.

John and Mary had eight children, of whom three daughters died in early childhood. William, their third child and eldest son, was born on 23rd April 1564 and baptised in Holy Trinity Church, Stratford, three days later. William's three younger brothers all died comparatively early: only Joan, a younger sister, outlived him.

John Shakespeare's fortunes evidently declined; in 1578 he mortgaged his wife's property at Wilmcote and later was unable to repay the money when it fell due. From 1576 he rarely attended Council meetings and his name was finally removed from the roll of aldermen for non-attendance 'of long time'.

William is likely to have attended Stratford Grammar School, where he would have received a grounding in the 'small Latin and less Greek' Ben Jonson credited him with. While only 18 he married Anne Hathaway, eight years his senior, the daughter of Richard Hathaway, a farmer of nearby Shottery. The marriage took place by licence from the Bishop of Worcester, dated 27th November 1582, probably to avoid delay, as Anne was already pregnant. Their first child, Susanna, born in the following year, was baptised on May 26th; and within two years twins, Hamnet and Judith, were born and were baptised on 2nd February 1585.

How William supported his family in these early years is unknown. With four younger children and a far from thriving business John Shakespeare would look to his eldest son to help in providing for their joint household. Stories told about Shakespeare during these 'lost years' between 1585 and 1592 rely largely on individuals' memories and cannot be verified. One belief is that he was 'a schoolmaster in the country'; another, that he was employed by a country attorney. The legend that he was obliged to leave Stratford after being caught deer-poaching at Charlecote by Sir Thomas Lucy persists, but is similarly unverified.

Whether Shakespeare decided to seek his fortune in London or joined one of the companies of travelling actors that visited Stratford from time to time and so migrated to the London stage, the first mention of him after the birth of his twins is a bitter attack on him by a London playwright, Robert Greene. In a pamphlet written in 1592 Greene warns his fellow playwrights of 'an upstart crow, beautified with our feathers, that with his *tiger's heart wrapped in a player's hide*' (a parody of a line in Shakespeare's *Henry VI Part 3*) 'supposes he is as well able to bombast out a blank verse as the best of you and . . . is in his own conceit the only Shake-scene in a country'. The allusions to Shakespeare are unmistakeable. Friends absolved him of the charge of plagiarism; but the attack reveals that he is already making a mark in the theatre.

In Shakespeare's time neither actors nor theatres were viewed with great favour by those in authority. Actors were obliged to belong to one of the acting companies operating under the protection of a nobleman, to avoid a charge of vagrancy under the Vagrancy Act. Shakespeare belonged to the Lord Chamberlain's Company (later The King's Men) performing before the Queen and Court when called upon. The Company were paid for plays acted at the Lord Chamberlain's behest, their main income coming from takings at performances in the theatres; in Shakespeare's case *The Theatre* in Finsbury; *The Rose* and *The Globe* on Bankside; and later *The Blackfriars Theatre*.

Theatres were considered possible sites of

unrest, vice and disease. Outbreaks of plague closed the theatres frequently. When this occurred in 1593 and 1594, halting the demand for plays, Shakespeare turned his hand to poetry, publishing his two long and successful poems *Venus and Adonis* and *The Rape of Lucrece*, dedicating them both to the influential young Earl of Southampton in terms indicating growing friendship.

In 1594 Shakespeare and Richard Burbage became full members of the Company, a progression that would normally follow an apprenticeship of seven years, though records so early have not survived. Each member held a share in the ownership of the Company, acting members receiving an actor's share of the takings in addition. Plays were written for the Company on contract and the playwright paid by fee, the plays becoming the property of the Company.

Unhappily Shakespeare's growing success in the theatre was marred by family tragedy. In August 1596 his only son Hamnet, one of the twins, died aged only 11; and sadly with him the male line of the Shakespeares died out. His death must have tempered the family's pleasure in the granting of a coat-of-arms to Shakespeare's father, entitling him and his son William to be styled 'Gentleman': a sure sign John Shakespeare's fortunes had recovered, and marking a milestone in our playwright's career. Next year William, then aged 33, bought New

Place, one of the largest houses in Stratford-upon-Avon; tangible proof of his increasing prosperity.

In 1597 theatres were closed by the Privy Council when a comedy *The Isle of Dogs* by Thomas Nashe and Ben Jonson, played at *The Rose* was deemed to be seditious. Jonson and two fellow actors were put in prison.

Shakespeare himself did not escape trouble. His disreputable character Falstaff was originally named Sir John Oldcastle, until Lord Cobham, whose family name was Oldcastle, objected; Shakespeare was obliged to change the name to Falstaff. His play *Richard II* was potentially more dangerous. Shakespeare's scenes leading to Richard II's deposition were thought by some to parallel the political situation of Queen Elizabeth, including the Queen herself. Friends of the Earl of Essex asked the Lord Chamberlain's Men to act *Richard II* in February 1601 on the day before the Earl's abortive uprising against the Queen, for which he was executed. The Privy Council questioned the players closely about the performance but took no action.

John Shakespeare died in 1601 and is buried in Holy Trinity churchyard. In the next few years William strengthened his ties with Stratford. In 1602 he bought a parcel of land in Old Stratford and a cottage in Chapel Lane. In 1605 for the large sum of £450 he was assigned one half of all the tithes of Stratford, Old Stratford, Welcombe and Bishopton, at an annual value of £60.

In 1607 Shakespeare's elder daughter Susanna married John Hall, a rising young physician who built up a substantial practice around Stratford. Their daughter Elizabeth was born next year, shortly before the death of Shakespeare's mother Mary, who is buried with her husband.

In 1608 Richard Burbage and the Company took over *The Blackfriars Theatre* for winter use. *The Globe Theatre* was open to the air and plays were acted by daylight, whereas *The Blackfriars Theatre*, enclosed, provided more comfort for audiences and, with the use of lighting, the opportunity for more elaborate stage effects.

Shakespeare is believed to have returned to live in his native Stratford in 1610 when he was 46, although he continued his association with the theatre for some years longer. It was during a performance of his play *King Henry VIII* in 1613 when cannons were fired at the entrance of the King, that *The Globe Theatre* caught fire and was burnt to the ground, destroying, it is believed, irreplaceable records relating to Shakespeare and The Company.

In 1613 Shakespeare bought a dwelling place near the theatre in Blackfriars, the only property he is known to have bought in London. He seems never to have lived in it and to have rented it to one John Robinson. William Johnson, host of the Mermaid Tavern, John Jackson and John Heminges are named with Shakespeare, but evidently only as trustees. In his will Shakespeare left the property to his daughter Susanna.

In February 1616 Shakespeare's younger daughter, the surviving twin Judith, married Thomas Quiney, the son of his old friend, Richard Quiney; though the revelation of young Quiney's responsibility for the pregnancy of a young woman, Mary Wheeler, clouded the occasion.

Evidently ailing, Shakespeare had given instructions for his will to be drawn up in January. Perhaps doubtful about his new son-in-law's suitability as a husband for Judith, he took steps when revising his will in March to safeguard her position, laying down that one half of her bequest would become payable only when Quiney had settled on his wife lands worth an equivalent amount. This episode and the death of his brother-in-law William Hart, husband of his sister Joan, at the house in Henley Street, may have affected Shakespeare's failing health. Hart was buried on 17th April. Shakespeare died six days later on 23rd April 1616, his 53rd birthday, and was buried on 26th April in the chancel of Holy Trinity Church. His wife survived him by seven years and is buried by his side. His gravestone bears the inscription:

Good friend for Jesus sake forbear
To dig the dust enclosed here:
Blest be the man that spares these stones,
And curst be he that moves my bones.

The popularity of Shakespeare's plays during his lifetime is apparent from the lasting success of the Company, of which he was leading playwright, his own growing prosperity, and the pleasure his plays evidently gave to the Courts of Queen Elizabeth and King James. Printed editions of some of his plays achieved large sales and several reprints.

In his choice of themes he appears to have sensed the moods of the time: the surge of interest in England's past following the defeat of the Armada; a renewed feeling of patriotic fervour and interest in wars at the time of the expedition to Ireland; the perennial enjoyment of comedy and romance; the fashion for plays in Italian settings. After the death of Elizabeth a more sombre outlook emerges; changing in the last group of plays to a mood in which alienation and conflict give way to hope and reconciliation.

The Lord Chamberlain's Company regularly acted before the Queen at Christmas-time. In *A Midsummer Night's Dream* Shakespeare paid a graceful tribute to Her Majesty. There is a tradition that the Queen so enjoyed his portrayal of Falstaff in *Henry IV Parts 1 and 2* that she commanded him to write another play showing Falstaff in love, and requiring it to be ready in a fortnight. Signs of haste in the play, *The Merry Wives of Windsor*, and allusions in the text to an impending great occasion lend colour to this story.

In 1598 Francis Meres, in his *Palladis Tamia*, praised 'mellifluous and honey-tongued Shakespeare' for his *Venus and Adonis, Lucrece* and 'sugared Sonnets', ranking his comedies (*Two Gentlemen of Verona, Comedy of Errors, Love's Labour's Lost, Midsummer Night's Dream* and *Merchant of Venice*) with those of Plautus, and his tragedies (*Richard II, Richard III, Henry IV, King John, Titus Andronicus* and *Romeo and Juliet*) with those of Seneca.

Upon the accession of King James in 1603 the Lord Chamberlain's Company was authorized to become the King's Men and to play Comedies, Tragedies, Histories, etc., within their usual house *The Globe* and elsewhere. Under King James, who took a keen interest in drama, the King's Men acted more frequently before the Court, performing several plays at Christmas-time. In 1613 *The Tempest* was played before the King for the marriage celebrations of the Princess Elizabeth.

Of the thirty-seven plays believed to be wholly or partly by Shakespeare, nineteen were published in separate quarto editions during his lifetime, *Othello* also being published in this format in 1622. After his death Shakespeare's fellow actors John Heminge, the Company's manager, and Henry Condell undertook the editing of his plays, which were published in one folio volume, The First Folio, in 1623. This volume, including seventeen plays published for the first time contains Shakespeare's complete output of plays, divided into Comedies, Histories and Tragedies; except *Pericles*, which was published in an unauthorized edition in 1609 but omitted from the First Folio.

Ben Jonson, Shakespeare's great rival and candid critic, addressed him in his poem for the First Folio as 'My Beloved, The Author William Shakespeare', writing of him:

'I confess thy writings to be such
As neither man nor muse can praise too much'

and declaring

'He was not of an age but for all time'.

Later critics, including Dryden, Dr. Johnson and Coleridge, in assessing his achievement, have ranked him among the greatest of poets and dramatists.

His appeal today probably owes much to his profound understanding of the human spirit and his ability to represent men's and women's struggles to surmount life's tribulations. His superb delineation of characters must rank among his greatest accomplishments. His foremost roles — Richard III, Macbeth, Hamlet, Falstaff, Othello, Shylock, Lear — are figures of commanding presence, with all their human frailties. Many less prominent figures have unmistakeable identities, delighting or disturbing us in their roles and their relationships with other characters. Shakespeare peopled his plays with heroes and villains; nobles and artisans; learned and simple; young and old; men and women. His soldiers and country-folk bear in their speech the certain stamp of their condition and origins.

Shakespeare's range of themes and dramatic encounters confronts us with moral issues as fresh today as in his own time. Cruelty, treachery, dishonesty and unkindness are starkly portrayed and their protagonists remitted to our judgement. Several plays treat of simple domestic conflicts and trace the uneasy course of true love. His scenes of tenderness reveal a sureness of touch rivalling his mastery of contention and battle. His wit and robust humour are seldom absent from the action even in his tragedies. The plays are written in powerful and rhythmic verse and prose, many including some of the finest passages in our language.

Shakespeare's reputation has grown with the years. His plays have been published in numerous editions, translated into many languages and acted in countries throughout the world. This edition is the first to provide readers with large print copies of his works.

K. J. Rider

From careful study of published texts, performances and associated evidence, the probable order and approximate dates of composition of Shakespeare's plays has been established. A table of his works is appended.

Approximate Dates of Composition of Shakespeare's Works

Plays

By 1592   Henry VI Part 1

By 1594   Henry VI Parts 2 and 3
Richard III
Titus Andronicus
The Comedy of Errors
Love's Labours Lost
The Two Gentlemen of Verona
The Taming of the Shrew

1594–1597 Romeo and Juliet
A Midsummer Night's Dream
Richard II
King John
The Merchant of Venice

1597–1600 Henry IV Parts 1 and 2
Henry V
Much Ado About Nothing
The Merry Wives of Windsor
As You Like It
Julius Caesar
Troilus and Cressida

1601–1603 Hamlet
Twelfth Night
Othello

1603–1608 Measure for Measure
All's Well That Ends Well
King Lear
Macbeth
Timon of Athens
Antony and Cleopatra
Coriolanus

After 1608 Pericles (omitted from the Folio)
Cymbeline
The Winter's Tale
The Tempest

1613 Henry VIII

Poems

KING RICHARD
THE SECOND

Characters

KING RICHARD
  THE SECOND.

JOHN OF GAUNT,
  Duke of Lancaster, ⎫
EDMUND OF LANGLEY, ⎬ uncles to the King.
  Duke of York, ⎭

HENRY, *surnamed*   Duke of Hereford, son
  BOLINGBROKE,   to John of Gaunt; after-
                       wards King Henry IV.

DUKE OF AUMERLE,   son to the Duke of York.

THOMAS MOWBRAY,   Duke of Norfolk.

DUKE OF SURREY.

EARL OF SALISBURY.

LORD BERKELEY.

BUSHY. ⎫
BAGOT, ⎬   supporters of King
GREEN. ⎭   Richard.

EARL OF
  NORTHUMBERLAND.

HENRY PERCY,   his son.

LORD ROSS.

LORD WILLOUGHBY.

LORD FITZWATER.

BISHOP OF CARLISLE.

ABBOT OF WESTMINSTER.

LORD MARSHAL.

SIR STEPHEN SCROOP.

SIR PIERCE OF EXTON.

CAPTAIN OF A BAND
OF WELSHMEN.

QUEEN,   to King Richard.

DUCHESS OF YORK.

DUCHESS OF   widow of Thomas of
GLOUCESTER,   Woodstock, Duke
                              of Gloucester.

LADIES,   attending on the Queen.

LORDS, HERALDS, OFFICERS, SOLDIERS, TWO
GARDENERS, KEEPER, MESSENGER, GROOM, *and
other* ATTENDANTS.

SCENE — England and Wales.

ACT I

Scene I.

London. KING RICHARD II'S palace.
Enter KING RICHARD II, JOHN OF GAUNT,
with other NOBLES *and* ATTENDANTS.

KING RICHARD II.
　Old John of Gaunt, time-honour'd Lancaster,
　Hast thou, according to thy oath and band,
　Brought hither Henry Hereford thy bold son,
　Here to make good the boisterous late appeal,
　Which then our leisure would not let us hear,
　Against the Duke of Norfolk, Thomas Mowbray?
JOHN OF GAUNT.
　I have, my liege.
KING RICHARD II.
　Tell me, moreover, hast thou sounded him,
　If he appeal the duke on ancient malice;
　Or worthily, as a good subject should,
　On some known ground of treachery in him?
JOHN OF GAUNT.
　As near as I could sift him on that argument, —
　On some apparent danger seen in him
　Aim'd at your highness, — no inveterate malice.

5

KING RICHARD II.

Then call them to our presence; face to face,
And frowning brow to brow, ourselves will hear
The accuser and the accused freely speak: —
High-stomach'd are they both, and full of ire,
In rage deaf as the sea, hasty as fire.

Enter BOLINGBROKE *and* MOWBRAY.

HENRY BOLINGBROKE.

Many years of happy days befall
My gracious sovereign, my most loving liege!

THOMAS MOWBRAY.

Each day still better other's happiness;
Until the heavens, envying earth's good hap,
Add an immortal title to your crown!

KING RICHARD II.

We thank you both: yet one but flatters us,
As well appeareth by the cause you come;
Namely to appeal each other of high treason. —
Cousin of Hereford, what dost thou object
Against the Duke of Norfolk, Thomas Mowbray?

HENRY BOLINGBROKE.

First, — heaven be the record to my speech! —
In the devotion of a subject's love,
Tendering the precious safety of my prince,
And free from other misbegotten hate,

6

Come I appellant to this princely presence. —
Now, Thomas Mowbray, do I turn to thee,
And mark my greeting well; for what I speak
My body shall make good upon this earth,
Or my divine soul answer it in heaven.
Thou art a traitor and a miscreant,
Too good to be so and too bad to live, —
Since the more fair and crystal is the sky,
The uglier seem the clouds that in it fly.
Once more, the more to aggravate the note,
With a foul traitor's name stuff I thy throat;
And wish, — so please my sovereign, — ere
  I move,
What my tongue speaks my right drawn sword
  may prove.

THOMAS MOWBRAY.

Let not my cold words here accuse my zeal:
'Tis not the trial of a woman's war,
The bitter clamour of two eager tongues,
Can arbitrate this cause betwixt us twain;
The blood is hot that must be cool'd for
  this:
Yet can I not of such tame patience boast
As to be hush'd and nought at all to say:
First, the fair reverence of your highness
  curbs me
From giving reins and spurs to my free
  speech;
Which else would post until it had return'd
These terms of treason doubled down his
  throat.
Setting aside his high blood's royalty,

And let him be no kinsman to my liege,
I do defy him, and I spit at him;
Call him a slanderous coward and a villain:
Which to maintain I would allow him odds,
And meet him, were I tied to run afoot
Even to the frozen ridges of the Alps,
Or any other ground inhabitable,
Where ever Englishman durst set his foot.
Meantime let this defend my loyalty, —
By all my hopes, most falsely doth he lie.

HENRY BOLINGBROKE.

Pale trembling coward, there I throw my gage,
Disclaiming here the kindred of the king,
And lay aside my high blood's royalty,
Which fear, not reverence, makes thee to except.
If guilty dread have left thee so much strength
As to take up mine honour's pawn, then stoop:
By that and all the rites of knighthood else,
Will I make good against thee, arm to arm,
What I have spoke, or thou canst worse devise.

THOMAS MOWBRAY.

I take it up; and by that sword I swear,
Which gently laid my knighthood on my shoulder,
I'll answer thee in any fair degree,
Or chivalrous design of knightly trial:
And when I mount, alive may I not light,
If I be traitor or unjustly fight!

KING RICHARD II.
   What doth our cousin lay to Mowbray's
   charge?
   It must be great that can inherit us
   So much as of a thought of ill in him.
HENRY BOLINGBROKE.
   Look, what I speak, my life shall prove it
   true: —
   That Mowbray hath received eight thousand
   nobles
   In name of lendings for your highness'
   soldiers,
   The which he hath detain'd for lewd
   employments,
   Like a false traitor and injurious villain.
   Besides, I say and will in battle prove, —
   Or here or elsewhere to the furthest verge
   That ever was survey'd by English eye, —
   That all the treasons for these eighteen years
   Complotted and contrived in this land
   Fetch from false Mowbray their first head and
   spring.
   Further, I say, — and further will maintain
   Upon his bad life to make all this good, —
   That he did plot the Duke of Gloucester's
   death,
   Suggest his soon-believing adversaries,
   And consequently, like a traitor coward,
   Sluiced out his innocent soul through streams
   of blood:
   Which blood, like sacrificing Abel's, cries,
   Even from the tongueless caverns of the earth,

To me for justice and rough chastisement;
And, by the glorious worth of my descent,
This arm shall do it, or this life be spent.

KING RICHARD II.

How high a pitch his resolution soars! —
Thomas of Norfolk, what say'st thou to this?

THOMAS MOWBRAY.

O, let my sovereign turn away his face
And bid his ears a little while be deaf,
Till I have told this slander of his blood,
How God and good men hate so foul a liar.

KING RICHARD II.

Mowbray, impartial are our eyes and ears:
Were he my brother, nay, my kingdom's
heir, —
As he is but my father's brother's son, —
Now, by my sceptre's awe, I make a vow,
Such neighbour nearness to our sacred blood
Should nothing privilege him, nor partialize
The unstooping firmness of my upright soul:
He is our subject, Mowbray; so art thou:
Free speech and fearless I to thee allow.

THOMAS MOWBRAY.

Then, Bolingbroke, as low as to thy heart,
Through the false passage of thy throat, thou
liest!
Three parts of that receipt I had for Calais
Disbursed I duly to his Highness' soldiers;
The other part reserved I by consent,
For that my sovereign liege was in my debt
Upon remainder of a dear account,
Since last I went to France to fetch his queen:

Now swallow down that lie. — For Gloucester's
death, —
I slew him not; but to my own disgrace
Neglected my sworn duty in that case. —
For you, my noble Lord of Lancaster,
The honourable father to my foe
Once did I lay an ambush for your life, —
A trespass that doth vex my grieved soul:
But ere I last received the sacrament
I did confess it, and exactly begg'd
Your Grace's pardon, and I hope I had it.
This is my fault: as for the rest appeal'd,
It issues from the rancour of a villain,
A recreant and most degenerate traitor:
Which in myself I boldly will defend;
And interchangeably hurl down my gage
Upon this overweening traitor's foot,
To prove myself a loyal gentleman
Even in the best blood chamber'd in his
bosom.
In haste whereof, most heartily I pray
Your highness to assign our trial day.

KING RICHARD II.

Wrath-kindled gentlemen, be ruled by me;
Let's purge this choler without letting blood:
This we prescribe, though no physician;
Deep malice makes too deep incision;
Forget, forgive; conclude and be agreed;
Our doctors say this is no month to bleed. —
Good uncle, let this end where it begun;
We'll calm the Duke of Norfolk, you your
son.

JOHN OF GAUNT.
To be a make-peace shall become my age: —
Throw down, my son, the Duke of Norfolk's
gage.

KING RICHARD II.
And, Norfolk, throw down his.

JOHN OF GAUNT.
                              When, Harry, when?
Obedience bids I should not bid again.

KING RICHARD II.
Norfolk, throw down; we bid; there is no
boot.

THOMAS MOWBRAY.
Myself I throw, dread sovereign, at thy foot.
My life thou shalt command, but not my
shame:
The one my duty owes; but my fair name —
Despite of death that lives upon my grave, —
To dark dishonour's use thou shalt not have.
I am disgraced, impeach'd and baffled here,
Pierced to the soul with slander's venom'd
spear,
The which no balm can cure but his
heart-blood
Which breathed this poison.

KING RICHARD II.
                              Rage must be withstood: —
Give me his gage: — lions make leopards
tame.

THOMAS MOWBRAY.
Yea, but not change his spots: take but my
shame.

And I resign my gage. My dear dear lord,
The purest treasure mortal times afford
Is spotless reputation; that away,
Men are but gilded loam or painted clay.
A jewel in a ten-times-barr'd-up chest
Is a bold spirit in a loyal breast.
Mine honour is my life; both grow in one:
Take honour from me, and my life is done:
Then, dear my liege, mine honour let me try;
In that I live and for that will I die.

KING RICHARD II.
Cousin, throw up your gage; do you begin.

HENRY BOLINGBROKE.
O, God defend my soul from such deep sin!
Shall I seem crest-fall'n in my father's sight?
Or with pale beggar-fear impeach my height
Before this out-dared dastard? Ere my tongue
Shall wound my honour with such feeble wrong,
Or sound so base a parle, my teeth shall tear
The slavish motive of recanting fear,
And spit it bleeding in his high disgrace,
Where shame doth harbour, even in Mowbray's face.

[*Exit* JOHN OF GAUNT.

KING RICHARD II.
We were not born to sue, but to command; —
Which since we cannot do to make you friends,
Be ready, as your lives shall answer it,

At Coventry, upon Saint Lambert's day:
There shall your swords and lances arbitrate
The swelling difference of your settled hate:
Since we can not atone you, we shall see
Justice design the victor's chivalry. —
Lord Marshal, command our officers-at-arms
Be ready to direct these home alarms.

[*Exeunt.*

Scene II.

The same. A room in the
DUKE OF LANCASTER'S palace.
Enter JOHN OF GAUNT *with* DUCHESS.

JOHN OF GAUNT.
Alas, the part I had in Woodstock's blood
Doth more solicit me than your exclaims,
To stir against the butchers of his life!
But since correction lieth in those hands
Which made the fault that we cannot correct,
Put we our quarrel to the will of heaven;
Who, when they see the hours ripe on earth,
Will rain hot vengeance on offenders' heads.
DUCHESS.
Finds brotherhood in thee no sharper spur?
Hath love in thy old blood no living fire?
Edward's seven sons, whereof thyself art one,
Were as seven vials of his sacred blood,
Or seven fair branches springing from one
root:
Some of those seven are dried by nature's
course,
Some of those branches by the Destinies cut;
But Thomas, my dear lord, my life, my
Gloucester,
One vial full of Edward's sacred blood,

15

One flourishing branch of his most royal
root:
Is crack'd, and all the precious liquor spilt,
Is hack'd down, and his summer leaves all
faded,
By envy's hand and murder's bloody axe.
Ah, Gaunt, his blood was thine! that bed, that
womb,
That metal, that self-mould, that fashion'd
thee
Made him a man; and though thou livest and
breathest,
Yet art thou slain in him: thou dost consent
In some large measure to thy father's death,
In that thou seest thy wretched brother die,
Who was the model of thy father's life.
Call it not patience, Gaunt; — it is despair:
In suffering thus thy brother to be slaughter'd,
Thou showest the naked pathway to thy life,
Teaching stern murder how to butcher thee:
That which in mean men we entitle patience
Is pale cold cowardice in noble breasts.
What shall I say? to safeguard thine own
life,
The best way is to venge my Gloucester's
death.

JOHN OF GAUNT.
God's is the quarrel; for God's substitute,
His deputy anointed in His sight,
Hath caused his death: the which if wrongfully,
Let heaven revenge; for I may never lift
An angry arm against His minister.

DUCHESS.
Where then, alas, may I complain myself?
JOHN OF GAUNT.
To God, the widow's champion and defence.
DUCHESS.
Why, then, I will. Farewell, old Gaunt.
Thou goest to Coventry, there to behold
Our cousin Hereford and fell Mowbray fight:
O, sit my husband's wrongs on Hereford's spear,
That it may enter butcher Mowbray's breast!
Or, if misfortune miss the first career,
Be Mowbray's sins so heavy in his bosom,
That they may break his foaming courser's back,
And throw the rider headlong in the lists,
A caitiff recreant to my cousin Hereford!
Farewell, old Gaunt: thy sometimes brother's wife
With her companion grief must end her life.
JOHN OF GAUNT.
Sister, farewell; I must to Coventry:
As much good stay with thee as go with me!
DUCHESS.
Yet one word more: — grief boundeth where it falls,
Not with the empty hollowness, but weight:
I take my leave before I have begun,
For sorrow ends not when it seemeth done.
Commend me to thy brother, Edmund York.
Lo, this is all: — nay, yet depart not so;
Though this be all, do not so quickly go;

I shall remember more. Bid him — ah,
what? —
With all good speed at Plashy visit me.
Alack, and what shall good old York there
see
But empty lodgings and unfurnish'd walls,
Unpeopled offices, untrodden stones?
And what hear there for welcome but my
groans?
Therefore commend me; let him not come
there,
To seek out sorrow that dwells every where.
Desolate, desolate, will I hence and die:
The last leave of thee takes my weeping eye.

[*Exeunt.*

Scene III.

Gosford Green, near Coventry.
The lists set out, and a throne; with
ATTENDANTS. *Enter the* LORD MARSHAL *and
the* DUKE OF AUMERLE.

LORD MARSHAL.
My Lord Aumerle, is Harry Hereford arm'd?
DUKE OF AUMERLE.
Yea, at all points; and longs to enter in.
LORD MARSHAL.
The Duke of Norfolk, sprightfully and bold,
Stays but the summons of the appellant's
trumpet.
DUKE OF AUMERLE.
Why, then, the champions are prepared, and
stay
For nothing but his majesty's approach.

The trumpets sound, and KING RICHARD
enters with his nobles, JOHN OF GAUNT,
BUSHY, BAGOT, GREEN, *and others. When they
are set, enter* THOMAS MOWBRAY *in arms,
defendant, with a* HERALD.

KING RICHARD II.
Marshal, demand of yonder champion

19

The cause of his arrival here in arms:
Ask him his name and orderly proceed
To swear him in the justice of his cause.

LORD MARSHAL.

In God's name and the King's, say who
thou art
And why thou comest thus knightly clad
in arms,
Against what man thou comest, and what thy
quarrel:
Speak truly, on thy knighthood and thy
oath;
As so defend thee heaven and thy valour!

THOMAS MOWBRAY.

My name is Thomas Mowbray, Duke of
Norfolk;
Who hither come engaged by my oath —
Which God defend a knight should violate! —
Both to defend my loyalty and truth
To God, my King and my succeeding issue,
Against the Duke of Hereford that appeals
me;
And, by the grace of God and this mine arm,
To prove him, in defending of myself,
A traitor to my God, my King, and me:
And as I truly fight, defend me heaven!

The trumpets sound. Enter BOLINGBROKE,
    appellant, in armour, with a HERALD.

KING RICHARD II.

Marshal, ask yonder knight in arms,

Both who he is and why he cometh hither
Thus plated in habiliments of war,
And formally, according to our law,
Depose him in the justice of his cause.

LORD MARSHAL.

What is thy name? and wherefore comest thou
hither,
Before King Richard in his royal lists?
Against whom comest thou? and what's thy
quarrel?
Speak like a true knight, so defend thee
heaven!

HENRY BOLINGBROKE.

Harry of Hereford, Lancaster and Derby
Am I; who ready here do stand in arms,
To prove, by God's grace and my body's
valour,
In lists, on Thomas Mowbray, Duke of
Norfolk,
That he is a traitor, foul and dangerous,
To God of heaven, King Richard and to
me;
And as I truly fight, defend me heaven!

LORD MARSHAL.

On pain of death, no person be so bold
Or daring-hardy as to touch the lists,
Except the marshal and such officers
Appointed to direct these fair designs.

HENRY BOLINGBROKE.

Lord Marshal, let me kiss my sovereign's
hand,
And bow my knee before his Majesty:

For Mowbray and myself are like two men
That vow a long and weary pilgrimage;
Then let us take a ceremonious leave
And loving farewell of our several friends.

LORD MARSHAL.

The appellant in all duty greets your Highness,
And craves to kiss your hand and take his
leave.

KING RICHARD II.

We will descend and fold him in our arms. —
Cousin of Hereford, as thy cause is right,
So be thy fortune in this royal fight!
Farewell, my blood; which if today thou
shed,
Lament we may, but not revenge thee dead.

HENRY BOLINGBROKE.

O let no noble eye profane a tear
For me, if I be gored with Mowbray's spear:
As confident as is the falcon's flight
Against a bird, do I with Mowbray fight. —
[to LORD MARSHAL] My loving lord, I take
my leave of you; —
Of you, my noble cousin, Lord Aumerle;
Not sick, although I have to do with death,
But lusty, young, and cheerly drawing
breath. —
Lo, as at English feasts, so I regreet
The daintiest last, to make the end most
sweet:
[to GAUNT] O thou, the earthly author of my
blood, —
Whose youthful spirit, in me regenerate,

Doth with a twofold vigour lift me up
To reach at victory above my head, —
Add proof unto mine armour with thy prayers;
And with thy blessings steel my lance's point,
That it may enter Mowbray's waxen coat,
And furbish new the name of John o' Gaunt,
Even in the lusty haviour of his son.

JOHN OF GAUNT.

God in thy good cause make thee prosperous!
Be swift like lightning in the execution;
And let thy blows, doubly redoubled,
Fall like amazing thunder on the casque
Of thy adverse pernicious enemy:
Rouse up thy youthful blood, be valiant and
live.

HENRY BOLINGBROKE.

Mine innocency and Saint George to thrive!

THOMAS MOWBRAY.

However God or fortune cast my lot,
There lives or dies, true to King Richard's
throne,
A loyal, just and upright gentleman:
Never did captive with a freer heart
Cast off his chains of bondage and embrace
His golden uncontroll'd enfranchisement,
More than my dancing soul doth celebrate
This feast of battle with mine adversary. —
Most mighty liege, and my companion peers,
Take from my mouth the wish of happy
years:
As gentle and as jocund as to jest
Go I to fight: truth hath a quiet breast.

KING RICHARD II.

Farewell, my lord: securely I espy
Virtue with valour couched in thine eye. —
Order the trial, Marshal, and begin.

LORD MARSHAL.

Harry of Hereford, Lancaster and Derby,
Receive thy lance; and God defend the right!

HENRY BOLINGBROKE.

Strong as a tower in hope, I cry amen.

LORD MARSHAL [*to an* OFFICER].

Go bear this lance to Thomas, Duke of
Norfolk.

FIRST HERALD.

Harry of Hereford, Lancaster and Derby,
Stands here for God, his sovereign and
himself,
On pain to be found false and recreant,
To prove the Duke of Norfolk, Thomas
Mowbray,
A traitor to his God, his King and him;
And dares him to set forward to the fight.

SECOND HERALD.

Here standeth Thomas Mowbray, Duke of
Norfolk,
On pain to be found false and recreant,
Both to defend himself and to approve
Henry of Hereford, Lancaster, and Derby,
To God, his sovereign and to him disloyal;
Courageously and with a free desire
Attending but the signal to begin.

LORD MARSHAL.

Sound, trumpets; and set forward, combatants.

[*A charge sounded.*

Stay, the king hath thrown his warder down.

KING RICHARD II.

Let them lay by their helmets and their
spears,
And both return back to their chairs again: —
Withdraw with us: — and let the trumpets
sound
While we return these dukes what we decree.

[*A long flourish.*

Draw near,
And list what with our council we have
done.
For that our kingdom's earth should not
be soil'd
With that dear blood which it hath fostered;
And for our eyes do hate the dire aspect
Of civil wounds plough'd up with neighbours'
sword;
And for we think the eagle-winged pride
Of sky-aspiring and ambitious thoughts,
With rival-hating envy, set on you
To wake our peace, which in our country's
cradle
Draws the sweet infant breath of gentle
sleep;
Which so roused up with boisterous untuned
drums,
With harsh-resounding trumpets' dreadful
bray,
And grating shock of wrathful iron arms,
Might from our quiet confines fright fair peace

25

And make us wade even in our kindred's
blood, —
Therefore we banish you our territories; —
You, cousin Hereford, upon pain of life,
Till twice five summers have enrich'd our
fields
Shall not regreet our fair dominions,
But tread the stranger paths of banishment.

HENRY BOLINGBROKE.

Your will be done: this must my comfort
be, —
That sun that warms you here shall shine
on me;
And those his golden beams to you here lent
Shall point on me and gild my banishment.

KING RICHARD II.

Norfolk, for thee remains a heavier doom,
Which I with some unwillingness pronounce:
The sly slow hours shall not determinate
The dateless limit of thy dear exile; —
The hopeless word of 'never to return'
Breathe I against thee, upon pain of life.

THOMAS MOWBRAY.

A heavy sentence, my most sovereign liege,
And all unlook'd for from your Highness'
mouth:
A dearer merit, not so deep a maim
As to be cast forth in the common air,
Have I deserved at your Highness' hands.
The language I have learn'd these forty
years,
My native English, now I must forego:

And now my tongue's use is to me no more
Than an unstringed viol or a harp,
Or like a cunning instrument cased up,
Or, being open, put into his hands
That knows no touch to tune the harmony:
Within my mouth you have engaol'd my tongue,
Doubly portcullis'd with my teeth and lips;
And dull unfeeling barren ignorance
Is made my gaoler to attend on me.
I am too old to fawn upon a nurse,
Too far in years to be a pupil now:
What is thy sentence then but speechless death,
Which robs my tongue from breathing native breath?

KING RICHARD II.
It boots thee not to be compassionate:
After our sentence plaining comes too late.

THOMAS MOWBRAY.
Then thus I turn me from my country's light,
To dwell in solemn shades of endless night.

KING RICHARD II.
Return again, and take an oath with thee.
Lay on our royal sword your banish'd hands;
Swear by the duty that you owe to God —
Our part therein we banish with yourselves —
To keep the oath that we administer: —
You never shall — so help you truth and God! —
Embrace each other's love in banishment;

27

Nor never look upon each other's face;
Nor never write, regreet, nor reconcile
This louring tempest of your home-bred hate;
Nor never by advised purpose meet
To plot, contrive, or complot any ill
'Gainst us, our state, our subjects, or our
land.

HENRY BOLINGBROKE.

I swear.

THOMAS MOWBRAY.

And I, to keep all this.

HENRY BOLINGBROKE.

Norfolk, so far as to mine enemy: —
By this time, had the King permitted us,
One of our souls had wander'd in the air.
Banish'd this frail sepulchre of our flesh,
As now our flesh is banish'd from this land:
Confess thy treasons ere thou fly the realm;
Since thou hast far to go, bear not along
The clogging burthen of a guilty soul.

THOMAS MOWBRAY.

No, Bolingbroke: if ever I were traitor,
My name be blotted from the book of
life,
And I from heaven banish'd as from hence!
But what thou art, God, thou, and I do
know;
And all too soon, I fear, the King shall
rue. —
Farewell, my liege. — Now no way can
I stray:
Save back to England, all the world's my
way.   [Exit.

KING RICHARD II.

   Uncle, even in the glasses of thine eyes
I see thy grieved heart: thy sad aspect
Hath from the number of his banish'd years
Pluck'd four away. — [*to* BOLINGBROKE] Six
frozen winter spent,
Return with welcome home from banishment.

HENRY BOLINGBROKE.

   How long a time lies in one little word!
Four lagging winters and four wanton springs
End in a word: such is the breath of kings.

JOHN OF GAUNT.

   I thank my liege, that in regard of me
He shortens four years of my son's exile:
But little vantage shall I reap thereby;
For, ere the six years that he hath to spend
Can change their moons and bring their
times about
My oil-dried lamp and time-bewasted light
Shall be extinct with age and endless night;
My inch of taper will be burnt and done,
And blindfold death not let me see my son.

KING RICHARD II.

   Why uncle, thou hast many years to live.

JOHN OF GAUNT.

   But not a minute, King, that thou canst
give:
Shorten my days thou canst with sullen
sorrow,
And pluck nights from me, but not lend a
morrow;
Thou canst help time to furrow me with age,

But stop no wrinkle in his pilgrimage;
Thy word is current with him for my death,
But dead, thy kingdom cannot buy my breath.

KING RICHARD II.

Thy son is banish'd upon good advice,
Whereto thy tongue a party-verdict gave:
Why at our justice seem'st thou, then, to
lour?

JOHN OF GAUNT.

Things sweet to taste prove in digestion
sour.
You urged me as a judge; but I had rather
You would have bid me argue like a father.
O, had it been a stranger, not my child,
To smooth his fault I should have been
more mild:
A partial slander sought I to avoid,
And in the sentence my own life destroy'd.
Alas, I look'd when some of you should say,
I was too strict to make mine own away;
But you gave leave to my unwilling tongue
Against my will to do myself this wrong.

KING RICHARD II.

Cousin, farewell; — and, uncle, bid him so:
Six years we banish him, and he shall go.
    [*Flourish. Exeunt* KING RICHARD *and* TRAIN.

DUKE OF AUMERLE.

Cousin, farewell: what presence must not
know,
From where you do remain let paper show.

LORD MARSHAL.

My lord, no leave take I; for I will ride,

As far as land will let me, by your side.
JOHN OF GAUNT.

O, to what purpose dost thou hoard thy
words,
That thou return'st no greeting to thy friends?
HENRY BOLINGBROKE.

I have too few to take my leave of you,
When the tongue's office should be prodigal
To breathe the abundant dolour of the heart.
JOHN OF GAUNT.

Thy grief is but thy absence for a time.
HENRY BOLINGBROKE.

Joy absent, grief is present for that time.
JOHN OF GAUNT.

What is six winters? they are quickly gone.
HENRY BOLINGBROKE.

To men in joy; but grief makes one hour
ten.
JOHN OF GAUNT.

Call it a travel that thou takest for pleasure.
HENRY BOLINGBROKE.

My heart will sigh when I miscall it so,
Which finds it an enforced pilgrimage.
JOHN OF GAUNT.

The sullen passage of thy weary steps
Esteem as foil wherein thou art to set
The precious jewel of thy home return.
HENRY BOLINGBROKE.

Nay, rather, every tedious stride I make
Will but remember me what a deal of world
I wander from the jewels that I love.
Must I not serve a long apprenticehood

To foreign passages, and in the end,
Having my freedom, boast of nothing else
But that I was a journeyman to grief?
JOHN OF GAUNT.
  All places that the eye of heaven visits
Are to a wise man ports and happy havens.
Teach thy necessity to reason thus;
There is no virtue like necessity.
Think not the King did banish thee,
But thou the King. Woe doth the heavier
   sit,
Where it perceives it is but faintly borne.
Go, say I sent thee forth to purchase honour
And not the King exiled thee; or suppose
Devouring pestilence hangs in our air
And thou art flying to a fresher clime:
Look, what thy soul holds dear, imagine it
To lie that way thou go'st, not whence thou
   comest:
Suppose the singing birds musicians,
The grass whereon thou tread'st the presence
   strew'd,
The flowers fair ladies, and thy steps no
   more
Than a delightful measure or a dance;
For gnarling sorrow hath less power to bite
The man that mocks at it and sets it light.
HENRY BOLINGBROKE.
  O, who can hold a fire in his hand
By thinking on the frosty Caucasus?
Or cloy the hungry edge of appetite
By bare imagination of a feast?

Or wallow naked in December snow
By thinking on fantastic summer's heat?
O, no! the apprehension of the good
Gives but the greater feeling to the worse:
Fell sorrow's tooth doth never rankle more
Than when he bites, but lanceth not the
sore.

JOHN OF GAUNT.

Come, come, my son, I'll bring thee on
thy way:
Had I thy youth and cause, I would not
stay.

HENRY BOLINGBROKE.

Then, England's ground, farewell; sweet soil,
adieu;
My mother, and my nurse, that bears me
yet!
Where'er I wander, boast of this I can, —
Though banish'd, yet a trueborn Englishman.
                                [*Exeunt.*

Scene IV.

The court.
Enter, from one side, KING RICHARD, BAGOT *and*
GREEN; *from the other* AUMERLE.

KING RICHARD II.
    We did observe. — Cousin Aumerle,
    How far brought you high Hereford on his
    way?

DUKE OF AUMERLE.
    I brought high Hereford, if you call him so,
    But to the next highway, and there I left
    him.

KING RICHARD II.
    And say, what store of parting tears were
    shed?

DUKE OF AUMERLE.
    Faith, none for me; except the north-east
    wind,
    Which then blew bitterly against our faces,
    Awaked the sleeping rheum, and so by chance
    Did grace our hollow parting with a tear.

KING RICHARD II.
    What said our cousin when you parted with
    him?

DUKE OF AUMERLE.
    'Farewell:'

And, for my heart disdained that my tongue
Should so profane the word, that taught me craft
To counterfeit oppression of such grief
That words seem'd buried in my sorrow's grave.
Marry, would the word 'farewell' have lengthen'd hours
And added years to his short banishment,
He should have had a volume of 'farewells;'
But since it would not, he had none of me.

KING RICHARD II.

He is our cousin, cousin; but 'tis doubt,
When time shall call him home from banishment,
Whether our kinsman come to see his friends.
Ourself and Bushy, Bagot here and Green
Observed his courtship to the common people;
How he did seem to dive into their hearts
With humble and familiar courtesy;
What reverence he did throw away on slaves;
Wooing poor craftsmen with the craft of smiles,
And patient underbearing of his fortune,
As 'twere to banish their affects with him.
Off goes his bonnet to an oyster-wench;
A brace of draymen bid God speed him well,
And had the tribute of his supple knee,
With 'Thanks, my countrymen, my loving friends;'
As were our England in reversion his,

And he our subjects' next degree in hope.

GREEN.

Well, he is gone; and with him go these
thoughts.
Now for the rebels which stand out in
Ireland, —
Expedient manage must be made, my liege,
Ere further leisure yield them further means
For their advantage and your Highness' loss.

KING RICHARD II.

We will ourself in person to this war:
And, for our coffers, with too great a court
And liberal largess, are grown somewhat
light,
We are enforced to farm our royal realm;
The revenue whereof shall furnish us
For our affairs in hand. If that come short,
Our substitutes at home shall have blank
charters;
Whereto, when they shall know what men
are rich,
They shall subscribe them for large sums
of gold
And send them after to supply our wants;
For we will make for Ireland presently.

Enter BUSHY.

Bushy, what news?

BUSHY.

Old John of Gaunt is grievous sick, my lord,
Suddenly taken; and hath sent post haste

To entreat your Majesty to visit him.

KING RICHARD II.

Where lies he?

BUSHY.

At Ely House.

KING RICHARD II.

Now put it, God, in the physician's mind
To help him to his grave immediately!
The lining of his coffers shall make coats
To deck our soldiers for these Irish wars. —
Come, gentlemen, let's all go visit him:
Pray God we may make haste, and come
too late!

ALL.

Amen.

[*Exeunt.*

ACT II

Scene I.

London. A room in Ely House.
Enter JOHN OF GAUNT *sick, with
the* DUKE OF YORK, *&c.*

JOHN OF GAUNT.
Will the king come, that I may breathe
my last
In wholesome counsel to his unstaid youth?
DUKE OF YORK.
Vex not yourself, nor strive not with your
breath;
For all in vain comes counsel to his ear.
JOHN OF GAUNT.
O, but they say the tongues of dying men
Enforce attention like deep harmony:
Where words are scarce, they are seldom spent
in vain;
For they breathe truth that breathe their words
in pain.
He that no more must say is listen'd more
Than they whom youth and ease have
taught to glose;
More are men's ends mark'd than their lives
before:
The setting sun, and music at the close,
As the last taste of sweets, is sweetest last,

Writ in remembrance more than things long
    past:
Though Richard my life's counsel would not
    hear,
My death's sad tale may yet undeaf his ear.
DUKE OF YORK.
No; it is stopp'd with other flattering sounds,
As, praises of his state: then there are found,
Lascivious metres, to whose venom sound
The open ear of youth doth always listen;
Report of fashions in proud Italy,
Whose manners still our tardy apish nation
Limps after in base imitation.
Where doth the world thrust forth a vanity —
So it be new, there's no respect how vile —
That is not quickly buzz'd into his ears?
Then all too late comes counsel to be heard,
Where will doth mutiny with wit's regard.
Direct not him whose way himself will choose:
'Tis breath thou lack'st, and that breath wilt
thou lose.
JOHN OF GAUNT.
Methinks I am a prophet new inspired
And thus expiring do foretell of him:
His rash fierce blaze of riot cannot last,
For violent fires soon burn out themselves;
Small showers last long, but sudden storms
are short;
He tires betimes that spurs too fast betimes;
With eager feeding food doth choke the
feeder:
Light vanity, insatiate cormorant,

Consuming means, soon preys upon itself.
This royal throne of kings, this sceptred isle,
This earth of majesty, this seat of Mars,
This other Eden, demi-paradise,
This fortress built by Nature for herself
Against infection and the hand of war,
This happy breed of men, this little world,
This precious stone set in the silver sea,
Which serves it in the office of a wall,
Or as a moat defensive to a house,
Against the envy of less happier lands;
This blessed plot, this earth, this realm, this
England,
This nurse, this teeming womb of royal
kings,
Fear'd by their breed and famous by their
birth,
Renowned for their deeds as far from
home, —
For Christian service and true chivalry, —
As is the sepulchre in stubborn Jewry,
Of the world's ransom, blessed Mary's Son; —
This land of such dear souls, this dear dear
land,
Dear for her reputation through the world,
Is now leased out, — I die pronouncing it, —
Like to a tenement or pelting farm:
England, bound in with the triumphant sea
Whose rocky shore beats back the envious
siege
Of watery Neptune, is now bound in with
shame,

With inky blots and rotten parchment bonds:
That England, that was wont to conquer others,
Hath made a shameful conquest of itself.
Ah, would the scandal vanish with my life,
How happy then were my ensuing death!

Enter KING RICHARD *and* QUEEN, AUMERLE,
BUSHY, GREEN, BAGOT, ROSS, *and* WILLOUGHBY.

DUKE OF YORK.
The King is come: deal mildly with his youth;
For young hot colts being raged do rage the more.

QUEEN.
How fares our noble uncle, Lancaster?

KING RICHARD II.
What comfort, man? how is't with aged Gaunt?

JOHN OF GAUNT.
O how that name befits my composition!
Old Gaunt indeed, and gaunt in being old:
Within me grief hath kept a tedious fast;
And who abstains from meat that is not gaunt?
For sleeping England long time have I watch'd;
Watching breeds leanness, leanness is all gaunt:
The pleasure that some fathers feed upon,
Is my strict fast, — I mean, my children's looks;

And therein fasting, hast thou made me
gaunt:
Gaunt am I for the grave, gaunt as a grave,
Whose hollow womb inherits nought but
bones.

KING RICHARD II.

Can sick men play so nicely with their
names?

JOHN OF GAUNT.

No, misery makes sport to mock itself:
Since thou dost seek to kill my name in me,
I mock my name, great King, to flatter thee.

KING RICHARD II.

Should dying men flatter with those that
live?

JOHN OF GAUNT.

No, no, men living flatter those that die.

KING RICHARD II.

Thou, now a-dying, say'st thou flatterest me.

JOHN OF GAUNT.

O, no! thou diest, though I the sicker be.

KING RICHARD II.

I am in health, I breathe, and see thee ill.

JOHN OF GAUNT.

Now He that made me knows I see thee ill;
Ill in myself to see, and in thee seeing ill.
Thy death-bed is no lesser than thy land
Wherein thou liest in reputation sick;
And thou, too careless patient as thou art,
Commit'st thy anointed body to the cure
Of those physicians that first wounded thee:
A thousand flatterers sit within thy crown,

Whose compass is no bigger than thy head;
And yet, incaged in so small a verge,
The waste is no whit lesser than thy land.
O, had thy grandsire with a prophet's eye
Seen how his son's son should destroy his
sons,
From forth thy reach he would have laid thy
shame,
Deposing thee before thou wert possess'd,
Which art possess'd now to depose thyself.
Why, cousin, wert thou regent of the world,
It were a shame to let this land by lease;
But for thy world enjoying but this land,
Is it not more than shame to shame it so?
Landlord of England art thou now, not king:
Thy state of law is bondslave to the law;
And thou —

KING RICHARD II.

A lunatic lean-witted fool,
Presuming on an ague's privilege,
Darest with thy frozen admonition
Make pale our cheek, chasing the royal blood
With fury from his native residence.
Now, by my seat's right royal majesty,
Wert thou not brother to great Edward's
son,
This tongue that runs so roundly in thy
head
Should run thy head from thy unreverent
shoulders.

JOHN OF GAUNT.

O, spare me not, my brother Edward's son,

For that I was his father Edward's son; —
That blood already, like the pelican,
Hast thou tapp'd out and drunkenly caroused:
My brother Gloucester, plain well-meaning
soul, —
Whom fair befall in heaven 'mongst happy
souls! —
May be a precedent and witness good
That thou respect'st not spilling Edward's
blood:
Join with the present sickness that I have;
And thy unkindness be like crooked age,
To crop at once a too long wither'd flower.
Live in thy shame, but die not shame with
thee! —
These words hereafter thy tormentors be! —
Convey me to my bed, then to my grave:
Love they to live that love and honour have.
          [*Exit, borne off by his* ATTENDANTS.
KING RICHARD II.

And let them die that age and sullens have;
For both hast thou, and both become the
grave.
DUKE OF YORK.

I do beseech your Majesty, impute his words
To wayward sickliness and age in him:
He loves you, on my life, and holds you
dear
As Harry Duke of Hereford, were he here.
KING RICHARD II.

Right, you say true: as Hereford's love, so
his;

As theirs, so mine; and all be as it is.

Enter NORTHUMBERLAND.

NORTHUMBERLAND.
My liege, old Gaunt commends him to your
Majesty.
KING RICHARD II.
What says he?
NORTHUMBERLAND.
                    Nay, nothing; all is said
His tongue is now a stringless instrument;
Words, life and all, old Lancaster hath spent.
DUKE OF YORK.
Be York the next that must be bankrupt so!
Though death be poor, it ends a mortal
woe.
KING RICHARD II.
The ripest fruit first falls, and so doth he;
His time is spent, our pilgrimage must be.
So much for that. — Now for our Irish
wars:
We must supplant those rough rug-headed
kerns,
Which live like venom where no venom
else
But only they have privilege to live.
And for these great affairs do ask some
charge,
Towards our assistance we do seize to us
The plate, coin, revenues and moveables,
Whereof our uncle Gaunt did stand possess'd.

DUKE OF YORK.

How long shall I be patient? ah, how long
Shall tender duty make me suffer wrong?
Not Gloucester's death, nor Hereford's banishment
Not Gaunt's rebukes, nor England's private wrongs,
Nor the prevention of poor Bolingbroke
About his marriage, nor my own disgrace,
Have ever made me sour my patient cheek,
Or bend one wrinkle on my sovereign's face.
I am the last of noble Edward's sons,
Of whom thy father, Prince of Wales, was first:
In war was never lion raged more fierce,
In peace was never gentle lamb more mild,
Than was that young and princely gentleman.
His face thou hast, for even so look'd he,
Accomplish'd with the number of thy hours;
But when he frown'd, it was against the French
And not against his friends; his noble hand
Did win what he did spend and spent not that
Which his triumphant father's hand had won:
His hands were guilty of no kindred's blood,
But bloody with the enemies of his kin.
O Richard! York is too far gone with grief,
Or else he never would compare between.

KING RICHARD II.

Why, uncle, what's the matter?

DUKE OF YORK.

O my liege,
Pardon me, if you please; if not, I, pleased
Not to be pardon'd, am content withal.
Seek you to seize and gripe into your hands
The royalties and rights of banish'd Hereford?
Is not Gaunt dead, and doth not Hereford
live?
Was not Gaunt just, and is not Harry true?
Did not the one deserve to have an heir?
Is not his heir a well-deserving son?
Take Hereford's rights away, and take from
Time
His charters and his customary rights;
Let not tomorrow then ensue today;
Be not thyself, — for how art thou a king
But by fair sequence and succession?
Now, afore God — God forbid I say true! —
If you do wrongfully seize Hereford's rights,
Call in the letters-patents that he hath
By his attorneys-general to sue
His livery, and deny his offer'd homage,
You pluck a thousand dangers on your head,
You lose a thousand well-disposed hearts
And prick my tender patience, to those
thoughts
Which honour and allegiance cannot think.

KING RICHARD II.
Think what you will, we seize into our
hands
His plate, his goods, his money and his
lands.

DUKE OF YORK.

I'll not be by the while: my liege, farewell:
What will ensue hereof, there's none can
tell;
But by bad courses may be understood
That their events can never fall out good.

[*Exit.*

KING RICHARD II.

Go, Bushy, to the Earl of Wiltshire straight:
Bid him repair to us to Ely House
To see this business. Tomorrow next
We will for Ireland; and 'tis time, I trow:
And we create, in absence of ourself,
Our uncle York Lord Governor of England;
For he is just and always loved us well. —
Come on, our Queen: tomorrow must we
part;
Be merry, for our time of stay is short

[*Flourish. Exeunt* KING RICHARD, QUEEN,
AUMERLE, BUSHY, GREEN, *and* BAGOT.

NORTHUMBERLAND.

Well, lords, the Duke of Lancaster is dead.

LORD ROSS.

And living too; for now his son is duke.

LORD WILLOUGHBY.

Barely in title, not in revenues.

NORTHUMBERLAND.

Richly in both, if justice had her right.

LORD ROSS.

My heart is great; but it must break with
silence,
Ere't be disburden'd with a liberal tongue.

NORTHUMBERLAND.

Nay, speak thy mind; and let him ne'er speak more

That speaks thy words again to do thee harm!

LORD WILLOUGHBY.

Tends that thou wouldst speak to the Duke of Hereford?

If it be so, out with it boldly, man;

Quick is mine ear to hear of good towards him.

LORD ROSS.

No good at all that I can do for him;

Unless you call it good to pity him,

Bereft and gelded of his patrimony.

NORTHUMBERLAND.

Now, afore God, 'tis shame such wrongs are borne

In him, a royal prince, and many moe

Of noble blood in this declining land.

The King is not himself, but basely led

By flatterers; and what they will inform,

Merely in hate, 'gainst any of us all,

That will the King severely prosecute

'Gainst us, our lives, our children, and our heirs.

LORD ROSS.

The commons hath he pill'd with grievous taxes,

And quite lost their hearts: the nobles hath he fined

For ancient quarrels, and quite lost their hearts.

LORD WILLOUGHBY.
And daily new exactions are devised, —
As blanks, benevolences, and I wot not what:
But what, o' God's name, doth become of
this?

NORTHUMBERLAND.
Wars have not wasted it, for warr'd he hath
not,
But basely yielded upon compromise
That which his noble ancestors achieved with
blows:
More hath he spent in peace than they
in wars.

LORD ROSS.
The Earl of Wiltshire hath the realm in farm.

LORD WILLOUGHBY.
The King's grown bankrupt, like a broken
man.

NORTHUMBERLAND.
Reproach and dissolution hangeth over him.

LORD ROSS.
He hath not money for these Irish wars,
His burthenous taxations notwithstanding,
But by the robbing of the banish'd duke.

NORTHUMBERLAND.
His noble kinsman: — most degenerate King!
But, lords, we hear this fearful tempest sing,
Yet see no shelter to avoid the storm;
We see the wind sit sore upon our sails,
And yet we strike not, but securely perish.

LORD ROSS.
We see the very wrack that we must suffer;

And unavoided is the danger now,
For suffering so the causes of our wrack.

NORTHUMBERLAND.

Not so; even through the hollow eyes of
death
I spy life peering; but I dare not say
How near the tidings of our comfort is.

LORD WILLOUGHBY.

Nay, let us share thy thoughts, as thou dost
ours.

LORD ROSS.

Be confident to speak, Northumberland:
We three are but thyself; and, speaking
so,
Thy words are but as thoughts; therefore,
be bold.

NORTHUMBERLAND.

Then thus: — I have from Port le Blanc, a
bay
In Brittany, received intelligence
That Harry Duke of Hereford, Rainold Lord
Cobham,
That late broke from the Duke of Exeter,
His brother, Archbishop late of Canterbury,
Sir Thomas Erpingham, Sir John Ramston,
Sir John Norbery, Sir Robert Waterton and
Francis Quoint, —
All these well furnish'd by the Duke of
Brittany
With eight tall ships, three thousand men
of war,
Are making hither with all due expedience

And shortly mean to touch our northern
shore:
Perhaps they had ere this, but that they stay
The first departing of the king for Ireland.
If then we shall shake off our slavish yoke,
Imp out our drooping country's broken wing,
Redeem from broking pawn the blemish'd
crown,
Wipe off the dust that hides our sceptre's
gilt
And make high majesty look like itself,
Away with me in post to Ravenspurgh;
But if you faint, as fearing to do so,
Stay and be secret, and myself will go.

LORD ROSS.

To horse, to horse! urge doubts to them
that fear.

LORD WILLOUGHBY.

Hold out my horse, and I will first be there.

[*Exeunt.*

Scene II.

The Court.
Enter QUEEN, BUSHY, *and* BAGOT.

BUSHY.

    Madam, your Majesty is too much sad:
    You promised, when you parted with the King,
    To lay aside life-harming heaviness
    And entertain a cheerful disposition.

QUEEN.

    To please the King I did; to please myself
    I cannot do it; yet I know no cause
    Why I should welcome such a guest as grief,
    Save bidding farewell to so sweet a guest
    As my sweet Richard: yet again, methinks,
    Some unborn sorrow, ripe in fortune's womb,
    Is coming towards me, and my inward soul
    With nothing trembles; at something it grieves,
    More than with parting from my lord the King.

BUSHY.

    Each substance of a grief hath twenty shadows,
    Which shows like grief itself, but is not so;
    For sorrow's eye, glazed with blinding tears,
    Divides one thing entire to many objects;

57

Like perspectives, which rightly gazed upon
Show nothing but confusion, — eyed awry
Distinguish form: so your sweet Majesty,
Looking awry upon your lord's departure,
Find shapes of grief, more than himself,
to wail;
Which, look'd on as it is, is nought but
shadows
Of what it is not. Then, thrice-gracious
Queen,
More than your lord's departure weep
not, — more's not seen;
Or if it be, 'tis with false sorrow's eye,
Which for things true weeps things imaginary.

QUEEN.
It may be so; but yet my inward soul
Persuades me it is otherwise: howe'er it be,
I cannot but be sad; so heavy sad
As, though, on thinking, on no thought I
think,
Makes me with heavy nothing faint and
shrink.

BUSHY.
'Tis nothing but conceit, my gracious lady.

QUEEN.
'Tis nothing less: conceit is still derived
From some forefather grief; mine is not so,
For nothing had begot my something grief;
Or something hath the nothing that I grieve:
'Tis in reversion that I do possess;
But what it is, that is not yet known; what
I cannot name; 'tis nameless woe, I wot.

Enter GREEN.

GREEN.

God save your Majesty! and well met, gentlemen:

I hope the King is not yet shipp'd for Ireland.

QUEEN.

Why hopest thou so? 'tis better hope he is;

For his designs crave haste, his haste good hope:

Then wherefore dost thou hope he is not shipp'd?

GREEN.

That he, our hope, might have retired his power,

And driven into despair an enemy's hope,

Who strongly hath set footing in this land:

The banish'd Bolingbroke repeals himself,

And with uplifted arms is safe arrived

At Ravenspurgh.

QUEEN.

Now God in heaven forbid!

GREEN.

Ah, madam, 'tis too true: and that is worse,

The Lord Northumberland, his son young Henry Percy,

The Lords of Ross, Beaumond, and Willoughby,

With all their powerful friends, are fled to him.

BUSHY.

Why have you not proclaim'd Northumberland
And all the rest revolted faction traitors?

GREEN.

We have: whereupon the Earl of Worcester
Hath broke his staff, resign'd his stewardship,
And all the household servants fled with him
To Bolingbroke.

QUEEN.

So, Green, thou art the midwife to my woe,
And Bolingbroke my sorrow's dismal heir:
Now hath my soul brought forth her prodigy,
And I, a gasping new-deliver'd mother,
Have woe to woe, sorrow to sorrow join'd.

BUSHY.

Despair not, madam.

QUEEN.

                              Who shall hinder me?
I will despair, and be at enmity
With cozening hope, — he is a flatterer,
A parasite, a keeper back of death,
Who gently would dissolve the bands of
life,
Which false hope lingers in extremity.

GREEN.

Here comes the Duke of York.

QUEEN.

With signs of war about his aged neck:
O, full of careful business are his looks!

Enter YORK.

Uncle, for God's sake, speak comfortable words.

DUKE OF YORK.

Should I do so, I should belie my thoughts:
Comfort's in heaven; and we are on the earth,
Where nothing lives but crosses, cares and grief.
Your husband, he is gone to save far off,
Whilst others come to make him lose at home:
Here am I left to underprop his land,
Who, weak with age, cannot support myself:
Now comes the sick hour that his surfeit made;
Now shall he try his friends that flatter'd him.

Enter a SERVANT.

SERVANT.

My lord, your son was gone before I came.

DUKE OF YORK.

He was? — Why, so! — go all which way it will! —
The nobles they are fled, the commons they are cold,
And will, I fear, revolt on Hereford's side. —
Sirrah, get thee to Plashy, to my sister Gloucester;
Bid her send me presently a thousand pound: —

Hold, take my ring.
SERVANT.
   My lord, I had forgot to tell your lordship,
   Today, as I came by, I called there; —
   But I shall grieve you to report the rest.
DUKE OF YORK.
   What is't, knave?
SERVANT.
   An hour before I came, the duchess died.
DUKE OF YORK.
   God for his mercy! what a tide of woes
   Comes rushing on this woeful land at once!
   I know not what to do: — I would to
   God, —
   So my untruth had not provoked him to
   it, —
   The King had cut off my head with my
   brother's. —
   What, are there no posts dispatch'd for
   Ireland? —
   How shall we do for money for these wars? —
   Come, sister, — cousin, I would say — pray,
   pardon me. —
   Go, fellow, get thee home, provide some
   carts
   And bring away the armour that is there.
                          [*Exit* SERVANT.
   Gentlemen, will you go muster men? If I
   Know how or which way to order these
   affairs
   Thus thrust disorderly into my hands,
   Never believe me. Both are my kinsmen: —

The one is my sovereign, whom both my oath
And duty bids defend; th'other again
Is my kinsman, whom the King hath wrong'd,
Whom conscience and my kindred bids to right.
Well, somewhat we must do. — Come, cousin, I'll
Dispose of you. — Gentlemen, go muster up your men,
And meet me presently at Berkeley.
I should to Plashy too; —
But time will not permit: — all is uneven,
And every thing is left at six and seven.

[*Exeunt* YORK *and* QUEEN.

BUSHY.

The wind sits fair for news to go to Ireland,
But none returns. For us to levy power
Proportionable to the enemy
Is all unpossible.

GREEN.

Besides, our nearness to the King in love
Is near the hate of those love not the King.

BAGOT.

And that's the wavering commons: for their love
Lies in their purses, and whoso empties them
By so much fills their hearts with deadly hate.

BUSHY.

Wherein the King stands generally condemn'd.

BAGOT.

If judgement lie in them, then so do we,
Because we ever have been near the King.

GREEN.

Well, I will for refuge straight to Bristol
Castle:
The Earl of Wiltshire is already there.

BUSHY.

Thither will I with you; for little office
The hateful commons will perform for us,
Except like curs to tear us all to pieces: —
Will you go along with us?

BAGOT.

No; I will to Ireland to his Majesty.
Farewell: if heart's presages be not vain,
We three here part that ne'er shall meet
again.

BUSHY.

That's as York thrives to beat back Bolingbroke.

GREEN.

Alas, poor duke! the task he undertakes
Is numbering sands and drinking oceans dry:
Where one on his side fights, thousands will
fly.
Farewell at once, — for once, for all, and
ever.

BUSHY.

Well, we may meet again.

BAGOT.

I fear me, never.
                                    [*Exeunt.*

Scene III.

The wilds in Gloucestershire.
Enter BOLINGBROKE *and* NORTHUMBERLAND,
with FORCES.

HENRY BOLINGBROKE.
How far is it, my lord, to Berkeley now?
NORTHUMBERLAND.
Believe me, noble lord,
I am a stranger here in Gloucestershire:
These high wild hills and rough uneven ways
Draws out our miles, and makes them
wearisome,
And yet your fair discourse hath been as
sugar,
Making the hard way sweet and delectable.
But I bethink me what a weary way
From Ravenspurgh to Cotswold will be found
In Ross and Willoughby, wanting your
company,
Which, I protest, hath very much beguiled
The tediousness and process of my travel:
But theirs is sweetened with the hope to
have
The present benefit which I possess;
And hope to joy is little less in joy
Than hope enjoy'd: by this the weary lords

Shall make their way seem short, as mine hath done
By sight of what I have, your noble company.

HENRY BOLINGBROKE.
Of much less value is my company
Than your good words. — But who comes here?

Enter HENRY PERCY.

NORTHUMBERLAND.
It is my son, young Harry Percy,
Sent from my brother Worcester, whence-soever.
Harry, how fares your uncle?

HENRY PERCY.
I had thought, my lord, to have learn'd his health of you.

NORTHUMBERLAND.
Why, is he not with the Queen?

HENRY PERCY.
No, my good Lord; he hath forsook the court,
Broken his staff of office and dispersed
The household of the King.

NORTHUMBERLAND.
                              What was his reason?
He was not so resolved when last we spake together.

HENRY PERCY.
Because your lordship was proclaimed traitor.
But he, my lord, is gone to Ravenspurgh,

To offer service to the Duke of Hereford,
And sent me over by Berkeley, to discover
What power the Duke of York had levied
there;
Then with directions to repair to Ravenspurgh.

NORTHUMBERLAND.

Have you forgot the Duke of Hereford,
boy?

HENRY PERCY.

No, my good lord, for that is not forgot
Which ne'er I did remember: to my knowledge,
I never in my life did look on him.

NORTHUMBERLAND.

Then learn to know him now; this is the
duke.

HENRY PERCY.

My gracious lord, I tender you my service,
Such as it is, being tender, raw and young:
Which elder days shall ripen and confirm
To more approved service and desert.

HENRY BOLINGBROKE.

I thank thee, gentle Percy; and be sure
I count myself in nothing else so happy
As in a soul remembering my good friends;
And, as my fortune ripens with thy love,
It shall be still thy true love's recompense:
My heart this covenant makes, my hand thus
seals it.

NORTHUMBERLAND.

How far is it to Berkeley? and what stir
Keeps good old York there with his men
of war?

HENRY PERCY.
There stands the castle, by yon tuft of trees,
Mann'd with three hundred men, as I have
heard;
And in it are the Lords of York, Berkeley,
and Seymour, —
None else of name and noble estimate.

NORTHUMBERLAND.
Here come the Lords of Ross and Willoughby,
Bloody with spurring, fiery-red with haste.

Enter ROSS *and* WILLOUGHBY.

HENRY BOLINGBROKE.
Welcome, my lords. I wot your love pursues
A banish'd traitor: all my treasury
Is yet but unfelt thanks, which more enrich'd
Shall be your love and labour's recompense.

LORD ROSS.
Your presence makes us rich, most noble
lord.

LORD WILLOUGHBY.
And far surmounts our labour to attain
it.

HENRY BOLINGBROKE.
Evermore thanks, the exchequer of the poor;
Which, till my infant fortune comes to years,
Stands for my bounty. — But who comes
here?

Enter BERKELEY.

NORTHUMBERLAND.

It is my Lord of Berkeley, as I guess.

LORD BERKELEY.

My Lord of Hereford, my message is to you.

HENRY BOLINGBROKE.

My lord, my answer is — 'to Lancaster;'
And I am come to seek that name in England;
And I must find that title in your tongue,
Before I make reply to aught you say.

LORD BERKELEY.

Mistake me not, my lord; 'tis not my meaning
To raze one title of your honour out: —
To you, my lord, I come, — what lord you will, —
From the most gracious regent of this land,
The Duke of York, to know what pricks you on
To take advantage of the absent time
And fright our native peace with self-born arms.

HENRY BOLINGBROKE.

I shall not need transport my words by you;
Here comes his Grace in person.

Enter YORK *attended.*

                         My noble uncle!
                              [*Kneels.*

DUKE OF YORK.

Show me thy humble heart, and not thy knee,

Whose duty is deceiveable and false.

HENRY BOLINGBROKE.

My gracious uncle —

DUKE OF YORK.

Tut, tut!
Grace me no grace, nor uncle me no uncle:
I am no traitor's uncle; and that word
'grace'
In an ungracious mouth is but profane.
Why have those banish'd and forbidden legs
Dared once to touch a dust of England's
ground?
But then more 'why?' why have they dared
to march
So many miles upon her peaceful bosom,
Frighting her pale-faced villages with war
And ostentation of despised arms?
Comest thou because the anointed King is
hence?
Why, foolish boy, the King is left behind,
And in my loyal bosom lies his power.
Were I but now the lord of such hot youth
As when brave Gaunt, thy father, and myself
Rescued the Black Prince, that young Mars
of men,
From forth the ranks of many thousand
French,
O, then how quickly should this arm of mine,
Now prisoner to the palsy, chastise thee
And minister correction to thy fault!

HENRY BOLINGBROKE.

My gracious uncle, let me know my fault:

On what condition stands it and wherein?

DUKE OF YORK.

Even in condition of the worst degree, —
In gross rebellion and detested treason:
Thou art a banish'd man; and here art come
Before the expiration of thy time,
In braving arms against thy sovereign.

HENRY BOLINGBROKE.

As I was banish'd, I was banish'd Hereford;
But as I come, I come for Lancaster.
And, noble uncle, I beseech your Grace
Look on my wrongs with an indifferent eye:
You are my father, for methinks in you
I see old Gaunt alive; O, then, my father,
Will you permit that I shall stand condemn'd
A wandering vagabond; my rights and
royalties
Pluck'd from my arms perforce and given
away
To upstart unthrifts? Wherefore was I born?
If that my cousin King be King of England,
It must be granted I am Duke of Lancaster.
You have a son, Aumerle, my noble cousin;
Had you first died, and he been thus trod
down,
He should have found his uncle Gaunt a
father,
To rouse his wrongs and chase them to
the bay.
I am denied to sue my livery here,
And yet my letters-patents give me leave.
My father's goods are all distrain'd and sold,

And these and all are all amiss employ'd.
What would you have me do? I am a
subject,
And I challenge law: attorneys are denied
me;
And therefore, personally I lay my claim
To my inheritance of free descent.

NORTHUMBERLAND.
The noble duke hath been too much abused.

LORD ROSS.
It stands your Grace upon to do him right.

LORD WILLOUGHBY.
Base men by his endowments are made
great.

DUKE OF YORK.
My lords of England, let me tell you this: —
I have had feeling of my cousin's wrongs
And laboured all I could to do him right;
But in this kind to come, in braving arms,
Be his own carver and cut out his way,
To find out right with wrong, — it may
not be;
And you that do abet him in this kind
Cherish rebellion and are rebels all.

NORTHUMBERLAND.
The noble duke hath sworn his coming is
But for his own; and for the right of that
We all have strongly sworn to give him aid;
And let him ne'er see joy that breaks that
oath!

DUKE OF YORK.
Well, well, I see the issue of these arms:

I cannot mend it, I must needs confess,
Because my power is weak and all ill left:
But if I could, by Him that gave me life,
I would attach you all and make you stoop
Unto the sovereign mercy of the King;
But since I cannot, be it known to you
I do remain as neuter. So, fare you well; —
Unless you please to enter in the castle
And there repose you for this night.

HENRY BOLINGBROKE.

An offer, uncle, that we will accept:
But we must win your Grace to go with us
To Bristol Castle, which they say is held
By Bushy, Bagot and their complices,
The caterpillars of the commonwealth,
Which I have sworn to weed and pluck
away.

DUKE OF YORK.

It may be I will go with you: — but yet I'll
pause;
For I am loath to break our country's laws.
Nor friends nor foes, to me welcome you
are:
Things past redress are now with me past
care.

                        [*Exeunt.*

Scene IV.

A camp in Wales.
Enter SALISBURY *and a* CAPTAIN.

CAPTAIN.

My lord of Salisbury, we have stay'd ten days,
And hardly kept our countrymen together,
And yet we hear no tidings from the King;
Therefore we will disperse ourselves: farewell.

EARL OF SALISBURY.

Stay yet another day, thou trusty Welshman:
The King reposeth all his confidence in thee.

CAPTAIN.

'Tis thought the King is dead; we will not stay.
The bay-trees in our country are all wither'd
And meteors fright the fixed stars of heaven;
The pale-faced moon looks bloody on the earth,
And lean-look'd prophets whisper fearful change;
Rich men look sad and ruffians dance and leap, —
The one in fear to lose what they enjoy,
The other to enjoy by rage and war:

These signs forerun the death or fall of
kings. —
Farewell: our countrymen are gone and fled,
As well assured Richard their King is dead.

                                                [Exit.

EARL OF SALISBURY.
Ah, Richard, with the eyes of heavy mind,
I see thy glory, like a shooting star,
Fall to the base earth from the firmament!
Thy sun sets weeping in the lowly west,
Witnessing storms to come, woe and unrest:
Thy friends are fled to wait upon thy foes;
And crossly to thy good all fortune goes.

                                                [Exit.

ACT III

ACT III

Scene I.

BOLINGBROKE'S camp at Bristol.
Enter BOLINGBROKE, YORK, NORTHUMBERLAND,
PERCY, WILLOUGHBY, *with* BUSHY
and GREEN, *prisoners.*

HENRY BOLINGBROKE.
Bring forth these men.
Bushy and Green, I will not vex your souls —
Since presently your souls must part your
bodies —
With too much urging your pernicious lives,
For 'twere no charity; yet, to wash your
blood
From off my hands, here in the view of men
I will unfold some causes of your deaths.
You have misled a prince, a royal king,
A happy gentleman in blood and lineaments,
By you unhappied and disfigured clean:
You have in manner with your sinful hours
Made a divorce betwixt his Queen and him;
Broke the possession of a royal bed
And stain'd the beauty of a fair queen's
cheeks
With tears drawn from her eyes by your foul
wrongs.
Myself, — a prince by fortune of my birth,

Near to the King in blood, and near in love
Till you did make him misinterpret me, —
Have stoop'd my neck under your injuries,
And sigh'd my English breath in foreign
    clouds,
Eating the bitter bread of banishment;
Whilst you have fed upon my signories,
Dispark'd my parks and fell'd my forest
    woods,
From my own windows torn my household
    coat,
Razed out my imprese, leaving me no sign,
Save men's opinions and my living blood,
To show the world I am a gentleman.
This and much more, much more than twice
    all this,
Condemns you to the death. — See them
    deliver'd over
To execution and the hand of death.
BUSHY.
More welcome is the stroke of death to me
Than Bolingbroke to England. — Lords,
    farewell.
GREEN.
My comfort is that heaven will take our
    souls
And plague injustice with the pains of hell.
HENRY BOLINGBROKE.
My Lord Northumberland, see them dispatch'd.
        [*Exeunt* NORTHUMBERLAND *and others,*
            with the PRISONERS.
Uncle, you say the Queen is at your house;

For God's sake, fairly let her be entreated:
Tell her I send to her my kind commends;
Take special care my greetings be deliver'd.
DUKE OF YORK.

A gentleman of mine I have dispatch'd
With letters of your love to her at large.
HENRY BOLINGBROKE.

Thanks, gentle uncle. — Come, lords, away.
To fight with Glendower and his complices:
Awhile to work, and after holiday.

[*Exeunt.*

Scene II.

The coast of Wales. A castle in view.
Drums; flourish and colours. Enter
KING RICHARD, *the* BISHOP OF CARLISLE,
AUMERLE, *and* SOLDIERS.

KING RICHARD II.
  Barkloughly Castle call they this at hand?
DUKE OF AUMERLE.
  Yea, my lord. How brooks your Grace the
    air,
  After your late tossing on the breaking seas?
KING RICHARD II.
  Needs must I like it well: I weep for joy
  To stand upon my kingdom once again.
  Dear earth, I do salute thee with my hand,
  Though rebels wound thee with their horses'
    hoofs:
  As a long-parted mother with her child
  Plays fondly with her tears and smiles in
    meeting,
  So, weeping, smiling, greet I thee, my earth,
  And do thee favours with my royal hands.
  Feed not thy sovereign's foe, my gentle
    earth,
  Nor with thy sweets comfort his ravenous
    sense;

83

But let thy spiders, that suck up thy venom,
And heavy-gaited toads lie in their way,
Doing annoyance to the treacherous feet
Which with usurping steps do trample thee:
Yield stinging nettles to mine enemies;
And when they from thy bosom pluck a flower,
Guard it, I pray thee, with a lurking adder
Whose double tongue may with a mortal touch
Throw death upon thy sovereign's enemies. —
Mock not my senseless conjuration, lords:
This earth shall have a feeling and these stones
Prove armed soldiers, ere her native King
Shall falter under foul rebellion's arms.

BISHOP OF CARLISLE.
Fear not, my lord: that Power that made you King
Hath power to keep you King in spite of all.
The means that heaven yields must be embraced,
And not neglected; else, if heaven would,
And we will not, heaven's offer we refuse,
The proffer'd means of succour and redress.

DUKE OF AUMERLE.
He means, my lord, that we are too remiss;
Whilst Bolingbroke, through our security,
Grows strong and great in substance and in friends.

KING RICHARD II.
Discomfortable cousin! know'st thou not

That when the searching eye of heaven is
hid,
Behind the globe, that lights the lower world,
Then thieves and robbers range abroad unseen
In murders and in outrage, boldly here;
But when from under this terrestrial ball
He fires the proud tops of the eastern pines
And darts his light through every guilty hole,
Then murders, treasons and detested sins,
The cloak of night being pluck'd from off
their backs,
Stand bare and naked, trembling at themselves?
So when this thief, this traitor, Bolingbroke, —
Who all this while hath revell'd in the night
Whilst we were wandering with the Antipodes,
Shall see us rising in our throne, the east,
His treasons will sit blushing in his face,
Not able to endure the sight of day,
But self-affrighted tremble at his sin.
Not all the water in the rough rude sea
Can wash the balm off from an anointed
king;
The breath of worldly men cannot depose
The deputy elected by the Lord:
For every man that Bolingbroke hath press'd
To lift shrewd steel against our golden crown,
God for his Richard hath in heavenly pay
A glorious angel: then, if angels fight,
Weak men must fall, for heaven still guards
the right.

Enter SALISBURY.

Welcome, my lord: how far off lies your power?

EARL OF SALISBURY.

Nor near nor farther off, my gracious lord,
Than this weak arm: discomfort guides my tongue
And bids me speak of nothing but despair.
One day too late, I fear me, noble lord,
Hath clouded all thy happy days on earth:
O, call back yesterday, bid time return,
And thou shalt have twelve thousand fighting men!
Today, today, unhappy day, too late,
O'erthrows thy joys, friends, fortune and thy state:
For all the Welshmen, hearing thou wert dead,
Are gone to Bolingbroke, dispersed and fled.

DUKE OF AUMERLE.

Comfort, my liege; why looks your Grace so pale?

KING RICHARD II.

But now the blood of twenty thousand men
Did triumph in my face, and they are fled;
And, till so much blood thither come again,
Have I not reason to look pale and dead?
All souls that will be safe fly from my side,
For time hath set a blot upon my pride.

DUKE OF AUMERLE.

Comfort, my liege; remember who you are.

KING RICHARD II.

I had forgot myself; am I not King?
Awake, thou coward majesty! thou sleepest.
Is not the King's name twenty thousand
names?
Arm, arm, my name! a puny subject strikes
At thy great glory. — Look not to the
ground,
Ye favourites of a king: are we not high?
High be our thoughts: I know my uncle
York
Hath power enough to serve our turn. —
But who comes here?

Enter SCROOP.

SIR STEPHEN SCROOP.

More health and happiness betide my liege
Than can my care-tuned tongue deliver him!

KING RICHARD II.

Mine ear is open and my heart prepared;
The worst is worldly loss thou canst unfold.
Say, is my kingdom lost? why, 'twas my care
And what loss is it to be rid of care?
Strives Bolingbroke to be as great as we?
Greater he shall not be; if he serve God,
We'll serve Him too and be his fellow so:
Revolt our subjects? that we cannot mend;
They break their faith to God as well as us:
Cry woe, destruction, ruin and decay;
The worst is death, and death will have
his day.

SIR STEPHEN SCROOP.
    Glad am I that your highness is so arm'd
    To bear the tidings of calamity.
    Like an unseasonable stormy day,
    Which makes the silver rivers drown their
    shores,
    As if the world were all dissolved to tears,
    So high above his limits swells the rage
    Of Bolingbroke, covering your fearful land
    With hard bright steel, and hearts harder
    than steel.
    White-beards have arm'd their thin and
    hairless scalps
    Against thy majesty; boys, with women's
    voices,
    Strive to speak big and clap their female
    joints
    In stiff unwieldy arms against thy crown;
    The very beadsmen learn to bend their bows
    Of double-fatal yew against thy state;
    Yea, distaff-women manage rusty bills
    Against thy seat: both young and old rebel,
    And all goes worse than I have power to
    tell.
KING RICHARD II.
    Too well, too well thou tell'st a tale so ill.
    Where is the Earl of Wiltshire? where is
    Bagot?
    What is become of Bushy? where is Green?
    That they have let the dangerous enemy
    Measure our confines with such peaceful
    steps?

If we prevail, their heads shall pay for it:
I warrant they have made peace with
Bolingbroke.

SIR STEPHEN SCROOP.

Peace have they made with him indeed, my
lord.

KING RICHARD II.

O villains, vipers, damn'd without redemption!
Dogs, easily won to fawn on any man!
Snakes, in my heart-blood warm'd, that sting
my heart!
Three Judases, each one thrice worse than
Judas!
Would they make peace? terrible hell make
war
Upon their spotted souls for this offence!

SIR STEPHEN SCROOP.

Sweet love, I see, changing his property,
Turns to the sourest and most deadly hate: —
Again uncurse their souls; their peace is made
With heads, and not with hands; those whom
you curse
Have felt the worst of death's destroying
wound
And lie full low, graved in the hollow ground.

DUKE OF AUMERLE.

Is Bushy, Green, and the Earl of Wiltshire
dead?

SIR STEPHEN SCROOP.

Ay, all of them at Bristol lost their heads.

DUKE OF AUMERLE.

Where is the duke my father with his power?

KING RICHARD II.

No matter where; — of comfort no man speak:
Let's talk of graves, of worms, and epitaphs;
Make dust our paper and with rainy eyes
Write sorrow on the bosom of the earth.
Let's choose executors and talk of wills:
And yet not so, — for what can we bequeath
Save our deposed bodies to the ground?
Our lands, our lives and all are Bolingbroke's,
And nothing can we call our own but death
And that small model of the barren earth
Which serves as paste and cover to our bones.
For God's sake, let us sit upon the ground
And tell sad stories of the death of kings: —
How some have been deposed; some slain in war,
Some haunted by the ghosts they have deposed;
Some poison'd by their wives; some sleeping kill'd;
All murder'd: — for within the hollow crown
That rounds the mortal temples of a king
Keeps Death his court and there the antic sits,
Scoffing his state and grinning at his pomp;
Allowing him a breath, a little scene,
To monarchize, be fear'd and kill with looks;
Infusing him with self and vain conceit, —
As if this flesh which walls about our life,
Were brass impregnable, and humour'd thus

Comes at the last and with a little pin
Bores through his castle wall, and — farewell
king!
Cover your heads and mock not flesh and
blood
With solemn reverence; throw away respect,
Tradition, form and ceremonious duty,
For you have but mistook me all this while:
I live with bread like you, feel want,
Taste grief, need friends: — subjected thus,
How can you say to me, I am a king?

BISHOP OF CARLISLE.

My lord, wise men ne'er sit and wail their
woes,
But presently prevent the ways to wail.
To fear the foe, since fear oppresseth strength,
Gives in your weakness strength unto your
foe,
And so your follies fight against yourself.
Fear and be slain; no worse can come to
fight:
And fight and die is death destroying death;
Where fearing dying pays death servile breath.

DUKE OF AUMERLE.

My father hath a power; inquire of him
And learn to make a body of a limb.

KING RICHARD II.

Thou chidest me well: — proud Bolingbroke,
I come
To change blows with thee for our day of
doom.
This ague fit of fear is over-blown;

An easy task it is to win our own. —
Say, Scroop, where lies our uncle with his
power?
Speak sweetly, man, although thy looks be
sour.

SIR STEPHEN SCROOP.

Men judge by the complexion of the sky
   The state and inclination of the day:
So may you by my dull and heavy eye,
   My tongue hath but a heavier tale to say.
I play the torturer, by small and small
To lengthen out the worst that must be
   spoken: —
Your uncle York is join'd with Bolingbroke,
And all your northern castles yielded up,
And all your southern gentlemen in arms
Upon his party.

KING RICHARD II.

            Thou hast said enough. —
[to AUMERLE]Beshrew thee, cousin, which
didst lead me forth
Of that sweet way I was in to despair!
What say you now? what comfort have we
now?
By heaven, I'll hate him everlastingly
That bids me be of comfort any more.
Go to Flint Castle: there I'll pine away;
A king, woe's slave, shall kingly woe obey.
That power I have, discharge; and let them
go
To ear the land that hath some hope to
grow,

For I have none: — let no man speak again
To alter this, for counsel is but vain.

DUKE OF AUMERLE.

My liege, one word.

KING RICHARD II.

                He does me double wrong
That wounds me with the flatteries of his
tongue.
Discharge my followers: let them hence away,
From Richard's night to Bolingbroke's fair
day.

                              [*Exeunt.*

Scene III.

Wales. Before Flint Castle.
Enter, with drum and colours, BOLINGBROKE,
YORK, NORTHUMBERLAND, *and* FORCES.

HENRY BOLINGBROKE.
So that by this intelligence we learn
The Welshmen are dispersed, and Salisbury
Is gone to meet the King, who lately landed
With some few private friends upon this
coast.
NORTHUMBERLAND.
The news is very fair and good, my lord:
Richard not far from hence hath hid his
head.
DUKE OF YORK.
It would beseem the Lord Northumberland
To say 'King Richard:' — alack the heavy day
When such a sacred king should hide his
head.
NORTHUMBERLAND.
Your Grace mistakes; only to be brief
Left I his title out.
DUKE OF YORK.
           The time hath been,
Would you have been so brief with him, he
would

Have been so brief with you, to shorten you,
For taking so the head, your whole head's
length.
HENRY BOLINGBROKE.
Mistake not, uncle, further than you should.
DUKE OF YORK.
Take not, good cousin, further than you
should,
Lest you mistake: the heavens are o'er our
heads.
HENRY BOLINGBROKE.
I know it, uncle, and oppose not myself
Against their will. — But who comes here?

Enter PERCY.

Welcome, Harry: what, will not this castle
yield?
HENRY PERCY.
The castle royally is mann'd, my lord,
Against thy entrance.
HENRY BOLINGBROKE.
Royally!
Why, it contains no king?
HENRY PERCY.
Yes, my good lord,
It doth contain a king; King Richard lies
Within the limits of yon lime and stone:
And with him are the Lord Aumerle, Lord
Salisbury,
Sir Stephen Scroop, besides a clergyman
Of holy reverence; who, I cannot learn.

NORTHUMBERLAND.
  O, belike it is the Bishop of Carlisle.
HENRY BOLINGBROKE.
  [*to* NORTHUMBERLAND] Noble lord,
Go to the rude ribs of that ancient castle;
Through brazen trumpet send the breath of parley
Into his ruin'd ears, and thus deliver: —
Henry Bolingbroke
On both his knees doth kiss King Richard's hand
And sends allegiance and true faith of heart
To his most royal person; hither come
Even at his feet to lay my arms and power,
Provided that my banishment repeal'd
And lands restored again be freely granted:
If not, I'll use the advantage of my power
And lay the summer's dust with showers of blood
Rain'd from the wounds of slaughter'd Englishmen:
The which, how far off from the mind of Bolingbroke
It is, such crimson tempest should bedrench
The fresh green lap of fair King Richard's land,
My stooping duty tenderly shall show.
Go, signify as much, while here we march
Upon the grassy carpet of this plain.
Let's march without the noise of threatening drum,
That from this castle's tatter'd battlements

Our fair appointments may be well perused.
Methinks King Richard and myself should
meet
With no less terror than the elements
Of fire and water, when their thundering
shock
At meeting tears the cloudy cheeks of heaven.
Be he the fire, I'll be the yielding water:
The rage be his, whilst on the earth I rain
My waters, — on the earth, and not on
him.
March on, and mark King Richard how he
looks.

Parle without, and answer within.
Then a flourish. Enter on the walls,
KING RICHARD, *the* BISHOP OF CARLISLE,
AUMERLE, SCROOP, *and* SALISBURY.

DUKE OF YORK.
See, see, King Richard doth himself appear,
As doth the blushing discontented sun
From out the fiery portal of the east,
When he perceives the envious clouds are bent
To dim his glory and to stain the track
Of his bright passage to the occident.
Yet looks he like a king: behold, his eye,
As bright as is the eagle's, lightens forth
Controlling majesty: — alack, alack, for woe,
That any harm should stain so fair a show!
KING RICHARD II [*to* NORTHUMBERLAND].
We are amazed; and thus long have we stood

To watch the fearful bending of thy knee,
Because we thought ourself thy lawful king:
And if we be, how dare thy joints forget
To pay their awful duty to our presence?
If we be not, show us the hand of God
That hath dismissed us from our stewardship;
For well we know, no hand of blood and
bone
Can gripe the sacred handle of our sceptre,
Unless he do profane, steal, or usurp.
And though you think that all, as you have
done,
Have torn their souls by turning them from
us,
And we are barren and bereft of friends;
Yet know, — my master, God omnipotent,
Is mustering in his clouds on our behalf
Armies of pestilence; and they shall strike
Your children yet unborn and unbegot,
That lift your vassal hands against my head
And threat the glory of my precious crown.
Tell Bolingbroke — for yond methinks he
stands —
That every stride he makes upon my land
Is dangerous treason: he is come to ope
The purple testament of bleeding war;
But ere the crown he looks for live in peace,
Ten thousand bloody crowns of mothers'
sons
Shall ill become the flower of England's face,
Change the complexion of her maid-pale
peace

To scarlet indignation and bedew
Her pastures' grass with faithful English
blood.

NORTHUMBERLAND.

The King of heaven forbid our lord the
King
Should so with civil and uncivil arms
Be rush'd upon! Thy thrice noble cousin
Harry Bolingbroke doth humbly kiss thy
hand;
And by the honourable tomb he swears,
That stands upon your royal grandsire's
bones,
And by the royalties of both your bloods, —
Currents that spring from one most gracious
head, —
And by the buried hand of warlike Gaunt,
And by the worth and honour of himself,
Comprising all that may be sworn or said, —
His coming hither hath no further scope
Than for his lineal royalties, and to beg
Enfranchisement immediate on his knees:
Which on thy royal party granted once,
His glittering arms he will commend to rust,
His barbed steeds to stables, and his heart
To faithful service of your majesty.
This swears he, as he is a prince, is just;
And, as I am a gentleman, I credit him.

KING RICHARD II.

Northumberland, say thus the King returns: —
His noble cousin is right welcome hither;
And all the number of his fair demands

Shall be accomplish'd without contradiction:
With all the gracious utterance thou hast
Speak to his gentle hearing kind commends. —
[*to* AUMERLE] We do debase ourselves, cousin,
do we not,
To look so poorly and to speak so fair?
Shall we call back Northumberland, and send
Defiance to the traitor, and so die?

DUKE OF AUMERLE.
No, good my lord; let's fight with gentle words
Till time lend friends and friends their helpful swords.

KING RICHARD II.
O God, O God! that e'er this tongue of mine,
That laid the sentence of dread banishment
On yon proud man, should take it off again
With words of sooth! O that I were as great
As is my grief, or lesser than my name!
Or that I could forget what I have been,
Or not remember what I must be now!
Swell'st thou, proud heart? I'll give thee scope
to beat,
Since foes have scope to beat both thee
and me.

DUKE OF AUMERLE.
Northumberland comes back from Bolingbroke.

KING RICHARD II.
What must the King do now? must he submit?

The King shall do it: must he be deposed?
The King shall be contented: must he lose
The name of king? o' God's name, let it go:
I'll give my jewels for a set of beads,
My gorgeous palace for a hermitage,
My gay apparel for an almsman's gown,
My figured goblets for a dish of wood,
My sceptre for a palmer's walking staff,
My subjects for a pair of carved saints,
And my large kingdom for a little grave,
A little little grave, an obscure grave; —
Or I'll be buried in the king's highway,
Some way of common trade, where subjects'
feet
May hourly trample on their sovereign's head;
For on my heart they tread now whilst
I live;
And buried once, why not upon my head? —
Aumerle, thou weep'st, — my tender-hearted
cousin! —
We'll make foul weather with despised tears;
Our sighs and they shall lodge the summer
corn,
And make a dearth in this revolting land.
Or shall we play the wantons with our woes,
And make some pretty match with shedding
tears?
As thus; — to drop them still upon one
place,
Till they have fretted us a pair of graves
Within the earth; and, therein laid, — 'There
lies

Two kinsmen digg'd their graves with weeping
eyes.'
Would not this ill do well? — Well, well, I
see
I talk but idly, and you laugh at me.
Most mighty prince, my Lord Northumberland,
What says King Bolingbroke? will his Majesty
Give Richard leave to live till Richard die?
You make a leg, and Bolingbroke says ay.

NORTHUMBERLAND.
My lord, in the base court he doth attend
To speak with you; — may it please you to
come down.

KING RICHARD II.
Down, down I come; like glistering Phaethon,
Wanting the manage of unruly jades.
In the base court? Base court, where kings
grow base,
To come at traitors' calls and do them
grace.
In the base court? Come down? Down, court!
down, king!
For night-owls shriek where mounting larks
should sing.
                              [*Exeunt from above.*

HENRY BOLINGBROKE.
What says his Majesty?

NORTHUMBERLAND.
                              Sorrow and grief of heart
Makes him speak fondly, like a frantic man:
Yet he is come.

Enter KING RICHARD *attended, below.*

HENRY BOLINGBROKE.
　　Stand all apart,
And show fair duty to his majesty. —
　　　　　　　　　　　[*He kneels down.*
My gracious lord, —
KING RICHARD II.
　　Fair cousin, you debase your princely knee
To make the base earth proud with kissing
　　it:
Me rather had my heart might feel your love
Than my unpleased eye see your courtesy.
Up, cousin, up; — your heart is up, I know,
Thus high at least [*touching his own head*],
　　although your knee be low.
HENRY BOLINGBROKE.
　　My gracious lord, I come but for mine own.
KING RICHARD II.
　　Your own is yours, and I am yours, and all.
HENRY BOLINGBROKE.
　　So far be mine, my most redoubted lord,
As my true service shall deserve your love.
KING RICHARD II.
　　Well you deserve.: — they well deserve to
　　have,
That know the strong'st and surest way to
　　get. —
Uncle, give me your hand: nay, dry your
　　eyes;
Tears show their love, but want their
　　remedies. —

Cousin, I am too young to be your father,
Though you are old enough to be my heir.
What you will have, I'll give, and willing too;
For do we must what force will have us do.
Set on towards London: — cousin, is it so?

HENRY BOLINGBROKE.

Yea, my good lord.

KING RICHARD II.

Then I must not say no.
                    [*Flourish. Exeunt.*

Scene IV.

Langley. The DUKE OF YORK'S garden.
Enter the QUEEN *and two* LADIES.

QUEEN.
What sport shall we devise here in this
garden,
To drive away the heavy thought of care?
LADY.
Madam, we'll play at bowls.
QUEEN.
'Twill make me think the world is full
of rubs,
And that my fortune rubs against the bias.
LADY.
Madam, we'll dance.
QUEEN.
My legs can keep no measure in delight,
When my poor heart no measure keeps in
grief:
Therefore, no dancing, girl; some other sport.
LADY.
Madam, we'll tell tales.
QUEEN.
Of sorrow or of joy?
LADY.
                    Of either, madam.

QUEEN.

   Of neither, girl:
For of joy, being altogether wanting,
It doth remember me the more of sorrow;
Or if of grief, being altogether had,
It adds more sorrow to my want of joy:
For what I have I need not to repeat;
And what I want it boots not to complain.

LADY.

   Madam, I'll sing.

QUEEN.

              'Tis well that thou hast cause;
But thou shouldst please me better, wouldst
thou weep.

LADY.

   I could weep, madam, would it do you
good.

QUEEN.

   And I could sing, would weeping do me
good,
And never borrow any tear of thee. —
But stay, here come the gardeners:
Let's step into the shadow of these trees.
My wretchedness unto a row of pins,
They'll talk of state; for every one doth so
Against a change: woe is forerun with woe.

              [QUEEN *and* LADIES *retire.*

Enter a GARDENER *and two* SERVANTS.

GARDENER.

   Go, bind thou up yon dangling apricocks,

Which, like unruly children, make their sire
Stoop with oppression of their prodigal weight:
Give some supportance to the bending twigs.
Go thou, and like an executioner,
Cut off the heads of too fast growing sprays,
That look too lofty in our commonwealth:
All must be even in our government. —
You thus employ'd, I will go root away
The noisome weeds, which without profit suck
The soil's fertility from wholesome flowers.

FIRST SERVANT.
Why should we in the compass of a pale
Keep law and form and due proportion,
Showing, as in a model, our firm estate,
When our sea-walled garden, the whole land,
Is full of weeds; her fairest flowers choked up,
Her fruit-trees all upturned, her hedges ruin'd,
Her knots disorder'd and her wholesome herbs
Swarming with caterpillars?

GARDENER.
                            Hold thy peace: —
He that hath suffer'd this disorder'd spring
Hath now himself met with the fall of leaf:
The weeds which his broad-spreading leaves did shelter,
That seem'd in eating him to hold him up,
Are pluck'd up root and all by Bolingbroke, —
I mean the Earl of Wiltshire, Bushy, Green.

FIRST SERVANT.

What, are they dead?

GARDENER.

         They are; and Bolingbroke
Hath seized the wasteful King. — O, what
pity is it
That he had not so trimm'd and dress'd
his land
As we this garden! We at time of year
Do wound the bark, the skin of our fruit-trees,
Lest, being over-proud in sap and blood,
With too much riches it confound itself:
Had he done so to great and growing men,
They might have lived to bear and he to
taste
Their fruits of duty. All superfluous branches
We lop away, that bearing boughs may live:
Had he done so, himself had borne the
crown,
Which waste of idle hours hath quite thrown
down.

FIRST SERVANT.

What, think you then the King shall be
deposed?

GARDENER.

Depress'd he is already, and deposed
'Tis doubt he will be: letters came last night
To a dear friend of the good Duke of
York's,
That tell black tidings.

QUEEN.

O, I am press'd to death through want of

speaking! —   [*Comes forward with* LADIES.
Thou, old Adam's likeness, set to dress this
garden,
How dares thy harsh rude tongue sound this
unpleasing news?
What Eve, what serpent, hath suggested thee
To make a second fall of cursed man?
Why dost thou say King Richard is deposed?
Darest thou, thou little better thing than
earth,
Divine his downfall? Say, where, when, and
how,
Camest thou by this ill tidings? speak, thou
wretch.

GARDENER.

Pardon me, madam: little joy have I
To breathe this news; yet what I say is true.
King Richard, he is in the mighty hold
Of Bolingbroke: their fortunes both are
weigh'd:
In your lord's scale is nothing but himself,
And some few vanities that make him light;
But in the balance of great Bolingbroke,
Besides himself, are all the English peers,
And with that odds he weighs King Richard
down.
Post you to London, and you will find it so;
I speak no more than every one doth know.

QUEEN.

Nimble mischance, that art so light of foot,
Doth not thy embassage belong to me,
And am I last that knows it? O, thou think'st

To serve me last, that I may longest keep
Thy sorrow in my breast. — Come. ladies, go,
To meet at London London's king in woe. —
What, was I born to this, that my sad look
Should grace the triumph of great Bolingbroke?
Gardener, for telling me these news of woe,
Pray God the plants thou graft'st may never grow.

                    [*Exeunt* QUEEN *and* LADIES.

GARDENER.
Poor Queen! so that thy state might be no worse,
I would my skill were subject to thy curse. —
Here did she fall a tear; here in this place
I'll set a bank of rue, sour herb of grace:
Rue, even for ruth, here shortly shall be seen,
In the remembrance of a weeping Queen.

                            [*Exeunt.*

ACT IV

ACT IV

Scene I.

Westminster Hall.

Enter, as to the Parliament, BOLINGBROKE,
AUMERLE, NORTHUMBERLAND, PERCY,
FITZWATER, SURREY, *another* LORD,
the BISHOP OF CARLISLE, *the* ABBOT OF
WESTMINSTER, *and* ATTENDANTS. HERALD,
OFFICERS, *and* BAGOT.

HENRY BOLINGBROKE.
  Call forth Bagot.
  Now, Bagot, freely speak thy mind;
  What thou dost know of noble Gloucester's
  death,
  Who wrought it with the King, and who
  perform'd
  The bloody office of his timeless end.
BAGOT.
  Then set before my face the Lord Aumerle.
HENRY BOLINGBROKE.
  Cousin, stand forth, and look upon that
  man.
BAGOT.
  My Lord Aumerle, I know your daring tongue
  Scorns to unsay what once it hath deliver'd.
  In that dead time when Gloucester's death
  was plotted,

115

I heard you say, — 'Is not my arm of length,
That reacheth from the restful English court
As far as Calais, to mine uncle's head?'
Amongst much other talk, that very time,
I heard you say that you had rather refuse
The offer of an hundred thousand crowns
Than Bolingbroke's return to England;
Adding withal how blest this land would be
In this your cousin's death.

DUKE OF AUMERLE.

      Princes and noble lords,
What answer shall I make to this base man?
Shall I so much dishonour my fair stars,
On equal terms to give him chastisement?
Either I must, or have mine honour soil'd
With the attainder of his slanderous lips. —
There is my gage, the manual seal of death,
That marks thee out for hell: I say, thou liest,
And will maintain what thou hast said is false
In thy heart-blood, though being all too base
To stain the temper of my knightly sword.

HENRY BOLINGBROKE.

Bagot, forbear; thou shalt not take it up.

DUKE OF AUMERLE.

Excepting one, I would he were the best
In all this presence that hath moved me so.

LORD FITZWATER.

If that thy valour stand on sympathy,
There is my gage, Aumerle, in gage to thine:

By that fair sun which shows me where thou
stand'st,
I heard thee say, and vauntingly thou spakest
it
That thou wert cause of noble Gloucester's
death.
If thou deny'st it twenty times, thou liest;
And I will turn thy falsehood to thy heart,
Where it was forged, with my rapier's point.

DUKE OF AUMERLE.

Thou darest not, coward, live to see that
day.

LORD FITZWATER.

Now by my soul, I would it were this hour.

DUKE OF AUMERLE.

Fitzwater, thou art damn'd to hell for this.

HENRY PERCY.

Aumerle, thou liest; his honour is as true
In this appeal as thou art all unjust;
And that thou art so, there I throw my gage,
To prove it on thee to the extremest point
Of mortal breathing: seize it, if thou darest.

DUKE OF AUMERLE.

An if I do not, may my hands rot off
And never brandish more revengeful steel
Over the glittering helmet of my foe!

ANOTHER LORD.

I task the earth to the like, forsworn Aumerle;
And spur thee on with full as many lies
As may be holloa'd in thy treacherous ear
From sun to sun: there is my honour's pawn;
Engage it to the trial, if thou darest.

DUKE OF AUMERLE.

Who sets me else? by heaven, I'll throw at all:
I have a thousand spirits in one breast,
To answer twenty thousand such as you.

DUKE OF SURREY.

My Lord Fitzwater, I do remember well
The very time Aumerle and you did talk.

LORD FITZWATER.

'Tis very true: you were in presence then;
And you can witness with me this is true.

DUKE OF SURREY.

As false, by heaven, as heaven itself is true.

LORD FITZWATER.

Surrey, thou liest.

DUKE OF SURREY.

                    Dishonourable boy!
That lie shall lie so heavy on my sword,
That it shall render vengeance and revenge
Till thou the lie-giver and that lie do lie
In earth as quiet as thy father's skull:
In proof whereof, there is my honour's pawn;
Engage it to the trial, if thou darest.

LORD FITZWATER.

How fondly dost thou spur a forward horse!
If I dare eat, or drink, or breathe, or live,
I dare meet Surrey in a wilderness,
And spit upon him, whilst I say he lies,
And lies, and lies: there is my bond of faith,
To tie thee to my strong correction. —
As I intend to thrive in this new world,
Aumerle is guilty of my true appeal:
Besides, I heard the banish'd Norfolk say

That thou, Aumerle, didst send two of thy
men
To execute the noble duke at Calais.

DUKE OF AUMERLE.

Some honest Christian trust me with a gage
That Norfolk lies: here do I throw down this,
If he may be repeal'd, to try his honour.

HENRY BOLINGBROKE.

These differences shall all rest under gage
Till Norfolk be repeal'd: repeal'd he shall be,
And, though mine enemy, restored again
To all his lands and signories: when he's
return'd,
Against Aumerle we will enforce his trial.

BISHOP OF CARLISLE.

That honourable day shall ne'er be seen.
Many a time hath banish'd Norfolk fought
For Jesu Christ in glorious Christian field,
Streaming the ensign of the Christian cross
Against black pagans, Turks, and Saracens:
And toil'd with works of war, retired himself
To Italy; and there at Venice gave
His body to that pleasant country's earth,
And his pure soul unto his captain Christ,
Under whose colours he had fought so long.

HENRY BOLINGBROKE.

Why, bishop, is Norfolk dead?

BISHOP OF CARLISLE.

As surely as I live, my lord.

HENRY BOLINGBROKE.

Sweet peace conduct his sweet soul to the
bosom

Of good old Abraham! — Lords appellants,
Your differences shall all rest under gage
Till we assign you to your days of trial.

Enter YORK, *attended.*

DUKE OF YORK.

Great Duke of Lancaster, I come to thee
From plume-pluck'd Richard; who with
willing soul
Adopts thee heir, and his high sceptre yields
To the possession of thy royal hand:
Ascend his throne, descending now from
him, —
And long live Henry, fourth of that name!

HENRY BOLINGBROKE.

In God's name, I'll ascend the regal throne.

BISHOP OF CARLISLE.

Marry. God forbid! —
Worst in this royal presence may I speak,
Yet best beseeming me to speak the truth.
Would God that any in this noble presence
Were enough noble to be upright judge
Of noble Richard! then true noblesse would
Learn him forbearance from so foul a wrong.
What subject can give sentence on his king?
And who sits here that is not Richard's
subject?
Thieves are not judged but they are by
to hear,
Although apparent guilt be seen in them;
And shall the figure of God's majesty,

His captain, steward, deputy-elect,
Anointed, crowned, planted many years,
Be judged by subject and inferior breath,
And he himself not present? O, forfend it,
God,
That in a Christian climate souls refined
Should show so heinous, black, obscene a
deed!
I speak to subjects, and a subject speaks,
Stirr'd up by God, thus boldly for his king.
My Lord of Hereford here, whom you call
king,
Is a foul traitor to proud Hereford's King;
And if you crown him, let me prophesy, —
The blood of English shall manure the
ground,
And future ages groan for this foul act;
Peace shall go sleep with Turks and infidels,
And in this seat of peace tumultuous wars
Shall kin with kin and kind with kind
confound;
Disorder, horror, fear and mutiny
Shall here inhabit, and this land be call'd
The field of Golgotha and dead men's skulls.
O, if you raise this house against this house,
It will the woefullest division prove
That ever fell upon this cursed earth.
Prevent it, resist it, let it not be so,
Lest child, child's children, cry against you
'woe!'

NORTHUMBERLAND.
Well have you argued, sir; and, for your pains,

Of capital treason we arrest you here. —
My Lord of Westminster, be it your charge
To keep him safely till his day of trial. —
May it please you, lords, to grant the
commons' suit.

HENRY BOLINGBROKE.

Fetch hither Richard, that in common view
He may surrender; so we shall proceed
Without suspicion.

DUKE OF YORK.

I will be his conduct.

[*Exit.*

HENRY BOLINGBROKE.

Lords, you that here are under our arrest,
Procure your sureties for your days of
answer. —
Little are we beholding to your love,

[*to* CARLISLE

And little look'd for at your helping hands.

Enter YORK, *with* KING RICHARD, *and*
OFFICERS *bearing the crown, &c.*

KING RICHARD II.

Alack, why am I sent for to a king,
Before I have shook off the regal thoughts
Wherewith I reign'd? I hardly yet have learn'd
To insinuate, flatter, bow, and bend my knee:
Give sorrow leave awhile to tutor me
To this submission. Yet I well remember
The favours of these men: were they not
mine?

Did they not sometime cry, 'All hail!' to
me?
So Judas did to Christ: but he, in twelve,
Found truth in all but one; I, in twelve
thousand, none.
God save the King! — Will no man say
amen?
Am I both priest and clerk? well then,
amen.
God save the King! although I be not he;
And yet, amen, if heaven do think him
me. —
To do what service am I sent for hither?

DUKE OF YORK.
To do that office of thine own good will
Which tired majesty did make thee offer, —
The resignation of thy state and crown
To Henry Bolingbroke.

KING RICHARD II.
Give me the crown. — Here, cousin, seize the
crown;
Here cousin:
On this side my hand, and on that side
yours.
Now is this golden crown like a deep well
That owes two buckets, filling one another;
The emptier ever dancing in the air,
The other down, unseen and full of water:
That bucket down and full of tears am
I,
Drinking my griefs, whilst you mount up
on high.

HENRY BOLINGBROKE.
  I thought you had been willing to resign.
KING RICHARD II.
  My crown I am; but still my griefs are
  mine:
  You may my glories and my state depose,
  But not my griefs; still am I king of those.
HENRY BOLINGBROKE.
  Part of your cares you give me with your
  crown.
KING RICHARD II.
  Your cares set up do not pluck my cares
  down.
  My care is loss of care, by old care done;
  Your care is gain of care, by new care won:
  The cares I give I have, though given away;
  They tend the crown, yet still with me they
  stay.
HENRY BOLINGBROKE.
  Are you contented to resign the crown?
KING RICHARD II.
  Ay, no; — no, ay; for I must nothing be;
  Therefore no no, for I resign to thee.
  Now mark me, how I will undo myself: —
  I give this heavy weight from off my head
  And this unwieldy sceptre from my hand,
  The pride of kingly sway from out my heart;
  With mine own tears I wash away my balm,
  With mine own hands I give away my crown,
  With mine own tongue deny my sacred
  state,
  With mine own breath release all duty's rites:

All pomp and majesty I do forswear;
My manors, rents, revenues I forego;
My acts, decrees, and statutes I deny:
God pardon all oaths that are broke to me!
God keep all vows unbroke that swear to
thee!
Make me, that nothing have, with nothing
grieved,
And thou with all pleased, that hast all
achieved!
Long mayst thou live in Richard's seat to
sit,
And soon lie Richard in an earthly pit!
God save King Henry, unking'd Richard
says,
And send him many years of sunshine days! —
What more remains?

NORTHUMBERLAND.
                              No more, but that you read
                                   [*Offering a paper.*
These accusations and these grievous crimes
Committed by your person and your followers
Against the state and profit of this land;
That, by confessing them, the souls of men
May deem that you are worthily deposed.

KING RICHARD II.
Must I do so? and must I ravel out
My weaved-up follies? Gentle Northumberland,
If thy offences were upon record,
Would it not shame thee in so fair a troop
To read a lecture of them? If thou wouldst,
There shouldst thou find one heinous article, —

Containing the deposing of a king
And cracking the strong warrant of an oath, —
Mark'd with a blot, damn'd in the book of
heaven: —
Nay, all of you that stand and look upon,
Whilst that my wretchedness doth bait
myself, —
Though some of you, with Pilate, wash your
hands
Showing an outward pity; yet you Pilates
Have here deliver'd me to my sour cross,
And water cannot wash away your sin.

NORTHUMBERLAND.

My lord, dispatch; read o'er these articles.

KING RICHARD II.

Mine eyes are full of tears, I cannot see:
And yet salt water blinds them not so much
But they can see a sort of traitors here.
Nay, if I turn mine eyes upon myself,
I find myself a traitor with the rest;
For I have given here my soul's consent
To undeck the pompous body of a king;
Made glory base and sovereignty a slave,
Proud majesty a subject, state a peasant.

NORTHUMBERLAND.

My lord, —

KING RICHARD II.

No lord of thine, thou haught insulting man,
Nor no man's lord; I have no name, no
title, —
No, not that name was given me at the
font, —

126

But 'tis usurp'd: — alack the heavy day,
That I have worn so many winters out,
And know not now what name to call myself!
O that I were a mockery king of snow,
Standing before the sun of Bolingbroke,
To melt myself away in water-drops! —
Good king, — great king, and yet not greatly good, —
An if my word be sterling yet in England,
Let it command a mirror hither straight,
That it may show me what a face I have,
Since it is bankrupt of his majesty.

HENRY BOLINGBROKE.

Go some of you and fetch a looking-glass.

                        [*Exit an* ATTENDANT.

NORTHUMBERLAND.

Read o'er this paper while the glass doth come.

KING RICHARD II.

Fiend, thou torment'st me ere I come to hell!

HENRY BOLINGBROKE.

Urge it no more, my Lord Northumberland.

NORTHUMBERLAND.

The commons will not then be satisfied.

KING RICHARD II.

They shall be satisfied: I'll read enough,
When I do see the very book indeed
Where all my sins are writ, and that's myself.

        Enter ATTENDANT, *with a glass.*

Give me the glass, and therein will I read. —
No deeper wrinkles yet? hath sorrow struck
So many blows upon this face of mine,
And made no deeper wounds? — O flattering glass,
Like to my followers in prosperity,
Thou dost beguile me! Was this face the face
That every day under his household roof
Did keep ten thousand men? was this the face
That, like the sun, did make beholders wink?
Was this the face that faced so many follies,
And was at last out-faced by Bolingbroke?
A brittle glory shineth in this face:
As brittle as the glory is the face;
         [*Dashes the glass against the ground.*
For there it is, crack'd in a hundred shivers. —
Mark, silent King, the moral of this sport, —
How soon my sorrow hath destroy'd my face.

HENRY BOLINGBROKE.

The shadow of your sorrow hath destroy'd
The shadow of your face.

KING RICHARD II.

                       Say that again.
The shadow of my sorrow! ha! let's see: —
'Tis very true, my grief lies all within;
And these external manners of lament
Are merely shadows to the unseen grief
That swells with silence in the tortured soul;
There lies the substance: and I thank thee, King,

For thy great bounty, that not only givest
Me cause to wail but teachest me the way
How to lament the cause. I'll beg one boon,
And then be gone and trouble you no more.
Shall I obtain it?

HENRY BOLINGBROKE.
                              Name it, fair cousin.

KING RICHARD II.
'Fair cousin'? I am greater than a king:
For when I was a king, my flatterers
Were then but subjects; being now a subject,
I have a king here to my flatterer.
Being so great, I have no need to beg.

HENRY BOLINGBROKE.
Yet ask.

KING RICHARD II.
And shall I have?

HENRY BOLINGBROKE.
You shall.

KING RICHARD II.
Then give me leave to go.

HENRY BOLINGBROKE.
Whither?

KING RICHARD II.
Whither you will, so I were from your sights.

HENRY BOLINGBROKE.
Go, some of you convey him to the Tower.

KING RICHARD II.
O, good! convey? — conveyers are you all,
That rise thus nimbly by a true king's fall.

  [*Exeunt* KING RICHARD, *some* LORDS, *and*
    a GUARD.

HENRY BOLINGBROKE.

   On Wednesday next we solemnly set down

   Our coronation: lords, prepare yourselves.

     [*Exeunt all except the* BISHOP OF CARLISLE,

       the ABBOT OF WESTMINSTER, *and* AUMERLE.

ABBOT OF WESTMINSTER.

   A woeful pageant have we here beheld.

BISHOP OF CARLISLE.

   The woe's to come; the children yet unborn,

   Shall feel this day as sharp to them as

   thorn.

DUKE OF AUMERLE.

   You holy clergymen, is there no plot

   To rid the realm of this pernicious blot?

ABBOT OF WESTMINSTER.

   My lord,

   Before I freely speak my mind herein,

   You shall not only take the sacrament

   To bury mine intents, but also to effect

   Whatever I shall happen to devise. —

   I see your brows are full of discontent,

   Your hearts of sorrow and your eyes of

   tears:

   Come home with me to supper; and I'll lay

   A plot shall show us all a merry day.

                       [*Exeunt.*

ACT V

Scene I.

London. A street leading to the Tower.
Enter QUEEN *and* LADIES.

QUEEN.

This way the King will come; this is the way
To Julius Caesar's ill-erected tower,
To whose flint bosom my condemned lord
Is doom'd a prisoner by proud Bolingbroke:
Here let us rest, if this rebellious earth
Have any resting for her true King's Queen. —
But soft, but see, or rather do not see,
My fair rose wither: yet look up, behold,
That you in pity may dissolve to dew,
And wash him fresh again with true-love
tears.

Enter KING RICHARD *and* GUARDS.

Ah, thou, the model where old Troy did
stand,
Thou map of honour, thou King Richard's
tomb,
And not King Richard; thou most beauteous
inn,
Why should hard-favour'd grief be lodged
in thee,

133

When triumph is become an alehouse guest?

KING RICHARD II.

Join not with grief, fair woman, do not so,
To make my end too sudden: learn, good soul,
To think our former state a happy dream;
From which awaked, the truth of what we are
Shows us but this: I am sworn brother, sweet,
To grim Necessity, and he and I
Will keep a league till death. Hie thee to France
And cloister thee in some religious house:
Our holy lives must win a new world's crown,
Which our profane hours here have stricken down.

QUEEN.

What, is my Richard both in shape and mind
Transform'd and weaken'd? hath Bolingbroke deposed
Thine intellect? hath he been in thy heart?
The lion dying thrusteth forth his paw,
And wounds the earth, if nothing else, with rage
To be o'erpower'd; and wilt thou, pupil-like,
Take thy correction mildly, kiss the rod,
And fawn on rage with base humility,
Which art a lion and a king of beasts?

KING RICHARD II.

A king of beasts, indeed; if aught but beasts,

I had been still a happy king of men.
Good sometime queen, prepare thee hence for
France:
Think I am dead: and that even here thou
takest,
As from my death-bed, thy last living leave.
In winter's tedious nights sit by the fire
With good old folks and let them tell thee
tales
Of woeful ages long ago betid;
And ere thou bid good night, to quit their
griefs
Tell thou the lamentable tale of me,
And send the hearers weeping to their beds:
For why, the senseless brands will sympathize
The heavy accent of thy moving tongue
And in compassion weep the fire out;
And some will mourn in ashes, some
coal-black,
For the deposing of a rightful king.

Enter NORTHUMBERLAND *attended.*

NORTHUMBERLAND.
My lord, the mind of Bolingbroke is changed:
You must to Pomfret, not unto the Tower. —
And, madam, there is order ta'en for you;
With all swift speed you must away to
France.
KING RICHARD II.
Northumberland, thou ladder wherewithal
The mounting Bolingbroke ascends my throne,

The time shall not be many hours of age
More than it is, ere foul sin gathering head
Shalt break into corruption: thou shalt think,
Though he divide the realm and give thee
half,
It is too little, helping him to all;
And he shall think that thou, which know'st
the way
To plant unrightful kings, wilt know again,
Being ne'er so little urged, another way
To pluck him headlong from the usurped
throne.
The love of wicked men converts to fear;
That fear to hate, and hate turns one or
both
To worthy danger and deserved death.

NORTHUMBERLAND.
My guilt be on my head, and there an end.
Take leave and part; for you must part
forthwith.

KING RICHARD II.
Doubly divorced! — Bad men, you violate
A twofold marriage, — 'twixt my crown and
me,
And then betwixt me and my married wife. —
Let me unkiss the oath 'twixt thee and me;
And yet not so, for with a kiss 'twas made. —
Part us, Northumberland; I toward the north,
Where shivering cold and sickness pines the
clime;
My wife to France, — from whence, set forth
in pomp,

She came adorned hither like sweet May,
Sent back like Hallowmas or short'st of day.

QUEEN.

And must we be divided? must we part?

KING RICHARD II.

Ay, hand from hand, my love, and heart from
heart.

QUEEN.

Banish us both and send the King with me.

NORTHUMBERLAND.

That were some love but little policy.

QUEEN.

Then whither he goes, thither let me go.

KING RICHARD II.

So two, together weeping, make one woe.
Weep thou for me in France, I for thee
here;
Better far off than near, be ne'er the near.
Go, count thy way with sighs; I mine with
groans.

QUEEN.

So longest way shall have the longest moans.

KING RICHARD II.

Twice for one step I'll groan, the way being
short,
And piece the way out with a heavy heart.
Come, come, in wooing sorrow let's be brief,
Since, wedding it, there is such length in
grief;
One kiss shall stop our mouths, and dumbly
part;
Thus give I mine, and thus take I thy heart.

[*They kiss.*

QUEEN.

Give me mine own again; 'twere no good part

To take on me to keep and kill thy heart.

[*They kiss again.*

So, now I have mine own again, be gone,

That I might strive to kill it with a groan.

KING RICHARD II.

We make woe wanton with this fond delay:

Once more, adieu; the rest let sorrow say.

[*Exeunt.*

Scene II.

The DUKE OF YORK'S palace.
Enter YORK *and his* DUCHESS.

DUCHESS OF YORK.
My lord, you told me you would tell the rest,
When weeping made you break the story off
Of our two cousins coming into London.

DUKE OF YORK.
Where did I leave?

DUCHESS OF YORK.
At that sad stop, my lord,
Where rude misgovern'd hands from windows' tops
Threw dust and rubbish on King Richard's head.

DUKE OF YORK.
Then, as I said, the duke, great Bolingbroke, —
Mounted upon a hot and fiery steed
Which his aspiring rider seem'd to know, —
With slow but stately pace kept on his course,
Whilst all tongues cried 'God save thee, Bolingbroke!'
You would have thought the very windows spake,

139

So many greedy looks of young and old
Through casements darted their desiring eyes
Upon his visage, and that all the walls
With painted imagery had said at once
'Jesu preserve thee! welcome, Bolingbroke!'
Whilst he, from the one side to the other turning,
Bareheaded, lower than his proud steed's neck,
Bespake them thus, — 'I thank you, countrymen:'
And thus still doing, thus he pass'd along.

DUCHESS OF YORK.

Alack, poor Richard! where rode he the whilst?

DUKE OF YORK.

As in a theatre, the eyes of men,
After a well-graced actor leaves the stage,
Are idly bent on him that enters next,
Thinking his prattle to be tedious;
Even so, or with much more contempt, men's eyes
Did scowl on gentle Richard; no man cried
'God save him!'
No joyful tongue gave him his welcome home:
But dust was thrown upon his sacred head;
Which with such gentle sorrow he shook off, —
His face still combating with tears and smiles,
The badges of his grief and patience, —
That had not God, for some strong purpose, steel'd

140

The hearts of men, they must perforce have melted
And barbarism itself have pitied him.
But heaven hath a hand in these events,
To whose high will we bound our calm contents.
To Bolingbroke are we sworn subjects now,
Whose state and honour I for aye allow.

DUCHESS OF YORK.
Here comes my son Aumerle.

DUKE OF YORK.
                              Aumerle that was;
But that is lost for being Richard's friend,
And, madam, you must call him Rutland now:
I am in Parliament pledge for his truth
And lasting fealty to the new-made King.

Enter AUMERLE.

DUCHESS OF YORK.
Welcome, my son: who are the violets now
That strew the green lap of the new come spring?

DUKE OF AUMERLE.
Madam, I know not, nor I greatly care not:
God knows I had as lief be none as one.

DUKE OF YORK.
Well, bear you well in this new spring of time,
Lest you be cropp'd before you come to prime.

What news from Oxford? hold those justs and
triumphs?

DUKE OF AUMERLE.

For aught I know, my lord, they do.

DUKE OF YORK.

You will be there, I know.

DUKE OF AUMERLE.

If God prevent not, I purpose so.

DUKE OF YORK.

What seal is that, that hangs without thy
bosom?

Yea, look'st thou pale? let me see the writing.

DUKE OF AUMERLE.

My lord, 'tis nothing.

DUKE OF YORK.

                    No matter, then, who see it;
I will be satisfied; let me see the writing.

DUKE OF AUMERLE.

I do beseech your grace to pardon me:
It is a matter of small consequence,
Which for some reasons I would not have
seen.

DUKE OF YORK.

Which for some reasons, sir, I mean to see.
I fear, I fear, —

DUCHESS OF YORK.

                    What should you fear?
'Tis nothing but some bond, that he is
enter'd into
For gay apparel 'gainst the triumph day.

DUKE OF YORK.

Bound to himself! what doth he with a bond

142

That he is bound to? Wife, thou art a fool. —

Boy, let me see the writing.

DUKE OF AUMERLE.

I do beseech you, pardon me; I may not show it.

DUKE OF YORK.

I will be satisfied; let me see it, I say.

[*He plucks it out of his bosom and reads it.*
Treason! foul treason! — Villain! traitor! slave!

DUCHESS OF YORK.

What is the matter, my lord?

DUKE OF YORK.

Ho! who is within there?

Enter a SERVANT.

           Saddle my horse. —
God for his mercy, what treachery is here!

DUCHESS OF YORK.

Why, what is it, my lord?

DUKE OF YORK.

Give me my boots, I say; saddle my horse, —
           [*Exit* SERVANT.
Now, by mine honour, by my life, by my troth,
I will appeach the villain.

DUCHESS OF YORK.

           What is the matter?

DUKE OF YORK.

Peace, foolish woman.

DUCHESS OF YORK.

I will not peace. — What is the matter,
Aumerle.

DUKE OF AUMERLE.

Good mother, be content; it is no more
Than my poor life must answer.

DUCHESS OF YORK.

Thy life answer!

DUKE OF YORK.

Bring me my boots: — I will unto the King.

His MAN *enters with his boots.*

DUCHESS OF YORK.

Strike him, Aumerle. — Poor boy, thou art
amazed. —
Hence, villain! never more come in my sight.

DUKE OF YORK.

Give me my boots, I say.

DUCHESS OF YORK.

Why, York, what wilt thou do?
Wilt thou not hide the trespass of thine
own?
Have we more sons? or are we like to have?
Is not my teeming date drunk up with time?
And wilt thou pluck my fair son from mine
age,
And rob me of a happy mother's name?
Is he not like thee? is he not thine own?

DUKE OF YORK.

Thou fond mad woman,
Wilt thou conceal this dark conspiracy?

A dozen of them here have ta'en the sacrament,
And interchangeably set down their hands,
To kill the King at Oxford.

DUCHESS OF YORK.

                          He shall be none;
We'll keep him here: then what is that to him?

DUKE OF YORK.

Away, fond woman! were he twenty times my son,
I would appeach him.

DUCHESS OF YORK.

                          Hadst thou groan'd for him
As I have done, thou wouldst be more pitiful.
But now I know thy mind; thou dost suspect
That I have been disloyal to thy bed,
And that he is a bastard, not thy son:
Sweet York, sweet husband, be not of that mind:
He is as like thee as a man may be,
Not like to me, or any of my kin,
And yet I love him.

DUKE OF YORK.

                          Make way, unruly woman!
                                          [*Exit.*

DUCHESS OF YORK.

After, Aumerle! mount thee upon his horse;
Spur post, and get before him to the King,
And beg thy pardon ere he do accuse thee.
I'll not be long behind; though I be old,

I doubt not but to ride as fast as York:
And never will I rise up from the ground
Till Bolingbroke have pardon'd thee. Away,
be gone!

[*Exeunt.*

Scene III.

Windsor Castle.
Enter BOLINGBROKE, PERCY, *and other* LORDS.

HENRY BOLINGBROKE.

Can no man tell me of my unthrifty son?
'Tis full three months since I did see him
last: —
If any plague hang over us, 'tis he.
I would to God, my lords, he might be
found:
Inquire at London, 'mongst the taverns there,
For there, they say, he daily doth frequent,
With unrestrained loose companions, —
Even such, they say, as stand in narrow
lanes,
And beat our watch, and rob our passengers;
Which he, young wanton and effeminate boy,
Takes on the point of honour to support
So dissolute a crew.

HENRY PERCY.

My lord, some two days since I saw the
Prince,
And told him of those triumphs held at
Oxford.

HENRY BOLINGBROKE.

And what said the gallant?

HENRY PERCY.

His answer was, — he would unto the stews,
And from the common'st creature pluck a glove,
And wear it as a favour; and with that
He would unhorse the lustiest challenger.

HENRY BOLINGBROKE.

As dissolute as desperate; yet through both
I see some sparks of better hope,
Which elder days may happily bring forth. —
But who comes here?

Enter AUMERLE, *amazed.*

DUKE OF AUMERLE.

Where is the King?

HENRY BOLINGBROKE.

What means
Our cousin, that he stares and looks so wildly?

DUKE OF AUMERLE.

God save your Grace! I do beseech your
Mmajesty,
To have some conference with your Grace alone.

HENRY BOLINGBROKE.

Withdraw yourselves, and leave us here alone.
                    [*Exeunt* PERCY *and* LORDS.
What is the matter with our cousin now?

DUKE OF AUMERLE.

For ever may my knees grow to the earth,
                                   [*Kneels.*

My tongue cleave to my roof within my
mouth
Unless a pardon ere I rise or speak.

HENRY BOLINGBROKE.

Intended or committed was this fault?
If on the first, how heinous e'er it be,
To win thy after-love I pardon thee.

DUKE OF AUMERLE.

Then give me leave that I may turn the key,
That no man enter till my tale be done.

HENRY BOLINGBROKE.

Have thy desire.

DUKE OF YORK [*within*].

My liege, beware; look to thyself;
Thou hast a traitor in thy presence there.

HENRY BOLINGBROKE.

Villain, I'll make thee safe.

[*Drawing*.

DUKE OF AUMERLE.

Stay thy revengeful hand; thou hast no cause
to fear.

DUKE OF YORK [*within*].

Open the door, secure, foolhardy King:
Shall I for love speak treason to thy face?
Open the door, or I will break it open.

Enter YORK.

HENRY BOLINGBROKE.

What is the matter, uncle? speak;
Recover breath; tell us how near is danger,
That we may arm us to encounter it.

DUKE OF YORK.
   Peruse this writing here, and thou shalt
   know
   The treason that my haste forbids me show.
DUKE OF AUMERLE.
   Remember, as thou read'st, thy promise
   pass'd:
   I do repent me; read not my name there
   My heart is not confederate with my hand.
DUKE OF YORK.
   It was, villain, ere thy hand did set it
   down. —
   I tore it from the traitor's bosom, King;
   Fear, and not love, begets his penitence:
   Forget to pity him, lest thy pity prove
   A serpent that will sting thee to the heart.
HENRY BOLINGBROKE.
   O heinous, strong and bold conspiracy! —
   O loyal father of a treacherous son!
   Thou sheer, immaculate and silver fountain,
   From when this stream through muddy
   passages
   Hath held his current and defiled himself!
   Thy overflow of good converts to bad;
   And thy abundant goodness shall excuse
   This deadly blot in thy digressing son.
DUKE OF YORK.
   So shall my virtue be his vice's bawd;
   And he shall spend mine honour with his
   shame,
   As thriftless sons their scraping fathers' gold.
   Mine honour lives when his dishonour dies,

Or my shamed life in his dishonour lies:
Thou kill'st me in his life; giving him breath,
The traitor lives, the true man's put to
death.

DUCHESS OF YORK [*within*].

What ho, my liege! for God's sake, let me
in.

HENRY BOLINGBROKE.

What shrill-voiced suppliant makes this eager
cry?

DUCHESS OF YORK [*within*].

A woman, and thy aunt, great King; 'tis I.
Speak with me, pity me, open the door:
A beggar begs that never begg'd before.

HENRY BOLINGBROKE.

Our scene is alter'd from a serious thing,
And now changed to 'The Beggar and the
King.' —
My dangerous cousin, let your mother in:
I know she is come to pray for your foul
sin.

DUKE OF YORK.

If thou do pardon, whosoever pray,
More sins for this forgiveness prosper may.
This fester'd joint cut off, the rest rest
sound;
This let alone will all the rest confound.

Enter DUCHESS.

DUCHESS OF YORK.

O King, believe not this hard-hearted man!

Love loving not itself none other can.

DUKE OF YORK.

Thou frantic woman, what dost thou make here?

Shall thy old dugs once more a traitor rear?

DUCHESS OF YORK.

Sweet York, be patient. — Hear me, gentle liege.

                           [*Kneels.*

HENRY BOLINGBROKE.

Rise up, good aunt.

DUCHESS OF YORK.

                     Not yet, I thee beseech:

For ever will I walk upon my knees,

And never see day that the happy sees,

Till thou give joy; until thou bid me joy,

By pardoning Rutland, my transgressing boy.

DUKE OF AUMERLE.

Unto my mother's prayers I bend my knee.

                           [*Kneels.*

DUKE OF YORK.

Against them both my true joints bended be.

                           [*Kneels.*

Ill mayst thou thrive, if thou grant any grace!

DUCHESS OF YORK.

Pleads he in earnest? look upon his face;

His eyes do drop no tears, his prayers are in jest;

His words come from his mouth, ours from our breast:

He prays but faintly and would be denied;

We pray with heart and soul and all beside:
His weary joints would gladly rise, I know;
Our knees shall kneel till to the ground
they grow:
His prayers are full of false hypocrisy;
Ours of true zeal and deep integrity.
Our prayers do out-pray his; then let them
have
That mercy which true prayer ought to have.

HENRY BOLINGBROKE.

Good aunt, stand up.

DUCHESS OF YORK.

             Nay, do not say, 'stand up;'
Say, 'pardon' first, and afterwards 'stand up.'
And if I were thy nurse, thy tongue to
teach,
'Pardon' should be the first word of thy
speech.
I never long'd to hear a word till now;
Say 'pardon,' King; let pity teach thee how:
The word is short, but not so short as
sweet;
No word like 'pardon' for kings' mouths
so meet.

DUKE OF YORK.

Speak it in French, King; say, *pardonne
moi*.

DUCHESS OF YORK.

Dost thou teach pardon pardon to destroy?
Ah, my sour husband, my hard-hearted lord,
That set'st the word itself against the word! —
Speak 'pardon' as 'tis current in our land;

The chopping French we do not understand.
Thine eye begins to speak; set thy tongue
there:
Or in thy piteous heart plant thou thine ear;
That hearing how our plaints and prayers do
pierce,
Pity may move thee 'pardon' to rehearse.
HENRY BOLINGBROKE.
Good aunt, stand up.
DUCHESS OF YORK.
                              I do not sue to stand;
Pardon is all the suit I have in hand.
HENRY BOLINGBROKE.
I pardon him, as God shall pardon me.
DUCHESS OF YORK.
O happy vantage of a kneeling knee!
Yet am I sick for fear: speak it again;
Twice saying 'pardon' doth not pardon twain,
But makes one pardon strong.
HENRY BOLINGBROKE.
                              With all my heart
I pardon him.
DUCHESS OF YORK.
                              A god on earth thou art.
HENRY BOLINGBROKE.
But for our trusty brother-in-law and the
abbot,
With all the rest of that consorted crew,
Destruction straight shall dog them at the
heels. —
Good uncle, help to order several powers
To Oxford, or where'er these traitors are:

They shall not live within this world, I
swear,
But I will have them, if I once know where.
Uncle, farewell: — and, cousin too, adieu:
Your mother well hath pray'd, and prove
you true.

DUCHESS OF YORK.

Come, my old son: — I pray God make
thee new.

[*Exeunt.*

Scene IV.

The same.
Enter SIR PIERCE OF EXTON *and a* SERVANT.

SIR PIERCE OF EXTON.
Didst thou not mark the King, what words
he spake,
'Have I no friend will rid me of this living
fear?'
Was it not so?
SERVANT.
These were his very words.
SIR PIERCE OF EXTON.
'Have I no friend?' quoth he: he spake it
twice,
And urged it twice together, — did he not?
SERVANT.
He did.
SIR PIERCE OF EXTON.
And speaking it, he wistly look'd on me,
As who should say, — 'I would thou wert
the man
That would divorce this terror from my
heart;' —
Meaning the king at Pomfret. Come, let's go:
I am the King's friend, and will rid his foe.
[*Exeunt.*

Scene V.

Pomfret Castle.
Enter KING RICHARD.

KING RICHARD II.

I have been studying how I may compare
This prison where I live unto the world:
And for because the world is populous
And here is not a creature but myself,
I cannot do it; — yet I'll hammer it out.
My brain I'll prove the female to my soul,
My soul the father; and these two beget
A generation of still-breeding thoughts,
And these same thoughts people this little
world;
In humours like the people of this world,
For no thought is contented. The better
sort, —
As thoughts of things divine, are intermix'd
With scruples and do set the word itself
Against the word:
As thus, 'Come, little ones;' and then again,
'It is as hard to come as for a camel
To thread the postern of a small needle's eye.'
Thoughts tending to ambition, they do plot
Unlikely wonders; how these vain weak nails
May tear a passage through the flinty ribs

Of this hard world, my ragged prison walls,
And, for they cannot, die in their own pride.
Thoughts tending to content flatter themselves
That they are not the first of fortune's
slaves,
Nor shall not be the last; like silly beggars,
Who sitting in the stocks refuge their shame,
That many have and others must sit there;
And in this thought they find a kind of ease,
Bearing their own misfortunes on the back
Of such as have before endured the like.
Thus play I in one person many people,
And none contented: sometimes am I king;
Then treasons make me wish myself a beggar,
And so I am: then crushing penury
Persuades me I was better when a king;
Then am I king'd again: and by and by
Think that I am unking'd by Bolingbroke,
And straight am nothing: — but whate'er I
be,
Nor I nor any man that but man is
With nothing shall be pleased, till he be
eased
With being nothing. — Music do I hear?
                                   [*Music.*
Ha, ha! keep time: — how sour sweet music
is,
When time is broke and no proportion kept!
So is it in the music of men's lives.
And here have I the daintiness of ear
To cheque time broke in a disorder'd string;
But for the concord of my state and time

Had not an ear to hear my true time broke.
I wasted time, and now doth time waste me;
For now hath time made me his numbering
clock;
My thoughts are minutes; and with sighs
they jar
Their watches on unto mine eyes, the outward
watch,
Whereto my finger, like a dial's point,
Is pointing still, in cleansing them from
tears.
Now sir, the sound that tells what hour it is
Are clamorous groans, which strike upon my
heart,
Which is the bell: so sighs and tears and
groans
Show minutes, times, and hours: — but my
time
Runs posting on in Bolingbroke's proud joy,
While I stand fooling here, his Jack o' the
clock.
This music mads me; let it sound no more;
For though it have holp madmen to their
wits,
In me it seems it will make wise men
mad.
Yet blessing on his heart that gives it me!
For 'tis a sign of love; and love to Richard
Is a strange brooch in this all-hating world.

Enter GROOM.

161

GROOM.

Hail, royal Prince!

KING RICHARD II.

Thanks, noble peer;
The cheapest of us is ten groats too dear.
What art thou? and how comest thou hither,
Where no man never comes but that sad dog
That brings me food to make misfortune live?

GROOM.

I was a poor groom of thy stable, King,
When thou wert king; who, travelling towards
York,
With much ado at length have gotten leave
To look upon my sometimes royal master's
face.
O, how it yearn'd my heart when I beheld
In London streets, that coronation-day,
When Bolingbroke rode on roan Barbary, —
That horse that thou so often hast bestrid,
That horse that I so carefully have dress'd!

KING RICHARD II.

Rode he on Barbary? Tell me, gentle friend,
How went he under him?

GROOM.

So proudly as if he disdain'd the ground.

KING RICHARD II.

So proud that Bolingbroke was on his back!
That jade hath eat bread from my royal hand;
This hand hath made him proud with clapping
him.
Would he not stumble? would he not fall
down, —

Since pride must have a fall, — and break
the neck
Of that proud man that did usurp his back?
Forgiveness, horse! why do I rail on thee,
Since thou, created to be awed by man,
Wast born to bear? I was not made a horse;
And yet I bear a burthen like an ass,
Spurr'd, gall'd and tired by jouncing Bolingbroke.

Enter KEEPER *with a dish.*

KEEPER [*to the* GROOM].
Fellow, give place; here is no longer stay.
KING RICHARD II.
If thou love me, 'tis time thou wert away.
GROOM.
What my tongue dares not, that my heart
shall say.   [*Exit.*
KEEPER.
My lord, will't please you to fall to?
KING RICHARD II.
Taste of it first, as thou art wont to do.
KEEPER.
My lord, I dare not. Sir Pierce of Exton,
Who lately came from the King, commands
the contrary.
KING RICHARD II.
The devil take Henry of Lancaster and thee!
Patience is stale, and I am weary of it.
                                    [*Beats the* KEEPER.
KEEPER.
Help, help, help!

Enter SIR PIERCE OF EXTON *and*
SERVANTS, *arm'd.*

KING RICHARD II.

How now! what means death in this rude
assault?

Villain, thy own hand yields thy death's
instrument.

[*Snatching a weapon and killing a* SERVANT.

Go thou, and fill another room in hell.

[*He kills another* SERVANT. *Then* EXTON
strikes him down.

That hand shall burn in never-quenching fire

That staggers thus my person. — Exton, thy
fierce hand

Hath with the King's blood stain'd the King's
own land.

Mount, mount, my soul! thy seat is up
on high;

Whilst my gross flesh sinks downward, here
to die.   [*Dies.*

EXTON.

As full of valour as of royal blood:

Both have I spill'd; — O would the deed
were good!

For now the devil, that told me I did well,

Says that this deed is chronicled in hell.

This dead king to the living king I'll bear: —

Take hence the rest, and give them burial
here.

[*Exeunt.*

Scene VI.

Windsor Castle.
Flourish. Enter BOLINGBROKE, YORK,
LORDS *and* ATTENDANTS.

HENRY BOLINGBROKE.
Kind uncle York, the latest news we hear
Is that the rebels have consumed with fire
Our town of Cicester in Gloucestershire;
But whether they be ta'en or slain we hear not.

Enter NORTHUMBERLAND.

Welcome, my lord: what is the news?
NORTHUMBERLAND.
First, to thy sacred state wish I all happiness.
The next news is, I have to London sent
The heads of Oxford, Salisbury, Blunt, and
Kent:
The manner of their taking may appear
At large discoursed in this paper here.
HENRY BOLINGBROKE.
We thank thee, gentle Percy, for thy pains;
And to thy worth will add right worthy
gains.

Enter FITZWATER.

LORD FITZWATER.

My lord, I have from Oxford sent to London
The heads of Brocas and Sir Bennet Seely,
Two of the dangerous consorted traitors
That sought at Oxford thy dire overthrow.

HENRY BOLINGBROKE.

Thy pains, Fitzwater, shall not be forgot;
Right noble is thy merit, well I wot.

Enter PERCY, *with the* BISHOP OF CARLISLE.

HENRY PERCY.

The grand conspirator, Abbot of Westminster,
With clog of conscience and sour melancholy
Hath yielded up his body to the grave;
But here is Carlisle living, to abide
Thy kingly doom and sentence of his pride.

HENRY BOLINGBROKE.

Carlisle, this is your doom: —
Choose out some secret place, some reverend
room,
More than thou hast, and with it joy thy
life;
So as thou livest in peace, die free from strife:
For though mine enemy thou hast ever been,
High sparks of honour in thee have I seen.

Enter SIR PIERCE OF EXTON, *with persons
bearing a coffin.*

SIR PIERCE OF EXTON.

Great King, within this coffin I present

Thy buried fear: herein all breathless lies
The mightiest of thy greatest enemies,
Richard of Bordeaux, by me hither brought.

HENRY BOLINGBROKE.

Exton, I thank thee not; for thou hast wrought
A deed of slander, with thy fatal hand,
Upon my head and all this famous land.

SIR PIERCE OF EXTON.

From your own mouth, my lord, did I this
deed.

HENRY BOLINGBROKE.

They love not poison that do poison need,
Nor do I thee: though I did wish him dead,
I hate the murderer, love him murdered.
The guilt of conscience take thou for thy
labour,
But neither my good word nor princely
favour:
With Cain go wander through shades of
night,
And never show thy head by day nor light. —
Lords, I protest, my soul is full of woe
That blood should sprinkle me to make me
grow:
Come, mourn with me for that I do lament,
And put on sullen black incontinent:
I'll make a voyage to the Holy Land,
To wash this blood off from my guilty
hand: —
March sadly after; grace my mournings here;
In weeping after this untimely bier.

[*Exeunt.*

Thy buried fear. Herein all breathless lies
The mightiest of thy greatest enemies,
Richard of Bordeaux, by me hither brought.

HENRY BOLINGBROKE.

Exton, I thank thee not; for thou hast wrought
A deed of slander with thy fatal hand
Upon my head and all this famous land.

SIR PIERCE OF EXTON.

From your own mouth, my lord, did I this
                    deed.

HENRY BOLINGBROKE.

They love not poison that do poison need,
Nor do I thee: though I did wish him dead,
I hate the murderer, love him murdered.
The guilt of conscience take thou for thy
                    labour,
But neither my good word nor princely
                    favour:
With Cain go wander through shades of
                    night,
And never show thy head by day nor light. —
Lords, I protest, my soul is full of woe,
That blood should sprinkle me to make me
                    grow.
Come, mourn with me for that I do lament,
And put on sullen black incontinent:
I'll make a voyage to the Holy Land,
To wash this blood off from my guilty
                    hand:—
March sadly after; grace my mournings here;
In weeping after this untimely bier.

[Exeunt.

Glossary

ABATE: to shorten. To cast down. To blunt.

ABATEMENT: diminution.

ABIDE: to sojourn. to expiate (a corruption of 'Aby').

ABLE: to uphold.

ABRIDGEMENT: a short play.

ABROOK: to brook, abide.

ABSEY-BOOK: a primer.

ABSOLUTE: positive, certain. Complete.

ABUSE: to deceive. Deception.

ABY: to expiate a fault.

ABYSM: abyss.

ACCITE: to cite, summon.

ACCUSE: accusation.

ACHIEVE: to obtain.

ACKNOWN: 'to be acknown' is to acknowledge.

ACQUITTANCE: a receipt or discharge.

ACTION-TAKING: litigious.

ACTURE: action.

ADDITION: title, attribute.

ADDRESS: prepare oneself.

ADVANCE: to prefer, promote to honour.

ADVERTISEMENT: admonition.

ADVERTISING: attentive.

ADVICE: consideration, discretion.

ADVISE: to consider, reflect.

169

ADVISED: considerate.

ADVOCATION: pleading, advocacy.

AFEARED: afraid.

AFFECT: to love.

AFFEERED: assessed, confirmed.

AFFY: to affiance. To trust.

AFRONT: in front.

AGAZED: looking in amazement.

AGLET-BABY: the small figure engraved on a jewel.

AGNISE: to acknowledge, confess.

A-GOOD: a good deal, plenteously.

A-HOLD: a sea-term.

AIM: a guess.

ALDER-LIEFEST: most loved of all.

ALE: alehouse.

ALLOW: to approve.

ALLOWANCE: approval.

AMES-ACE: two aces, the lowest throw of the dice.

AMORT: dead, dejected.

AN: if.

ANCHOR: an anchorite, hermit.

ANCIENT: an ensign-bearer.

ANGEL: a coin, bearing the image of an angel.

ANIGHT: by night.

ANSWER: retaliation.

ANTHROPOPHAGINIAN: a cannibal.

ANTICK: the fool in the old plays.

ANTRE: a cave.

APPARENT: heir-apparent.

APPEAL: accusation. Accuse.

APPEARED: made apparent.

APPLE-JOHN: a kind of apple.

APPOINTMENT: preparation.

APPREHENSION: opinion.

APPREHENSIVE: apt to apprehend or understand.

APPROBATION: probation.

APPROOF: approbation, proof.

APPROVE: to prove. To justify, make good.

APPROVER: one who proves or tries.

ARCH: chief.

ARGAL: ergo, therefore.

ARGENTINE: silver.

ARGIER: Algiers.

ARGOSY: a merchant ship, originally of Ragusa.

ARGUMENT: subject.

ARMIGERO: Esquire.

AROINT: get thee gone.

A-ROW: in a row.

ARTICULATE: to enter into articles of agreement.

ASK: to require.

ASPECT: regard, looks.

ASPERSION: sprinkling; hence blessing, generally accompanied by the sprinkling of holy water.

ASSAY: attempt, test, make proof of.

ASSINEGO: an ass.

ASSUBJUGATE: to subjugate.

ASSURANCE: deed of assurance.

ASSURED: betrothed.

ATOMY: an atom, a small person.

ATONE: to put people at one, to reconcile.

ATTACH: to seize, lay hold on.

ATTASKED: taken to task, reprehended.

ATTEND: to listen to.

ATTENT: attentive.

ATTORNEY: an agent.

ATTORNEY: to employ as an agent. To perform by an agent.

AUDACIOUS: spirited, daring.

AUGUR: augury.

AUTHENTIC: clothed with authority.

AVAUNT: be gone, a word of abhorrence.

AVE: hail.

AVE-MARY: salutation addressed to the Blessed Virgin Mary.

AVERRING: confirming.

AWFUL: worshipful.

AWKWARD: contrary.

BACCARE: keep back.

BACKWARD: the hinder part; the past.

BALKED: heaped, as on a ridge.

BALLOW: a cudgel.

BALM: the oil of consecration.

BAN: to curse.

BANK: to sail by the banks.

BARM: yeast.

BARN: a child.

BARNACLE: a shellfish, supposed to produce the sea-bird of the same name.

BASE: a game, sometimes called Prisoners' base.

BASES: an embroidered mantle worn by knights on horseback, reaching below the knees.

BASILISK: a kind of ordnance.

BASTA: (Italian), enough.

172

BASTARD: raisin wine.

BATE: to flutter, as a hawk. To abate.

BAT-FOWLING: catching birds with a clap-net by night.

BATLET: a small bat, used for beating clothes.

BATTLE: army.

BAVIN: like brushwood, blazing and instantly dying.

BAWCOCK: a fine fellow.

BAY: the space between the roof timbers.

BEADSMAN: one who says prayers for another.

BEARING-CLOTH: a christening robe.

BEAT: to flutter as a falcon, to meditate, consider earnestly.

BEAVER: the lower part of a helmet.

BEETLE: a mallet.

BEING: dwelling.

BE-METE: to measure.

BE-MOILED: daubed with dirt.

BENVENUTO: (Italian), welcome.

BERGOMASK: a rustic dance.

BESHREW: evil befall; a plague upon.

BESTRAUGHT: distraught, distracted.

BETEEM: to pour out. To allow.

BETID: happened.

BEZONIAN: a beggarly fellow.

BIDING: abiding-place.

BIGGEN: a night-cap.

BILBERRY: the whortleberry.

BILBO: a sword, from Bilbao in Spain.

BILBOES: fetters or stocks.

BILL: a bill-hook, a weapon.

BIN: been, are.

BIRD-BOLT: an arrow for shooting at birds.

BIRDING: hawking at partridges.

BISSON: blind.

BLANK: the white mark in the middle of a target.

BLENCH: to start aside, flinch.

BLENT: blended.

BLOOD-BOLTERED: smeared with blood.

BLOW: to inflate.

BOARD: to accost.

BOB: a blow, or hit; a gibe. To cheat.

BODGE: to botch, bungle.

BODIKIN: 'Od's Bodikin', God's little body.

BOITIER VERT: (French), green box.

BOLLEN: swollen.

BOLTED: sifted, refined.

BOLTER: a sieve.

BOLTING-HUTCH: a container for sifting meal.

BOMBARD: a barrel, a drunkard.

BOMBAST: padding.

BONA-ROBA: a harlot.

BOND: that to which one is bound.

BOOK: a paper of conditions.

BOOT: help, use.

BOOTS: bots, a kind of worm.

BORE: calibre of a gun; hence, metaph. size, weight, importance.

BOSKY: covered with underwood.

BOSOM: wish, heart's desire.

BOTS: worms which infest horses.

BOURN: a boundary. A brook.

BRACE: armour for the arm, state of defence.

BRACH: a hound bitch.

BRAID: deceitful.

BRAVE: handsome, well-dressed.

BRAVE: boast.

BRAVERY: finery. Boastfulness.

BRAWL: a kind of dance.

BREAST: voice.

BREATHE: to exercise.

BREECHING: liable to be whipped.

BREED-BATE: a fomenter of trouble or debate.

BREESE: the gadfly.

BRIBE-BUCK: a buck given away in presents.

BRING: to attend one on a journey.

BROCK: a badger.

BROKE: to act as a procurer.

BROKEN: having lost some teeth by age.

BROKEN MUSIC: the music of stringed instruments.

BROKER: an agent.

BROTHERHOOD: trading company.

BROWNIST: a sectary, a follower of Brown, the founder of the Independents.

BRUIT: noise, report, rumour.

BRUSH: rude assault.

BUCK: suds or lye for washing clothes in.

BUCK-BASKET: a soiled clothes basket.

BUCKING: washing.

BUCK-WASHING: washing in lye.

BUG: a bugbear, a spectre.

BULLY-ROOK: a bragging cheater.

BURGONET: a kind of helmet.

BURST: to break.

BUSKY: bushy.

BUTT-SHAFT: a light arrow for shooting at a target.

BUXOM: obedient.

BY'RLAKIN: by our little Lady: an oath.

CADDIS: worsted galloon, or trimming tape.

CADE: a cask or barrel.

CAGE: a prison.

CAIN-COLOURED: red (applied to hair).

CAITIFF: a captive, a slave; a mean fellow.

CALCULATE: prophesy.

CALIVER: a hand-gun.

CALLET: a trull.

CALLING: appellation.

CALM: qualm.

CAN: to know, be skilful in.

CANAKIN: a little can.

CANARY: a wine brought from the Canary Islands.

CANDLE-WASTERS: persons who sit up all night to drink.

CANKER: a caterpillar. The dog-rose.

CANSTICK: a candlestick.

CANTLE: a slice, corner.

CANTON: a canto.

CANVAS: to sift: hence, metaphorically, to prove.

CAPABLE: subject to. Intelligent. Capable of inheriting. Ample, capacious.

CAPITULATE: make a combined force.

CAPOCCHIA: a simpleton.

CAPRICIO: (Italian), caprice.

176

CAPRICIOUS: lascivious.

CAPTIOUS: capacious.

CARACK: a large ship of burden.

CARBONADO: meat scotched for broiling.

CARD: the diagram of points on a mariner's compass.

CAREIRE: the curvetting of a horse.

CARKANET: a necklace.

CARL: a churl, a husbandman.

CARLOT: a churl, a husbandman.

CASTILIAN: a native of Castile; used as a cant term.

CASTILIANO VULGO: a cant term, meaning, apparently, to use discreet language.

CATAIAN: a native of Cathay, Chinese.

CATLING: cat-gut.

CAUTEL: deceit.

CAUTELOUS: insidious.

CAVALERO: a cavalier, gentleman.

CAVIARE: the roe of sturgeon pickled; metaph. a delicacy not appreciated by the vulgar.

CEASE: decease.

CENSURE: judgment. To judge, criticise.

CEREMONY: a ceremonial rite or vestment.

CERTES: certainly.

CESS: rate, reckoning.

CHACE: a term at tennis.

CHAMBER: a species of great gun.

CHAMBERER: an effeminate man.

CHANSON: a song.

CHARACT: affected quality.

CHARACTER: handwriting. Write, engrave.

CHARACTERY: handwriting. That which is written.

CHARE: a turn of work, a chore.

CHARGE-HOUSE: a free-school.

CHARLES' WAIN: the Great Bear, the Plough.

CHARNECO: a species of sweet wine.

CHAUDRON: entrails.

CHEATER: for escheator, an officer who collected the fines to be paid into the Exchequer.

CHECK AT: in falconry, when a falcon foresakes her proper quarry for baser game.

CHEER: fortune, countenance.

CHERRY-PIT: a game played with cherrystones.

CHEVERIL: kid leather.

CHEWIT: a cough, a chatterer.

CHILDING: pregnant.

CH'ILL: vulgar for 'I will'.

CHIRURGEONLY: in a manner becoming a surgeon.

CHOPIN: a high shoe or clog.

CHRISTENDOM: the state of being a Christian.

CHRISTOM: clothed with a chrisom, the white garment put on newly-baptized children.

CHUCK: chicken, a term of endearment.

CHUFF: a coarse blunt clown.

CINQUE PACE: a kind of dance.

CIPHER: to decipher.

CIRCUMSTANCE: an argument.

CITAL: recital.

CITE: to incite.

CITTERN: a guitar.

CLACK-DISH: a beggar's dish.

CLAP I' THE CLOUT: to shoot an arrow into the

bull's eye of the target.

CLAW: to flatter.

CLEPE: to call.

CLIFF: clef, the key in music.

CLING: to starve.

CLINQUANT: glittering.

CLIP: to embrace, enclose.

CLOUT: the mark in the middle of a target.

COAST: to advance, approach.

COBLOAF: a big loaf.

COCK: a cockboat.

COCK: a euphemism for God.

COCKLE: tares or darnel.

COCKNEY: a milksop.

COCK-SHUT-TIME: the twilight, when cocks and hens go to roost.

COG: to cheat, dissemble.

COGNIZANCE: badge, token.

COIGN: projecting corner stone.

COIL: tumult, turmoil.

COISTREL: a cowardly knave.

COLLECTION: drawing a conclusion.

COLLIED: blackened, clouded.

COLOUR: pretence.

COLOURABLE: specious, plausible.

COLT: to defraud, befool.

CO-MART: a joint bargain.

COMBINATE: betrothed.

COMMODITY: interest, profit.

COMMONTY: used ludicrously for comedy.

COMPACT: compacted, composed.

COMPETITOR: an associate, a partner.

179

COMPLEMENT: accomplishment.

COMPLEXION: humour.

COMPOSE: to agree.

COMPOSTION: composition, agreement.

COMPTIBLE: tractable.

CON: to learn by heart. To acknowledge.

CONCEIT: conception, opinion, fancy.

CONCUPY: concubine.

CONDITION: temper, quality.

CONDOLEMENT: grief.

CONFECT: to make up into sweetmeats.

CONFOUND: to consume, destroy.

CONJECT: conjecture.

CONSIGN: to sign a common bond, to confederate.

CONSORT: to accompany.

CONSTANCY: consistency, fidelity.

CONSTANT: settled, determined.

CONSTER: to construe.

CONTEMPTIBLE: contemptuous.

CONTINENT: that which contains.

CONTINUATE: uninterrupted.

CONTRACTION: the marriage contract.

CONTRARY: to oppose.

CONTRIVE: to spend (time).

CONTROL: to confute.

CONVENT: to convene, summon, to be convenient.

CONVERTITE: a convert.

CONVEY: to manage. To filch.

CONVINCE: to conquer, subdue.

CONVIVE: to feast together.

CONY-CATCH: to cheat, to dupe.

COOLING CARD: anything that dashes hopes.

COPATAIN HAT: a high-crowned hat.

COPE: to reward, to give in return.

COPPED: rising to a cop or head.

COPY: theme, example.

CORAGIO: (Italian) courage!

CORAM: an ignorant mistake for Quorum.

CORANTO: lively dance.

CORINTH: a cant term for a brothel.

CORINTHIAN: a wencher.

CORKY: dry like cork, withered.

CORNUTO: (Italian) a cuckold.

COROLLARY: surplus, additional.

CORPORAL: corporeal, bodily.

CORPORAL OF THE FIELD: an aide-de-camp.

CORRIVAL: rival.

COSTARD: the head.

COSTER-MONGER: peddling, mercenary.

COTE: a cottage.

COTE: to come alongside, overtake. To quote.

COT-QUEAN: an effeminate man, molly-coddle.

COUNT CONFECT: an affected nobleman.

COUNTENANCE: pretend; give support to.

COUNTERFEIT: portrait. A piece of base coin.

COUNTERPOINT: a counterpane.

COUNTERVAIL: to counterpoise, outweigh.

COUNTY: count, earl.

COUPLEMENT: union.

COURT HOLY-WATER: flattery.

COVENT: a convent.

COVER: to lay the table for dinner.

COWISH: cowardly.

COWL-STAFF: the staff for carrying a tub.

181

COX MY PASSION: an oath, for 'God's Passion'.
COY: to stroke, fondle. To show disdain.
COZEN: to cheat.
COZIER: a tailor or cobbler.
CRACK: to boast.
CRACK: a loud noise, clap. A forward boy.
CRACK-HEMP: a gallows-bird.
CRANK: a winding passage. To twist and turn.
CRANTS: garlands.
CRARE: a ship of burden.
CRAVEN: a dunghill cock, a coward.
CREATE: formed, compounded.
CREDENT: creditable. Credible. Credulous.
CRESCIVE: increasing.
CRESTLESS: not entitled to bear arms, lowborn.
CRISP: curled, winding.
CROSS: a coin stamped with a cross.
CROW-KEEPER: one who scares crows.
CROWNER: a coroner.
CROWNET: a coronet.
CRY: a pack of hounds or knaves.
CRY AIM: to encourage.
CUE: the last words of an actor's speech, the signal for the next actor to begin.
CUISSES: pieces of armour to cover the thighs.
CULLION: a base fellow.
CUNNING: skill, skilful.
CURB: to bend, truckle.
CURRENTS: occurrences.
CURST: shrewish, sharp tempered.
CURTAIL: a cur.
CURTAL: a docked horse.

182

CURTAL-AXE: a cutlass.

CUSTALORUM: a ludicrous mistake for Custos Rotulorum, a chief justice.

CUSTARD-COFFIN: the crust of a custard-pudding.

CUSTOMER: a common woman.

CUT: a cheat. 'To draw cuts' is to draw lots.

CYPRESS: a kind of crape.

DAFF: to befool. To put off.

DANGER: reach, control, power.

DANSKER: a Dane.

DARRAIGN: to set in array.

DAUB: to disguise.

DAUBERY: imposition, falsehood.

DEARN: hidden, solitary.

DEBOSHED: debauched, drunken.

DECK: to bedew, to adorn.

DECLINE: to enumerate.

DEEM: doom, judgment.

DEFEAT: to undo, destroy. Destruction.

DEFEATURE: disfigurement.

DEFENCE: art of fencing.

DEFEND: to forbid.

DEFY: renounce.

DEGREE: relative position or rank.

DEMERIT: merit, desert.

DENAY: denial.

DENIER: the 12th part of a French sou coin.

DENY: to refuse.

DEPEND: to be in service.

DEROGATE: degraded, debased.

DESCANT: comment on a given theme.

DETECT: to charge, blame.

DETERMINE: to conclude.

DICH: may it do.

DIFFUSED: confused.

DIGRESSION: transgression.

DIG-YOU-GOOD-DEN: give you good evening.

DILDO: the chorus or burden of a song.

DINT: stroke, impression.

DIRECTION: judgment, skill.

DISABLE: to disparage.

DISAPPOINTED: unprepared.

DISCASE: to undress.

DISCONTENT: a malcontent.

DISCOURSE: power of reasoning.

DISLIMN: to disfigure, transform, efface.

DISME: a tenth or tithe.

DISPARK: to destroy a park.

DISPONGE: to squeeze out as from a sponge.

DISPOSE: disposal, disposition. To arrange.

DISPOSITION: arrangement; behaviour.

DISPUTABLE: disputatious.

DISSEMBLY: used ridiculously for assembly.

DISTASTE: to offend the taste, disgust.

DISTEMPERED: discontented, disturbed.

DISTRACTION: a detached troop or company of soldiers.

DIVISION: a phrase or passage in a melody.

DOFF: to take off, remove. To put off with an excuse.

DOIT: a small Dutch coin, a trifle.

184

DOLE: portion dealt. Grief, lamentation.

DOTANT: one who dotes, a dotard.

DOUT: to quench.

DOWLAS: a kind of coarse sacking.

DOWLE: feather.

DOWN-GYVED: hanging down like gyves or fetters.

DRAB: a harlot.

DRAUGHT: a privy.

DRAWN: having his sword drawn.

DRIBBLING: falling wide of the mark.

DROLLERY: a puppet-show.

DRUMBLE: to dawdle.

DUC-DAME: duc-ad-me, bring him to me.

DUDGEON: hilt of a dagger.

DULL: soothing.

DUMP: sad tune.

DUP: lift up, undo.

EAGER: harsh, cutting, sour.

EANLING: a yeanling, a lamb.

EAR: to plough.

ECHE: to eke out.

ECSTACY: madness.

EFT: ready, convenient.

EISEL: vinegar.

ELD: old age.

EMBOSSED: swollen; foaming from exertion (of a hound).

EMBOWELLED: disembowelled.

EMBRASURE: embrace.

EMPERY: empire.

EMULATION: jealousy.

EMULOUS: jealous, ambitious.

ENCAVE: to place in a cave, to hide.

ENFEOFF: to hand over, surrender.

ENGINE: a machine of war.

ENGLUT: to swallow speedily.

ENGROSS: to make gross or fat.

ENGROSSMENT: immoderate acquisition.

ENKINDLE: to make keen.

ENMEW: to shut up, coop up.

ENSCONCE: to cover as with a fort; to take shelter.

ENSEAMED: fat, greasy.

ENSHIELD: guard, protect.

ENTERTAIN: take into service.

ENTERTAINMENT: treatment; reception.

ENTREATMENT: entreating.

EPHESIAN: a toper, a cant term.

EQUIPAGE: attendance, retinue.

EREWHILE: a short time since.

ESCOT: to pay a man's reckoning, to maintain.

ESPERANCE: hope, used as a war-cry.

ESPIAL: a scout or spy.

ESTIMATION: conjecture.

ESTRIDGE: ostrich.

EXCREMENT: outgrowths from the body like hair or nails.

EXECUTOR: an executioner.

EXEMPT: excluded, separated.

EXERCISE: a religious service.

EXHALE: to draw the sword.

EXHIBITION: allowance, pension.

EXIGENT: death, ending; emergency.
EXION: ridiculously used for 'action'.
EXPEDIENCE: purpose requiring haste.
EXPEDIENT: expeditious, swift.
EXPIATE: completed, fully arrived.
EXPOSTULATE: to expound, discuss.
EXPOSTURE: exposure.
EXPRESS: well made.
EXPULSE: to expel.
EXSUFFLICATE: contemptible, puffed out.
EXTEND: to seize, to magnify.
EXTERN: outward.
EXTIRP: to extirpate.
EXTRAUGHT: extracted, descended.
EXTRAVAGANT: foreign, wandering.
EYAS: a nestling hawk.
EYAS-MUSKET: a young sparrow-hawk, a sprightly boy.
EYE: a shade of colour, as in shot silk.
EYNE: eyes.

FACINOROUS: wicked.
FACT: guilt, crime.
FACTIOUS: instant, importunate.
FACULTY: essential virtue or power.
FADGE: to suit, turn out.
FADING: a kind of ending to a song.
FAIN: glad, gladly.
FAIR: beauty.
FAITOR: imposter, cheat.
FALLOW: fawn-coloured.
FALSING: deceptive.

FAMILIAR: a familiar spirit.

FANCY-FREE: untouched by love.

FANG: to seize.

FANTASTIC: a fantastical person.

FAP: drunk.

FARCED: stuffed out.

FARDEL: a burden.

FARTUOUS: used ridiculously for 'virtuous'.

FAT: hot; vat.

FAVOUR: countenance. Complexion. Quality.

FEAR: to frighten.

FEAT: dexterous, neat, becoming.

FEAT: to mirror, reflect.

FEATLY: nimbly, daintily.

FEATURE: beauty.

FEDERARY: confederate, accomplice.

FEEDER: agent, servant.

FEE-GRIEF: a private grief.

FEERE: a companion, spouse.

FEHEMENTLY: used ridiculously for 'vehemently'.

FELL: the hide.

FENCE: art or skill in defence.

FEODARY: one who holds an estate by suit or service to a superior lord; a dependant.

FESTINATELY: quickly.

FET: fetched.

FICO: a fig.

FIG: to insult.

FIGHTS: screens round a ship to conceal the men from the enemy.

FILE: to defile, pollute.

FILL-HORSE: shaft-horse.

FILLS: the shafts.

FINE: end.

FINELESS: endless.

FIRAGO: ridiculously used for 'Virago'.

FIRE-DRAKE: meteor;(slang) man with red nose.

FIRE-NEW: brand-new.

FIRK: to chastise.

FIT: a canto or division of a song. A trick or habit. A spasm.

FITCHEW: a polecat.

FIVES: a disease incident to horses.

FLAP-DRAGON: raisins in burning brandy.

FLAP-JACK: a pan-cake.

FLATNESS: depth.

FLAW: a gust of wind, or sudden emotion, fragment.

FLAW: to make a flaw in, to break.

FLECKED: spotted, streaked.

FLEET: to float. To pass away, to pass the time.

FLEETING: inconstant.

FLESHMENT: excitement arising from success.

FLEWED: with hanging chops, like hounds.

FLIGHT: archery contest.

FLIRT-GILL: a light woman.

FLOTE: wave, sea.

FLOURISH: ornament.

FLUSH: fresh, full of vigour, in full bloom.

FOIL: defeat, disadvantage.

FOIN: to fence, fight.

FOISON: plenty, abundance.

FOND: foolish, foolishly affectionate.

FOOT-CLOTH: a saddle-cloth hanging down to the ground.

FORBID: accursed, outlawed.

FORBODE: forbidden.

FORCE: to stuff, to cram.

FORDO: to kill, destroy. To weary.

FOREIGN: obliged to live abroad.

FOREPAST: former.

FORESLOW: to delay.

FORFEND: to forbid.

FORGETIVE: inventive.

FORKED: horned. Two-legged.

FORMAL: regular, normal.

FORSPEAK: to speak against.

FORSPENT: exhausted, weary.

FORTHRIGHT: a straight path.

FORWEARY: to weary, exhaust.

FOSSET-SELLER: seller of taps (faucets) for barrels.

FOX: a sword; a cant word.

FOX-SHIP: the cunning of the fox.

FRAMPOLD: peevish, disagreeable.

FRANK: the feeding place of swine, sty.

FRANKED: confined.

FRANKLIN: a freeholder, a small squire.

FRAUGHT: freight, the cargo of a ship.

FRAUGHTING: freight, the cargo of a ship.

FRESH: a spring of fresh water.

FRET: the stop of a musical instrument.

FRET: to wear away. To variegate, adorn.

FRIEND: to befriend.

FRIPPERY: an old-clothes shop.

FRONT: to affront, oppose.

FRONTIER: fortress.

FRONTLET: that which is worn on the forehead.

FRUSH: to break or bruise.

FRUSTRATE: frustrated.

FUB OFF: to put off.

FULFIL: to fill full.

FULLAM: a loaded die.

FULSOME: lustful, offensive.

GABERDINE: a loose outer coat, or smock frock.

GAD: a pointed instrument. Upon the gad, with impetuous haste, on the spur of the moment.

GAIN-GIVING: misgiving.

GALLIARD: a kind of dance.

GALLIASSE: a kind of ship.

GALLIMAUFRY: a ridiculous medley.

GALLOW: to scare.

GALLOWGLASS: the irregular infantry of Ireland, and the Highlands of Scotland.

GAMESTER: a frolicsome person. A loose woman.

GARBOIL: disorder, uproar.

GARNER: to lay by, as corn in a barn.

GAST: frightened.

GAUDY: festive.

GAZE: an object of wonder.

GEAR: matter of business of any kind.

GECK: a fool, butt.

GENERAL: the generality, the people.

GENEROSITY: noble birth.

GENEROUS: noble.

GENTILITY: good manners.

GENTLE: noble, well-born. To ennoble.

GENTRY: gentlemanly behaviour.

GERMAN: akin. Appropriate.

GERMEN: seed, embryo.

GEST: period; deed.

GIB: a he-cat.

GIFTS: talents, endowment.

GIGLOT: a wanton girl.

GILDER: a coin of the value of 1s. 6d. or 2s.

GIMMAL: double, jointed.

GIMMOR: contrivance.

GING: gang.

GLEEK: to scoff.

GLOSE: to comment; to intercept.

GLUT: to swallow.

GNARL: to snarl.

GOOD-DEED: indeed.

GOOD-DEN: good-evening.

GOOD-YEAR!: an oath (What the good year!)

GORBELLIED: corpulent.

GOURD: false dice.

GOUT: a drop.

GOVERNMENT: discretion, control.

GRACIOUS: abounding in grace.

GRAINED: engrained, dyed.

GRAMERCY: much thanks.

GRANGE: the farmstead attached to a monastery, a solitary farm-house.

GRATILLITY: a nonce-word: 'gratuity'.

GRATULATE: to congratulate.

GRAVE: to bury.

GREASILY: grossly.
GREEK: a bawd, buffoon.
GREENLY: foolishly.
GREET: to weep.
GRIZE: a step.
GROUNDLING: one who frequents the pit of a theatre.
GUARD: decoration, ornament.
GUARDAGE: guardianship.
GUINEA-HEN: a courtesan.
GULES: red, a term in heraldry.
GUN-STONE: a cannon ball.
GUST: taste, relish.
GYVE: to fetter.

HACK: to become common.
HAGGARD: a wild or unreclaimed hawk.
HAG-SEED: seed or offspring of a hag.
HAIR: grain, nature.
HALIDOM: holiness, used as an oath.
HALLOWMAS: All Hallows' Day.
HAP: chance, fortune.
HAPPILY: accidentally.
HANDSAW: perhaps a corruption of heronshaw; a heron.
HARDIMENT: defiance, brave deeds.
HARRY: to annoy, harass.
HAUGHT: haughty.
HAUNT: company.
HAVING: property, fortune.
HAVIOUR: behavior.
HAY: a term in fencing; a dance.

HEADY: violent, headlong.

HEBENON: henbane.

HEFT: a heaving.

HELM: to steer, manage.

HENCE: henceforward.

HENCHMAN: a page or attendant.

HENT: grasp, occasion for seizing.

HERMIT: a beadsman.

HEST: command, behest.

HIGHT: called.

HILD: pp. held.

HILDING: a paltry fellow.

HIREN: a prostitute, with a pun on the word 'iron'.

HOISE: to hoist, heave up on high.

HOIST: hoisted.

HOLP: helped.

HOME: to the utmost, fully.

HONEST: chaste, modest.

HONESTY: chastity.

HONEY-STALKS: red clover.

HOODMAN-BLIND: blindman's-buff.

HORN-MAD: furious, enraged.

HOROLOGE: a clock.

HOT-HOUSE: a brothel.

HOX: to hamstring.

HUGGER-MUGGER: secrecy.

HULL: to drift on the sea like a wrecked ship.

HUMOROUS: humid; full of humours.

HUNT-COUNTER: to follow the scent the wrong way.

HUNTS-UP: a hunting cry for daybreak.

HURLY: noise, confusion.

HURTLE: to clash noisily.

HUSBANDRY: frugality. Management.

HUSWIFE: a jilt.

ICE-BROOK: an icy-cold brook to temper steel.

I'FECKS: in faith, a euphemism.

IGNOMY: ignominy.

IMAGE: representation.

IMBARE: to bare, lay open.

IMMEDIACY: close connexion.

IMMOMENT: unimportant.

IMP: to graft, to splice a falcon's broken feathers.

IMP: a scion, a child.

IMPAWN: to stake, to risk.

IMPEACH: to bring into question. Impeachment.

IMPEACHMENT: cause of censure, hindrance.

IMPERCEIVERANT: undiscerning.

IMPETICOS: to pocket.

IMPORTANCE: importunity.

IMPORTANT: importunate.

IMPOSITION: command.

IMPRESE: a device with a motto.

IMPRESS: to compel to serve.

INCAPABLE: unconscious, unaware.

INCARNARDINE: to dye red.

INCENSED: incited, enraged.

INCH-MEAL: inch by inch.

INCLINING: inclination; compliant.

INCLIP: to embrace.

INCLUDE: conclude.

INCONY: fine, delicate.

INCORRECT: ill-regulated.

IND: India.

INDENT: to compound or bargain.

INDEX: a preface, contents.

INDIFFERENT: ordinary.

INDIGEST: shapeless mass.

INDITE: to invite. To convict.

INDUCTION: introduction, beginning.

INHABITABLE: uninhabitable.

INHERIT: to possess.

INHOOPED: penned up in hoops.

INKHORN-MATE: a contemptuous term for an ecclesiastic, or man of learning.

INKLE: a narrow fillet or tape.

INLAND: civilized, well-educated.

INLY: inwardly.

INSANE: that which causes insanity.

INSTANCE: example. Information. Reason, proof.

INTEND: to pretend.

INTENDMENT: intention.

INTENTIVELY: attentively.

INTERESSED: allied, interested.

INTRINSE: intricate.

INTRINSICATE: intricate.

INVENTION: imagination.

INWARD: an intimate friend; intimate.

INWARDNESS: intimacy.

IRREGULOUS: lawless, licentious.

JACK: a mean fellow.

JACK-A-LENT: a puppet thrown at in Lent.

JACK GUARDANT: a jack in office.

JADE: to whip, to treat with contempt.

JAR: the ticking of a clock.

JAUNCE: to cause a horse to prance; to trudge about.

JESS: a strap attached to the talons of a hawk.

JEST: to tilt in a tournament, to joust.

JET: to strut.

JOURNAL: daily.

JOVIAL: appertaining to Jove.

JUDICIOUS: critical.

JUMP: hazard.

JUMP: exactly, nicely.

JUT: to encroach.

JUTTY: jut out beyond; projection.

JUVENAL: youth, young man.

KAM: crooked, twisted.

KECKSY: hemlock-like weed.

KEECH: a lump of tallow.

KEEL: to skim, to cool.

KERN: the rude foot soldiers of the Irish.

KIBE: a chilblain.

KICKSHAWS: fancy trifles of food; frivolities.

KICKSY WICKSY: a wife, used in disdain.

KILN-HOLE: oven.

KINDLE: to bring forth young; used only of beasts.

KINDLESS: unnatural.

KINDLY: natural, generous.

KIRTLE: a gown.

KNAP: to snap, knock.

KNAVE: a boy. A serving-man.

KNOT: flower bed.

LABRAS: lips.
LACED-MUTTON: a courtezan.
LAG: the lowest of the people.
LAG: late, behindhand.
LAKIN: ladykin, little lady, 'By'r lakin': an oath.
LAND-DAMN: a term of abuse.
LAPSED: taken, apprehended.
LARGE: licentious, free.
LARGESS: a present.
LASS-LORN: deserted by a mistress.
LATCH: to smear. To catch.
LATED: belated.
LATTEN: made of brass.
LAUND: lawn, clearing in a forest.
LAVOLTA: a dance.
LAY: wager.
LEAGUE: besieging army.
LEASING: lying.
LEATHER-COATS: russet apples.
LEECH: a physician.
LEER: countenance, complexion.
LEET: a manor court.
LEGE: to allege.
LEGERITY: lightness.
LEIGER: an ambassador resident abroad.
LEMAN: a lover or mistress.
LENTEN: meagre; appropriate to Lent.
L'ENVOY: the final stanza of a poem.
LET: hindrance; to hinder.

LETHE: death. A river in Hades.

LEVEL: to aim.

LEWD: ignorant, base.

LEWDSTER: a lewd person.

LIBBARD: a leopard.

LIBERAL: licentious.

LIBERTY: libertinism.

LIEF: dear. Willingly.

LIFTER: a thief.

LIGHT O' LOVE: a tune so called.

LIGHTLY: easily, generally.

LIKE: to liken, compare.

LIKE: likely.

LIKING: condition.

LIMBECK: an alembick, a still.

LIMBO: the abode of the just who died before Christ's coming; slang for prison.

LIME: to entangle as with bird-lime. To mix lime with beer or other liquor.

LIMN: to draw or paint.

LINE: support.

LINSTOCK: a staff with a match at the end used by gunners in firing cannon.

LIST: a strip of cloth: an enclosure for tilting.

LITHER: lazy.

LITTLE: miniature.

LIVELIHOOD: appearance of life.

LIVERY: legal proceedings to recover an inheritance.

LOB: a lout.

LOCKRAM: a sort of coarse linen.

LODE-STAR: the leading-star, pole-star.

LOGGATS: the game called nine-pins.

LOOF: to luff, bring a vessel up to the wind.

LOON: a low contemptible fellow.

LOTTERY: a prize.

LOUT: to treat one as a lout, with contempt.

LOZEL: a rascal.

LUBBER: a lout, a clumsy fellow.

LUCE: the pike or jack, a fresh-water fish.

LUNES: fits of lunacy.

LURCH: to outdo, to deprive of all chance.

LURE: a dummy bird to attract a hawk.

LUXURIOUS: lascivious.

LUXURY: lust.

LYM: a bloodhound.

MAGNIFICO: a Venetian nobleman.

MAGGOT-PIE: a magpie.

MAIL: cover as with a coat of mail.

MAIN-COURSE: the mainsail.

MAKE: to do up, bar.

MALKIN: a servant wench.

MALLECHO: mischief.

MAMMERING: hesitating.

MAMMET: a doll, a puppet.

MAMMOCK: tear to pieces.

MAN: to tame a hawk.

MANAGE: management, control of a horse.

MANDRAGORA or MANDRAKE: a plant of soporiferous quality, supposed to resemble a man.

MANKIND: having a masculine nature.

MARCHES: frontiers, borders.

MARCHPANE: a sweetmeat like marzipan.

200

MARGENT: margin.

MARRY: an exclamation of surprise, indignation, etc.

MARTLEMAS: Martinmas, 11th November, a word applied derisively to an old man.

MATCH: a compact, agreement.

MATE: to confound, dismay.

MEACOCK: tame, cowardly.

MEALED: mingled, stained.

MEAN: instrument used to promote an end; opportunity.

MEAN: the tenor part in a harmony.

MEASURE: traverse. A stately dance.

MEAZEL: a leper.

MEDAL: a portrait in a locket.

MEDICINE: a physician.

MEED: reward, hire. Merit.

MEINY: retinue.

MELL: to mix, to meddle.

MEMORISE: to cause to be remembered.

MEPHISTOPHILUS: the name of a familiar spirit.

MERCATANTE: (Italian), a foreign trader.

MESS: a company of four.

METAPHYSICAL: supernatural.

METE-YARD: measuring-wand.

MEW UP: to confine.

MICHER: a truant.

MILL-SIXPENCE: a milled sixpence.

MINCING: affected.

MISCREATE: illegitimate, deformed.

MISERY: avarice.

MISPRISE: to despise. To mistake.

MISPRISION: mistaking, scorning.

MISSIVE: messenger.

MISTEMPERED: tempered for an evil purpose.

MISTHINK: to think ill of.

MISTRESS: the jack in bowling.

MOBLED: muffled, veiled.

MODERN: commonplace.

MODULE: a model, image.

MOIETY: a portion.

MOME: a stupid person.

MONTHS-MIND: a monthly commemoration of the dead, a strong desire.

MOON-CALF: a nick-name applied to Caliban.

MOONISH: inconstant.

MOP: grimace.

MORISCO: a morris-dancer.

MORRIS-PIKE: Moorish-pike.

MORT: death, applied to animals of the chase.

MORTIFIED: ascetic.

MOSE: applied to disease in a horse.

MOTION: a puppet-show.

MOTLEY: the many-coloured coat of a fool; one who plays the fool.

MOTLEY-MINDED: foolish.

MOUSE-HUNT: a weasel. A woman chaser.

MOW: to make grimaces.

MOY: the French 'Moi', misinterpreted by Pistol as a coin.

MUCH: significant of contempt.

MUCH: used ironically.

MURE: a wall.

MUSS: a scramble, a children's game.

MUTINE: to mutiny; a mutineer.

NAPKIN: a handkerchief.
NAYWARD: towards denial, or unbelief.
NAYWORD: a catch-word, by-word.
NEB: beak, mouth.
NEELD: a needle.
NEIF: hand.
NEPHEW: a grandson, kinsman.
NETHER-STOCKS: stockings, the stocks.
NICK: score or reckoning.
NICK: to brand with folly.
NIGHTED: black as night.
NIGHT-RULE: nightly revel.
NINE MEN'S MORRIS: a game in which each side has nine pieces, 'men'; the area in which it is played.
NINNY: a fool, a simpleton.
NOBLE: a coin, worth 6s. 8d.
NODDY: a dolt, simpleton.
NONCE: for the nonce, for the occasion.
NOOK-SHOTTEN: indented with bays and creeks.
NOURISH: nurse.
NOVUM: a game at dice.
NUTHOOK: a hook for pulling down nuts, a beadle.

O: a circle, the globe.
OAR: to row as with oars.
OBSEQUIOUS: a dutiful observance of funeral.
OBSTACLE: obstinate.
OCCUPATION: working men.

OCCURENT: an incident.

OD'S: interj. euphemism for God's.

OD'S BODY: God's body.

OD'S PITTIKINS: God's pity.

OEILLIAD: an amorous glance.

O'ERPARTED: having too important a part to act.

OFFICE: function, service, office-holder.

OLD: slang; great, fine.

ONEYER: a banker. A doubtful word.

OPEN: to give tongue as a hound.

OPERANT: active.

OPPOSITE: adversary.

OPPOSITION: combat.

OR: before.

ORDINANCE: rank, order. That which is ordained.

ORGULOUS: proud.

ORT: leaving, refuse, fragment.

OSTENT: show, appearance.

OSTENTATION: show, appearance.

OUNCE: a beast of prey, a lynx.

OUPHE: a fairy, elf.

OUSEL-COCK: the blackbird.

OUT: in error, at variance.

OUT-LOOK: to face down, to outstare.

OUTWARD: outside, external appearance.

OWE: to own.

PACK: to plot, be in league.

PADDOCK: a toad.

PALABRAS: words, a cant term, from the Spanish.

PALE: an inclosure; to enclose.

PALL: to wrap as with a pall. To fail, be ruined.

PALMER: one who bears a palm-branch, in token of having made a pilgrimage to the Holy Land.

PALMY: flourishing.

PARCELLED: belonging to individuals.

PARD: the leopard.

PARITOR: an apparitor, summoner to a bishop's court.

PARLE: talk, parley.

PARLOUS: perilous. keen, shrewd.

PARTED: endowed, gifted.

PARTISAN: a pike.

PASH: the head.

PASH: to strike violently, to bruise, crush.

PASSANT: (of heraldic figures), walking.

PASSING: surpassingly, exceedingly.

PASSION: pain, compassion, grief.

PASSY-MEASURE: a stately dance, a pavane.

PASTRY: the room where pastry was made.

PATCH: a mean fellow, a clown.

PATCHERY: trickery.

PATH: to walk.

PATIENT: to make patient, to compose.

PATINE: the metal dish on which the bread is placed in the administration of the Eucharist.

PAUCA VERBA: few words.

PAUCAS: few, a cant word.

PAVIN: a dance, a pavane.

PAX: a small image of Christ.

205

PEAT: a term of endearment for a child.

PEDASCULE: a pedant, schoolmaster.

PEIZE: to balance, weigh down.

PELTING: paltry.

PERDU: lost. A sentry in a perilous post.

PERDURABLE: everlasting.

PERDY: a euphemism for Par Dieu.

PERFECT: certain, fully prepared.

PERIAPTS: charms worn round the neck.

PERJURE: a perjured person.

PERSPECTIVE: a telescope, or some sort of optical device.

PEW-FELLOW: a comrade.

PHEEZE: beat, chastise, settle.

PIA-MATER: the brain.

PICK: to pitch, throw.

PICKERS: (and stealers), the fingers, hands.

PICKT-HATCH: a place noted for brothels.

PIELED: shaven.

PILCHER: a scabbard. A pilchard.

PILL: to pillage.

PIN: a malady of the eye. The centre of a target.

PINFOLD: a pound, a place to confine lost cattle.

PIONED: meaning doubtful; perhaps trenched.

PLACKET: a petticoat-front. A woman.

PLAIN SONG: a simple air, the simple truth.

PLANCHED: made of boards.

PLANTATION: colonizing, planting a colony.

PLAUSIVE: plausible, acceptable.

PLEACHED: interwoven, folded.

POINT: a lace to hold up breeches.
POINT-DEVICE: derived from the French, faultless.
POISE: balance, weight, importance.
POLLED: shorn.
POMANDER: a perfumed ball.
POMEWATER: a kind of apple.
POOR-JOHN: salted fish.
POPINJAY: a parrot, a fop.
PORT: pomp, state, bearing. A gate.
PORTABLE: bearable.
PORTANCE: conduct, behavior.
POSSESS: to inform.
POTCH: to push violently, stab.
POTENT: a potentate.
POUNCET-BOX: a box for holding perfumes.
PRACTISE: wicked stratagem.
PRACTISANT: a confederate, conspirator.
PRANK: to dress up.
PRECEPT: a justice's summons, a warrant.
PREGNANT: fertile of invention. Ready. Obvious.
PRENOMINATE: to name beforehand, to prophesy.
PRE-ORDINANCE: old-established law.
PRESENCE: the presence-chamber. High bearing.
PREST: ready.
PRETENCE: design, plan.
PRETEND: to portend. To intend.
PREVENT: to anticipate.
PRICK: the mark denoting the hour on a dial.
PRICK: to incite. To mark off on a list.
PRICK-SONG: music sung in parts by note.
PRICKET: a stag of two years.
PRIG: thief.

PRIME: rank, lecherous.

PRIMERO: a game at cards.

PRINCIPALITY: one of the orders of angels.

PRINCOX: a coxcomb, forward fellow.

PRIZER: a prize-fighter.

PROCURE: to bring.

PROFACE: interj. may it do you good.

PROGRESS: a royal ceremonial journey.

PROJECT: to shape or contrive.

PROMPTURE: suggestion.

PRONE: ready, willing.

PROOF: strength of manhood.

PROPAGATE: to advance, to forward.

PROPAGATION: augmentation.

PROPER-FALSE: handsome deceiver.

PROPERTIED: endowed with the properties of. Treated as a property.

PROPOSE: To converse. To purpose.

PROROGUE: to defer.

PROVAND: provender.

PUCELLE: a virgin, the maid Joan of Arc.

PUDENCY: modesty.

PUGGING: thieving.

PUN: to pound.

PURCHASE: acquire, gain.

PUTTER-ON: an instigator.

PUTTER-OUT: one who lends money at interest.

PUTTOCK: a kite.

QUAIL: be afraid: to cause to quail. A loose woman.

QUAINT: curiously beautiful. Clever.

QUALIFY: to moderate.
QUALITY: Rank or condition. Natural gifts, skill.
QUARRY: game, a heap of game.
QUARTER: area assigned to a body of troops. Watch, guard.
QUAT: a pimple; used in contempt of a person.
QUEASY: squeamish, unsettled, ticklish.
QUELL: murder, slaughter.
QUENCH: to grow cool.
QUERN: a hand-mill.
QUEST: search, inquest, jury.
QUESTRIST: one who goes in search of another.
QUICK: living, pregnant, enlivening.
QUICKEN: to come to life.
QUIDDITY: subtlety, argument.
QUILLET: legal quibble.
QUINTAIN: a post for tilting at.
QUIP: sharp jest, a taunt.
QUIT: to requite, release, remit, pay back.
QUITTANCE: requital.
QUIVER: active, nimble.
QUOTE: to note, set down.

RABATO: a ruff, a collar.
RABBIT-SUCKER: a weasel, a baby rabbit.
RACE: breed; inherited nature, origin.
RACK: wreck, stretch, cause pain, misrepresent.
RACK: drifting cloud.
RAPTURE: a fit. Seizure, force of movement.
RASCAL: a lean deer.
RASH: quick, violent. To thrust in.

RATE: opinion, judgment, estimation.

RATE: to assign, to value. To scold.

RATOLORUM: corruption of Custos Rotulorum (Keeper of the Rolls).

RAUGHT: past tense of to reach.

RAVIN: ravenous. Devour.

RAWNESS: unprovided state, unprotected.

RAYED: arrayed, served, dirtied.

RAZED: slashed, cut ornamentally.

REBATE: to deprive of keenness.

REBECK: a three-stringed fiddle.

RECHEAT: to call back the hounds.

RECORD: to sing.

RECORDER: a flute.

RECURE: to cure, recover.

RED-LATTICE: suitable to an ale-house.

REDUCE: to bring back.

REECHY: smoky, dirty.

REFELL: to refute.

REFER: hand over, transfer.

REGIMENT: government.

REGREET: to salute, greet.

REGUERDON: requital, reward.

REMEMBER: to remind.

REMORSE: pity.

REMORSEFUL: full of pity, compassionate.

REMOTION: removal, remoteness.

REMOVED: remote, secluded.

RENDER: account, admission. To declare.

RENEGE: to renounce, to deny.

REPAIR: comfort. Resort, return.

REPEAL: to reverse the sentence of exile.

REPROOF: confutation.
REPUGN: to resist.
REQUIEM: mass for the dead.
RESOLVE: to satisfy. To dissolve.
RESPECT: consideration, comparison, esteem.
RESPECTIVE: respectful, thoughtful.
RETIRE: retreat, withdraw.
REVERB: to echo, reverberate.
REVOLT: a rebel.
RIB: to enclose as within ribs.
RIGGISH: wanton.
RIGOL: a circle.
RIPE: ready, mature.
RIVAGE: the shore.
RIVAL: a partner.
RIVALITY: equal rank.
RIVE: to fire, to split.
ROAD: a prostitute.
ROISTING: roistering, rousing.
ROMAGE: unusual stir, turmoil.
RONYON: a term of contempt used to a woman.
ROOD: the crucifix.
ROOK: a cheat.
ROPERY: roguery.
ROPE-TRICKS: trickery, roguery.
ROUND: to be with child.
ROUND: unceremonious.
ROUNDEL: a dance or song.
ROUNDURE: an enclosure; roundness.
ROUSE: carousal.
ROYNISH: mangy, scurvy.
RUBIOUS: ruddy, ruby-red.

RUDDOCK: the redbreast.
RUSH: a ring made of rushes.

SACRING-BELL: the little bell rung at mass to give notice that the elements are consecrated.
SAD: serious.
SAFE: sane, sound, secure.
SALT: lascivious, biting, tearful.
SANDED: sand coloured.
SANS: without.
SAUCY: lascivious.
SAW: a moral saying, a proverb.
SAY: assay, taste. Silken.
SCAFFOLDAGE: the gallery of a theatre.
SCALD: scurvy, scabby.
SCALE: to weigh in scales.
SCALL: a scab, a word of reproach.
SCAMBLE: to scramble.
SCAMEL: possibly sea-mel, or sea-mew.
SCAN: to examine carefully.
SCANT: to cut short, to spare; scanty.
SCANTLING: a small portion, sample.
SCAPE: to escape.
SCATHE: injury, injure.
SCATHFUL: destructive, harmful.
SCONCE: the head, protection, a fort.
SCOTCH: to bruise or cut slightly.
SCRIMER: a fencer.
SCROYLE: a scabby fellow, scoundrel.
SCULL: a shoal of fish.
SEAL: set one's seal to a deed; confirm. A token.

SEAM: fat.

SEAMY: showing the seam, the worst side.

SEAR: scorched, withered. To dry up.

SEARCH: to probe (a wound).

SECT: a cutting or scion. A political party.

SEEL: to sew up the eyes, to blind.

SEEMING: outward manner and appearance.

SEEN: versed, instructed.

SELD: seldom.

SELF-BOUNTY: native goodness.

SEMBLABLY: alike.

SENIORY: seniority.

SENNET: a flourish of trumpets.

SEPULCHRE: to bury.

SEQUESTRATION: separation.

SERE: dry, withered.

SERJEANT: a bailiff.

SERPICO: a skin disease.

SERVICEABLE: diligent in service.

SETEBOS: a fiend feared by Caliban.

SETTER: a spy for thieves.

SEVERAL: privately owned land; enclosed pasture.

SHARDS: shreds, broken fragments of pottery.

SHARDS: the wing cases of beetles.

SHARKED: snatched up, collected hastily.

SHEER: pure. Unmixed.

SHENT: rebuked, blamed. Hurt.

SHERIFF'S-POST: a post at the door of a sheriff, to which royal proclamations were fixed.

SHIVE: slice.

SHOT: the reckoning at an ale-house.

SHOUGHS: shaggy dogs.

213

SHOVEL-BOARD: game played by sliding metal pieces along a board at a mark.

SHREWD: mischievous, shrewish.

SHRIFT: confession. Absolution.

SHRIVE: to hear or make confession.

SHROUD: protect, cover, hide.

SIEGE: seat. Stool. Rank.

SIGHT: an aperture in a helmet. A visor.

SIGHTLESS: invisible. Unsightly.

SILLY: simple, rustic.

SIMULAR: counterfeit, feigned. A simulator.

SINGLE: feeble.

SIR: a title often applied to a bachelor of arts and priests as well as to knights.

SITH: since.

SITHENCE: since.

SIZES: allowances.

SKAINS-MATES: scapegraces.

SKILL: to be of importance, to matter.

SKIMBLE-SKAMBLE: rambling, disjointed.

SKINKER: a drawer of liquor.

SKIRR: to scour.

SLAVE: to enslave.

SLEAVE: skein of silk.

SLEDDED: sledged.

SLEIDED: untwisted, raw, applied to silk.

SLIP: a counterfeit coin.

SLIPPER: slippery.

SLIVER: split, tear off. A branch.

SLOPS: loose breeches.

SLUBBER: to perform hurriedly. To smear.

SMOOTH: to flatter.

214

SNEAP: rebuke, snub, pinch.

SNECK-UP: go hang!

SNUFF: anger. 'Take in snuff', take offence.

SOFTLY: gently.

SOIL: spot, tarnish.

SOLICIT: solicitation.

SOLIDARE: a small coin.

SOMETIMES: formerly, former.

SOOTH: truth. Conciliation.

SOREL: a buck of the third year.

SORRY: sorrowful, dismal.

SORT: a company. Rank, condition. Lot. 'In a sort', in a manner.

SORT: to choose. to suit. To consort. To ordain.

SOT: fool, drunkard.

SOUL-FEARING: terrifying.

SOWL: to lug, drag.

SOWTER: name of a dog.

SPED: settled, done for.

SPEED: fortune.

SPERR: to bolt, fasten.

SPIAL: spy.

SPILL: to destroy.

SPILTH: spilling.

SPLEEN: violent feeling; anger, irritability, laughter.

SPRAG: quick.

SPRINGHALT: stringhalt, a disease of horses.

SPRITED: haunted.

SPURS: roots of trees.

SQUARE: to quarrel, measure.

SQUARE: the front part of a woman's dress.

SQUARE: fair, straightforward.

SQUARER: quarreller, swaggerer.

SQUASH: an unripe peascod.

SQUIER: a square or rule.

SQUINY: to squint.

STAGGERS: a disease in horses, attended with giddiness.

STAIN: to disfigure, tarnish.

STALE: a decoy. A gull. A prostitute.

STALE: urine.

STANIEL: an inferior kind of hawk.

STATE: a canopied chair.

STATION: attitude, stance.

STATIST: a statesman.

STATUTE-CAPS: woollen caps worn by citizens.

STEAD: to help, to act instead.

STEELED: set or fixed, delineated.

STERNAGE: steerage, course.

STICKLER: an arbitrator in combats.

STIGMATIC: branded by deformity.

STILL: constant.

STILLY: softly, silently.

STINT: to stop, to check.

STITHY: a smith's forge. To forge.

STOCCADO: a stoccata, or thrust in fencing.

STOCK: thrust.

STOMACH: courage. Appetite, inclination.

STONE-BOW: a cross-bow for throwing stones.

STOUP: a cup, flagon.

STOVER: fodder.

STRAIGHT: immediately.

STRAIN: lineage. Disposition. To embrace.

STRANGE: foreign. Coy, reserved. Marvellous.
STRANGENESS: coyness, reserve.
STRANGER: foreigner.
STRAPPADO: a kind of punishment.
STRICTURE: strictness.
STROSSERS: trousers.
STUCK: a sword-thrust (from stoccata).
STY: to lodge as in a sty.
SUBSCRIBE: to yield, succumb, write down.
SUCCESS: issue, consequence. Succession.
SUDDEN: hasty, rash.
SUFFERANCE: suffering, forbearance.
SUGGEST: to tempt, entice, persuade.
SUGGESTION: temptation, incitement.
SUITED: dressed.
SULLEN: doleful, melancholy.
SUMPTER: a pack-horse, drudge.
SUPPOSE: supposition, substitution.
SUPPOSED: counterfeit.
SURCEASE: cessation, death.
SURPRISE: to capture by surprise.
SUR-REINED: over-worked.
SUSPECT: suspicion.
SUSPIRE: to breathe.
SWABBER: a sweeper of the deck of a ship.
SWARTH: black.
SWARTH: quantity of grass cut down by one
   sweep of the scythe.
SWASHER: swaggerer.
SWATH: The same as 'swarth'.
SWATHLING: swaddling.
SWAY: to move on, advance.

SWIFT: ready, quick.
SWINGE-BUCKLER: a bully, a swashbuckler.

TABLE: a tablet, note-book, painting surface.
TABLES: the game of backgammon. A note-book.
TABOR: a small side-drum.
TABOURINE: tambourine, drum.
TAG: the rabble.
TAINT: stain, defile; be infected by.
TAINTURE: defilement.
TAKE: to infect, bewitch.
TAKE OUT: to copy.
TAKE UP: to borrow money, or buy on credit. To make up a quarrel.
TAKING: infection, malignant influence.
TAKING OFF: murder.
TALE: counting, reckoning.
TALL: strong, valiant.
TALLOW-CATCH: a lump of tallow.
TANG: twang, sound.
TANLING: anything tanned by the sun.
TARRE: to excite, urge on.
TARRIANCE: delay.
TARTAR: Tartarus, hell.
TASK: to employ. Challenge.
TASKING: challenging.
TASTE: enjoy sexually.
TAWDRY-LACE: a rustic necklace.
TAXATION: satire, sarcasm. Demand.
TAXING: satire, censure.
TEEN: grief.

TELL: to count.

TEMPER: to mix, to soften.

TEMPERANCE: temperature.

TEND: to attend to.

TENDER: offer, desire, esteem. To have consideration for.

TENT: to probe as a wound.

TERCEL: the male of the goshawk.

TERMAGANT: a ranting character in old plays.

TESTED: pure, assayed.

TESTERN: to reward with a tester, or six-pence.

THARBOROUGH: (corrupted from 'third-borough') a constable.

THEORICK: theory.

THEWS: sinews, muscles.

THICK: (of speech) huskily.

THICK-PLEACHED: thickly intertwined.

THIRD-BOROUGH: a constable.

THOUGHT: anxiety, grief.

THRASONICAL: boastful.

THREE-MAN BEETLE: a wooden mallet worked by three men.

THREE-MAN-SONG-MEN: singers of glees in three parts.

THREE-PILE: three-piled velvet.

THRENE: lament.

THRID: thread, fibre.

THROE: to put in agonies, cause pain.

THRUM: the tufted end of a thread in weaving.

THRUMMED: made of coarse ends or tufts.

TICKLE: ticklish.

TIGHT: nimble, active. Water-tight.

TIKE: a cur.

TILLY-VALLY: an exclamation of contempt.

TILTH: tillage.

TIMELESS: untimely.

TINCT: stain, dye.Colour of the elixir of life.

TIRE: attire, head-dress.

TIRE: to tear as a bird of prey. Devour.

TIRE: attire, headdress.

TOD: a tod of wool (28lbs).

TOKENED: marked with plague spots.

TOKENS: plague spots; marks of infection.

TOLL: to exact toll. To pay toll.

TOPLESS: supreme, without superior.

TOUCH: touchstone. Trait. An acute feeling.

TOUCHED: pricked, infected.

TOUSE: to pull, tear.

TOWARD: nearly ready, impending.

TOYS: trifles, foolish tricks.

TRADE: beaten path.

TRAJECT: a ferry.

TRANSLATED: transformed.

TRASH: to check, as a huntsman his hounds.

TRAY-TRIP: an old game played with dice.

TREACHERS: traitors, deceivers.

TREATIES: entreaties.

TRENCHED: carved, engraved.

TRICK: fashion. Distinguishing characteristic. Knack.

TRICK: to dress up.

TRICKED: blazoned, spotted.

TRICKING: ornament, costumes.

TRICKSY: elegantly.

TRIPLE: third.

TROJAN: a cant word for a thief.

TROLL-MY-DAMES: (Fr. *trou-madame*;) a game like bagatelle.

TROTH-PLIGHT: betrothed.

TROW: to trust, think.

TRUE: honest.

TRUNDLE-TAIL: a long-tailed dog.

TUCKET-SONANCE: a flourish on the trumpet.

TUNDISH: a funnel.

TURLYGOOD: bedlam-beggars, gypsies.

TWIGGEN: made of twigs, wicker.

TWILLED: Retained by woven branches.

TWINK: a twinkling.

TWIRE: to peep.

UMBERED: stained, dark, as with umber.

UNANELED: without extreme unction.

UNAVOIDED: unavoidable.

UNBARBED: uncovered, bare.

UNBATED: unblunted.

UNBOLT: to disclose, explain.

UNBOLTED: unsifted, unrefined.

UNBREATHED: unpractised.

UNCAPE: to throw off the hounds.

UNCHARGED: undefended, acquitted.

UNCLEW: to unravel, undo.

UNCOINED: unalloyed, unfeigned.

UNDERGO: to undertake.

UNDERTAKER: one who takes up another's quarrel.

UNDER-WROUGHT: undermined.

UNEATH: hardly.

UNEXPRESSIVE: inexpressible, beyond praise.

UNFAIR: to deprive of beauty.

UNHATCHED: undisclosed.

UNHOUSELED: without receiving the sacrament.

UNIMPROVED: undisciplined, inexperienced.

UNION: a pearl.

UNKIND: unnatural.

UNLIVED: bereft of life.

UNMANNED: untamed, applied to a hawk.

UNOWED: unowned.

UNPREGNANT: unready to act.

UNPROPER: common to all, not one's own.

UNQUESTIONABLE: averse to questioning.

UNREADY: undressed.

UNRESPECTIVE: inconsiderate. Undiscriminating.

UNSISTING: unresisting.

UNSTANCHED: incontinent.

UNTEMPERING: unsoftening.

UNTENTED: unsearchable, incurable.

UNTRADED: unused, uncommon.

UNVALUED: priceless. Of little value.

UPSPRING REEL: a boisterous dance.

URCHIN: the hedge-hog.

USANCE: usury.

USE: interest, custom, trust.

UTIS: merriment which accompanied a festival.

UTTER: to expel, put forth, sell.

UTTERANCE: extremity, the bitter end.

VADE: to fade.

VAIL: to lower, submit. Sinking.

VALANCED: fringed (with a beard).

VALIDITY: value, worth.

VANTAGE: advantage.

VANTBRACE: armour for the forearm.

VARLET: a servant, valet. A rascal.

VAST: waste, desert.

VASTIDITY: immensity.

VASTY: vast, immense.

VAUNT: the van, the beginning.

VAUNT-COURIERS: forerunners.

VAWARD: the van, vanguard, advanced guard.

VEGETIVES: herbs, vegetables.

VELURE: velvet.

VELVET-GUARDS: velvet trimmings; applied metaphorically to the citizens who wore them.

VENEW: a bout in fencing, a term applied to repartee and sallies of wit.

VENGE: to avenge.

VENTAGES: holes in a flute or flageolet.

VERY: true, real.

VIA: away!

VICE: the buffoon in the old morality plays.

VIE: to challenge a term at cards. To compete.

VIEWLESS: invisible.

VILLAIN: a lowborn man: a scoundrel.

VINEWED: mouldy.

VIOL-DE-GAMBOYS: a bass viol.

VIRGINALLING: playing with the fingers, as on the virginals.

VIRTUE: the essential excellence. Valour.

VIRTUOUS: excellent, potent.

VIZAMENT: advisement, counsel.
VOLUBLE: fickle.
VOTARIST: votary, one who has taken a vow.
VULGAR: the common people.
VULGARLY: publicly.

WAFT: to wave, beckon. To turn, carry by sea.
WAFTAGE: passage by water.
WAFTURE: waving, beckoning.
WAGE: to reward as with wages.
WAILFUL: lamentable.
WAIST: the middle of a ship.
WANNION: 'With a wannion' — 'with a vengeance'.
WAPPENED: withered, overworn.
WARD: guard. Prison. Safety.
WARDEN: a large pear used for baking.
WARDER: truncheon, staff.
WARN: to summon.
WASSAIL: a drinking bout. Festivity.
WAT: a familiar word for a hare.
WATCH: a watch light. Wakefulness.
WATCH: to tame by keeping constantly awake.
WATER-GALL: a secondary rainbow.
WATER-RUG: a kind of dog.
WATER-WORK: painting in distemper or water colour.
WAX: to grow.
WEATHER-FEND: defend from the weather, shelter.
WEB AND PIN: the cataract in the eye.
WEE: to think.
WEED: garment.

224

WEET: to know.

WELKIN: the sky; sky-blue.

WELL-LIKING: in good condition, plump.

WEND: to go.

WESAND: the wind-pipe.

WHELK: a weal, pimple.

WHELKED: marked with whelks or protuberances.

WHEN: an exclamation of impatience.

WHIFFLER: an officer who clears the way in processions.

WHILE-ERE: a little while ago.

WHILES: until.

WHIP-STOCK: handle of a whip.

WHIST: hushed, silent.

WHITE: the centre of an archery butt.

WHITELY: pale-faced.

WHITING-TIME: bleaching time.

WHITSTER: bleacher.

WHITTLE: a clasp knife.

WHOO-BUB: hubbub.

WIDOW: to endow with a widow's right.

WIDOWHOOD: widow's jointure.

WIGHT: person.

WILDERNESS: wildness.

WIMPLED: veiled, hooded, blindfolded.

WINDOW-BARS: lattice-work across a woman's stomacher.

WINDRING: winding.

WINTER-GROUND: to protect (a plant) from frost.

WIS: in the compound 'I wis', certainly.

WISTLY: wistfully.

WIT: knowledge, wisdom.
WITHOUT: beyond.
WITS: five, the five senses.
WITTOL: a contented cuckold.
WITTY: intelligent.
WOMAN-TIRED: hen-pecked.
WONDERED: marvellously gifted.
WOOD: mad.
WOODCOCK: a simpleton.
WOODMAN: a hunter; so, of women.
WOOLWARD: shirtless.
WORD: flatter or put off with words. The Bible.
WORLD: 'To go to the world', to get married; 'a woman of the world', a married woman.
WORM: a serpent.
WORTS: cabbages.
WOT: to know.
WOUND: twisted about.
WREAK: vengeance. To avenge.
WREAKFUL: revengeful, avenging.
WREST: an instrument for tuning a harp. To devise, pervert.
WRIT: gospel, truth. Document.
WRITHLED: shrivelled, wrinkled.
WROTH: misfortune.
WRUNG: twisted, strained.
WRY: to swerve, to go astray.

YARE: ready, swift, easily handled.
YARELY: readily, nimbly.
Y-CLAD: clad.

Y-CLEPED: called, named.

YEARN: to grieve, vex.

YELLOWNESS: jealousy.

YELLOWS: a disease of horses.

YEOMAN: a sheriff's officer. A freeholder or farmer.

YIELD: to reward. To report.

YOND: yonder.

ZANY: a clown, gull. A fool's stooge.

Notes

Notes